# Epistle to Gregory and Origen's Commentary on the Gospel of John

# Epistle to Gregory and Origen's Commentary on the Gospel of John

# Epistle to Gregory and Origen's Commentary on the Gospel of John

© Lighthouse Publishing 2025

Written by: Origen of Alexandria (185-253 AD)
Translated by: Allan Menzies (1845-1916)
Updated into Modern U.S English: A.M. Overett (b.1960)

All rights reserved. Without limiting the rights under copyright reserved above, no part of this publication may be reproduced, stored in a retrieval system, or transmitted, in any form or by any means (electronic, mechanical, photocopying, recording or otherwise), without the prior written permission of the copyright owner of this book.

Published by
Lighthouse Publishing
SAN 257-4330
228 Freedom Parkway
Hoschton, GA 30548
United States of America

www.lighthousechristianpublishing.com

Commentaries of Origen.

Introduction.

For a general account of Origen and of his works we may refer to Dr. Crombie's *Life of Origen*, in vol. iv. of this series (xxiii. in Clark's issue). The principal facts of his career are as follows: He was born of Christian parents at Alexandria about the year 185 a.d., and from his earliest youth devoted himself to the study of Scripture in such a way as to suggest that he was destined for a great career. His father suffered martyrdom in the year 202, and Origen very soon afterwards succeeded the great Clement as head of the school at Alexandria. Thirteen years after, the persecution of Caracalla drove him from his own country to Cæsarea, where though still a layman he preached at church meetings. Recalled to Alexandria, he labored there for fifteen years further as teacher and author, till in the year 231 his ordination at Cæsarea to the office of presbyter drew upon him the condemnation of the bishop of Alexandria and became the occasion of his permanent withdrawal from the place of his birth. At Cæsarea he now formed a new school of Christian training similar to that from which he had been driven. At this time, as well as in the earlier period of his life, he made various journeys to different parts of the world. His death was brought about by sufferings inflicted on him in the persecution of Decius, and took place at Tyre, probably in the year 254.

Part of the Commentary on John, the first great work of Christian interpretation, and part of that on Matthew, written by the father at a later period of his life, are here presented to the reader; and a few words of introduction may be added on Origen's work as an expositor and on these two works in particular.

Though Origen was the first great interpreter of Scripture in the Church, commentaries had been written before his. He speaks of those who had preceded him in this activity; and though but little survives of the labors of these earlier expositors, we know that the work of commenting on Scripture was zealously carried on in the Gnostic churches in the latter part of the second century, and several of the older exegetes in the Church are also known to us by name and reputation. Heracleon the Gnostic commentator on John, who is often cited and often rather unfairly dealt with by Origen, as he follows him over the same ground, belonged to the Valentinian school. Many of his comments the reader will find to be very just and shrewd; but the tenets of his school led him into many extravagances. Of Pantænus, head of the catechetical school at Alexandria in the end of the second and early years of the third century, we hear that he interpreted many of the books of Scripture. We also learn that he preceded Clement and Origen, his successors in office, in the application of Gentile learning to Christian studies; the broad and liberal tone of Alexandrian theology may be due in part to his influence. Much of his exegetical work was still extant in the days of Jerome, who, however, reports that he did more for the Church as a teacher than as a writer. Only fragments of his Commentaries now remain. In Clement's works, on the contrary, we find, if not any set commentaries, various extended discussions of particular texts. We also find in him a theory of Scripture, its inspiration and its nature, which is followed also by Origen, and which determines the whole character of Alexandrian exegesis. In accordance with the general tendency of that age, which witnessed a reaction from the independence of philosophy and an appeal in many quarters to the authority of ancient oracles and writings, the Alexandrian school treats Scripture as an inspired and infallible storehouse of truth,—of truth, however, not patent to the simple reader, but requiring the spiritual man to discern its mystic import. Clement discusses the question why divine things are wrapped up in mysteries, and holds that all who have spoken of such things have dealt with them in this way. Everything in Scripture, therefore, has a mystical in addition to its obvious meaning. Every minute particular about the tabernacle and its furniture is charged with an unseen truth. The effect of such a view of Scripture on exegesis is necessarily that the interpreter finds in the inspired words not what they plainly convey, but what most interests his own mind. In assigning to each verse its spiritual meaning, he is neither guided nor restrained by any rule or system, but enjoys complete liberty. The natural good sense of these great scholars curbed to some extent the license of their theory; but with such a view of Scripture they could not but run into many an extravagance; and the allegorical method of interpretation, which so long prevailed in Christendom and is still practiced in some quarters, dates from Alexandria. The roots of it lie further back, in Jewish rabbinical treatment of the Old Testament, and in the Greek philosophy of Alexandria. In Philo, the great contemporary of Christ at Alexandria, rabbinical and Greek learning met, and Scripture being a divine authority and having to furnish evidence of Greek philosophical doctrines, the allegorical method of interpretation was called to perform large services. To Philo's eyes all wisdom was contained in the Pentateuch, and many an idea of which Moses never dreamed had to be extracted from that ancient record. The method was older than Clement and Origen, but it was through them that it became so firmly established in the Church.

In Origen we first find a great teacher who deliberately sets himself to the task of explaining Scripture. He became, at the early age of eighteen, the head of the catechetical school at Alexandria, an institution which not only trained catechumens but provided open lectures, on every part of Christian learning, and from that time to his death, at the age of sixty-nine, he was constantly engaged in the work of public exposition. At Alexandria his expositions took place in the school, but at Cæsarea they formed part of the church services, so that the reports of those belonging to the Cæsarean period provide us with the earliest examples we possess of the discourse at Christian meetings. In an activity which he practiced so much Origen acquired extraordinary skill and facility, and gained the highest reputation, even beyond the limits of the Church. It is no wonder, therefore, if he succeeded in treating nearly the whole Bible in this way, a thing which might no doubt be said of many a Christian teacher since his day; for he was not one who was apt to repeat himself, but was constantly pressing on to break new ground.

But the reported homilies form only a part—and that not the most important part—of his exegetical works. What he gave in his homilies was necessarily designed for edification; it had to be plain enough to be understood by a mixed audience, and serviceable to their needs. Origen believed, however, that there was very much in Scripture that lay beyond the capacity of the ordinary mind, and that the highest way of treating Scripture was not that of practical application, but that of searching after its hidden sense. In the fourth book of his *De Principiis* (vol. x. of Clark's set) he sets forth his views about the Scriptures. "As man," he there says, "consists of body, soul, and spirit, so in the same way does Scripture, which has been arranged to be given by God for the salvation of man." Scripture, therefore, has three senses, the bodily (somatic) or the obvious matter-of-fact sense, the psychical or moral sense, which serves for edification of the pious, and, highest of all, the spiritual sense. For this latter sense of Scripture Origen has many names,—as many as forty have been counted,—he calls it the heavenly sense, the intellectual, the anagogical, the mystic, the hidden. This is what chiefly engages his interest in the work of expounding. Scripture is to him full of mysteries, every jot and tittle has its secret, and to read these heavenly mysteries is the highest object of the interpreter. In addition, therefore, to his oral expositions (ὁμιλίαι) and the short notes (σημειώσεις) which are generally reckoned as a third class of his exegetical works, we have the written commentaries, books, or τόμοι of Origen, in which he discusses Scripture without being hampered by the requirements of edification, according to the method which alone he recognizes as adequate. He was enabled to devote himself to this labor by the generosity of a rich friend, Ambrosius, who urged him to undertake it, and provided funds for the payment of shorthand writers and copyists. We are told that seven of the former were at one time placed at his disposal. The work which he was thus led to undertake Origen felt to be very responsible and burdensome; it was not to be approached without fervent prayer, and he sometimes complains that it is too much for him, and that it is only the urgent commands of Ambrosius that make him go on with it. (See the opening chapters of the various books on John.)

What has been said will to some extent explain the nature of these commentaries, parts of which are now for the first time presented to the English reader. There is a side of them, however, of which we have not yet spoken. Origen was a great scholar as well as a great theologian; and he thought it right, as the reader may see from the letter to Gregory also here given, that scholarship should contribute all it could to the study of Scripture. Of his multifarious knowledge and of his easy command of all the science and philosophy of his day, the reader may judge for himself even from what is now presented to him. His work on the words of Scripture has a value quite independently of his theological views. Some of the most important qualifications of the worthy interpreter of Scripture he possesses in a supreme degree. His knowledge of Scripture is extraordinary both for its range and its minute accuracy. He had no concordance to help him; but he was himself a concordance. Whatever word occurs he is able to bring from every part of Scripture the passages in which it is used. He quotes passages, it is true, which are only verbally connected with the text before him and have no affinity of idea; the wealth of illustration he has at his command does not always assist, but sometimes, as the reader will see, impedes his progress: yet the wonder is not diminished of such a knowledge of all parts of the Bible as is probably without parallel. It has to be added that he is strong in grammar, and has a true eye for the real meaning of his text; the discussions in which he does this often leave nothing to be desired. In defining his terms he often goes far astray; he has to define them according to the science of his day; but he is not guilty of loose construction of sentences. Another matter in which he is distinguished is that of textual criticism. He is the first great textual critic of the Church. That his name occurs more frequently than that of any other father in the digests of early readings of the text of the New Testament, is due no doubt to the fact that he is the earliest writer of commentaries which have been preserved; his commentaries contain complete texts of the portions of Scripture commented on, as well as copious quotations from other parts of Scripture. But he was keenly interested in the text of the New Testament for its own sake. He tells us that many variations already existed in his day in different copies. And he preserves many readings which afterwards disappeared from the Bible. It has also to be said that he often quotes the same text differently in different passages, so that it appears probable that he used several copies of the N.T. books, and that these copies differed from each other. If, therefore, as Tischendorf suggests, Origen made a collation of the various texts of the N.T. with which he was acquainted, as he did with his texts of the O.T. in his Hexapla, he had no strong views as to which text was to be followed. He sometimes expresses an opinion as to which is the true reading (pp. 368 sq.), but he does so on grounds which the textual critics of the present day could not approve.

It may be stated here that the translators of Origen in this volume have sought to represent their author's critical position with regard to Scripture by translating his Scripture quotations from his text. As he used the Septuagint version of the Old Testament, many of his quotations from that part of Scripture appear in a form unfamiliar to the English reader. In the New Testament, also, his text is also very different from that which afterwards prevailed in the Church.

The weakness of Origen as an interpreter is his want of historical feeling or of any conception of such a thing as growth or development in revelation. His mind slips incessantly away from the real scenes and events recorded in Scripture, to the ideal region where he conceives that the truths reside which these prefigure. Scripture is to him not a record of actual occurrences which took place as they are narrated, but a storehouse of types of heavenly things, which alone are real. He scoffs at the notion that historical facts should be regarded as the chief outcome of a Scripture narrative (John, book x. 15–17, pp. 389–394). When he does treat the facts as facts he has many a shrewd observation and many a beautiful application. But the facts are to a large extent in his way; they have to give place to something more important. He sees very well how the synoptic narratives clash with that of John; no better demonstration of this need be looked for than he gives in the tenth book of his John; from this, however, he infers not that the books must have had different sources of information, but that the literal meaning of the passages must be altogether disregarded, and their true purport looked for, not in the things of history, but in the things of the Spirit. The water-pots at the feast in Cana (*De Principiis*), the shoe latchet of the Savior (John, book vi. 17), the ass and foal (John, book x. 18), each must receive a transcendent application.

It follows from this that the commentaries are deficient in order and sequence. The method which calls the writer to look at every step for spiritual meanings, combined with his own extraordinary fertility of imagination and wealth of matter, makes these books very disconnected. At each point a number of questions suggests itself as to possible meanings; a host of texts is brought at once from every part of Scripture to afford illustration, and these again have to be considered. Very modestly are the questions and themes introduced. The tone is as far as possible from being *ex cathedra*; it is rather that of a student groping his way, and asking at each step for assistance. And the great mass of the questions thus raised is left, apparently, unanswered. So that the work as a whole is rather a great collection of materials for future consideration than a finished treatise.

Such being the characteristics of Origen's commentaries, they have by many been regarded as unsuitable for the general reader, and unfavorably compared with those of later writers, to whom the interpretation of Scripture was not weighted with such difficulties as Origen had to contend with. Our author does not carry us along in his commentaries with a stream of golden eloquence; his interests are intellectual more than literary or practical, his work is scientific rather than popular. Perhaps the historical student has more to gain from them than the preacher. But among the pages which witness chiefly to restless intellectual energy and unwearied diligence, there are also many passages of rare and touching beauty, when the writer realizes the greatness of the Christian salvation, or when the heavenly things to the search for which all his labor is devoted shine by their own brightness on his sight.

The Commentaries on John are the earliest work of Christian exegesis which has come down to us, and are therefore placed in this volume before those on Matthew. The first five books on John were written at Alexandria before Origen's compulsory withdrawal from that city to Cæsarea in 231. In chaps. 4 and 8 of the first book he speaks of this work as being the first fruits of his activity as a writer on Holy Scripture. The sixth book, as he tells us in VI. 1, had been begun at Alexandria, but the manuscript had been left behind, so that a new beginning had to be made at Cæsarea. The work was again interrupted by the persecution of Maximian in 238; the volumes from the twenty-second to the last were written after that date. At the end of the thirty-second volume, which is the last we now possess, the writer has only reached John xiii. 33, but he tells us in his Commentary on Matthew that he has spoken of the two thieves in his work on John. In the time of Eusebius only twenty-two books survived out of the whole number, which seems to have been thirty-nine. We now possess books I., ii., vi., x., xiii., xix., xx., xxviii., xxxii., some of which, however, are not complete, and a few fragments. The thirteenth book begins in the middle of the story of the Samaritan woman. Ambrosius had wished that story to be completed in the twelfth book, but Origen did not like to make his books too long, and on this point disregarded the authority of his mentor. The nineteenth and twentieth books are both occupied with the eighth chapter of John, which, if it was all treated on the same scale, must have occupied two more books in addition to these. The thirty-second book scarcely completes the thirteenth chapter of the Gospel; and if the remaining chapters only occupied seven books, the treatment of these must have been much more condensed.

Two Latin translations of Origen's John were made in the sixteenth century, one by Ambrosius

Ferrarius of Milan from the Venice Codex, the other by Joachim Perionius.

The Commentaries on John and on Matthew are both embraced in several manuscripts. Of those on John, Mr. A. E. Brooke (*Texts and Studies*, vol. i. No. 4; *The Fragments of Heracleon*, pp. 1–30; "the mss. of Origen's Commentaries on S. John") enumerates eight or nine. The Munich ms. of the thirteenth century is the source of all the rest. Huet, the first editor (1668), used the Codex Regius (Paris) of the sixteenth century, which is in many passages mutilated and disfigured. The brothers Delarue (1733–1759) used the mss. Barberinus and Bodleianus, which are more complete, and Lommatzsch (1831) follows his predecessors. The present translations are from the text of Lommatzsch, which is in many places very defective.

### Letter of Origen to Gregory.

When and to whom the Learning derived from Philosophy may be of Service for the Exposition of the Holy Scriptures; with a lively Personal Appeal.

This letter to Gregory, afterwards bishop of Cæsarea, and called Thaumaturgus, was preserved in the Philocalia, or collection of extracts from Origen's works drawn up by Gregory of Nyssa and Basil of Cæsarea. It is printed by Delarue and Lommatzsch in the forefront of their editions of the works. It forms a good preface to the commentaries, as it shows how Origen considered the study of Scripture to be the highest of all studies, and how he regarded scientific learning, in which he was himself a master, as merely preparatory for this supreme learning. Dräseke has shown that it was written about 235, when

Origen, after having had Gregory as his pupil at Cæsarea for some years, had fled before the persecution under Maximinus Thrax to Cappadocia; while Gregory, to judge from the tenor of this Epistle, had gone to Egypt. The Panegyric on Origen, pronounced by Gregory at Cæsarea about 239, when the school had reassembled there after the persecution, shows that the master's solicitude for his pupil's true advancement was not disappointed.

1. Gregory is Urged to Apply His Gentile Learning to the Study of Scripture.

All hail to thee in God, most excellent and reverend Sir, son Gregory, from Origen. A natural quickness of understanding is fitted, as you are well aware, if it be diligently exercised, to produce a work which may bring its owner so far as is possible, if I may so express myself, to the consummation of the art the which he desires to practice, and your natural aptitude is sufficient to make you a consummate Roman lawyer and a Greek philosopher too of the most famous schools. But my desire for you has been that you should direct the whole force of your intelligence to Christianity as your end, and that in the way of production. And I would wish that you should take with you on the one hand those parts of the philosophy of the Greeks which are fit, as it were, to serve as general or preparatory studies for Christianity, and on the other hand so much of Geometry and Astronomy as may be helpful for the interpretation of the Holy Scriptures. The children of the philosophers speak of geometry and music and grammar and rhetoric and astronomy as being ancillary to philosophy; and in the same way we might speak of philosophy itself as being ancillary to Christianity.

## 2. This Procedure is Typified by the Story of the Spoiling of the Egyptians.

It is something of this sort perhaps that is enigmatically indicated in the directions God is represented in the Book of Exodus as giving to the children of Israel. They are directed to beg from their neighbors and from those dwelling in their tents vessels of silver and of gold, and raiment; thus they are to spoil the Egyptians, and to obtain materials for making the things they are told to provide in connection with the worship of God. For out of the things of which the children of Israel spoiled the Egyptians the furniture of the Holy of Holies was made, the ark with its cover, and the cherubim and the mercy-seat and the gold jar in which the manna, that bread of angels, was stored. These probably were made from the finest of the gold of the Egyptians, and from a second quality, perhaps, the solid golden candlestick which stood near the inner veil, and the lamps on it, and the golden table on which stood the shewbread, and between these two the golden altar of incense. And if there was gold of a third and of a fourth quality, the sacred vessels were made of it. And of the Egyptian silver, too, other things were made; for it was from their sojourn in Egypt that the children of Israel derived the great advantage of being supplied with such a quantity of precious materials for the use of the service of God. Out of the Egyptian raiment probably were made all those requisites named in Scripture in embroidered work; the embroiderers working with the wisdom of God, such garments for such purposes, to produce the hangings and the inner and outer courts. This is not a suitable opportunity to enlarge on such a theme or to show in how many ways the children of Israel found those things useful which they got from the Egyptians. The Egyptians had not made a proper use of them; but the Hebrews used them, for the wisdom of God was with them, for religious purposes. Holy Scripture knows, however, that it was an evil thing to descend from the land of the children of Israel into Egypt; and in this a great truth is wrapped up. For some it is of evil that they should dwell with the Egyptians, that is to say, with the learning of the world, after they have been enrolled in the law of God and in the Israelite worship of Him. Ader the Edomite, as long as he was in the land of Israel and did not taste the bread of the Egyptians, made no idols; but when he fled from the wise Solomon and went down into Egypt, as one who had fled from the wisdom of God he became connected with Pharaoh, marrying the sister of his wife, and begetting a son who was brought up among the sons of Pharaoh. Therefore, though he did go back to the land of Israel, he came back to it to bring division into the people of God, and to cause them to say to the golden calf, "These are thy gods, O Israel, which brought thee up out of the land of Egypt." I have learned by experience and can tell you that there are few who have taken of the useful things of Egypt and come out of it, and have then prepared what is required for the service of God; but Ader the Edomite on the other hand has many a brother. I mean those who, founding on some piece of Greek learning, have brought forth heretical ideas, and have as it were made golden calves in Bethel, which is, being interpreted, the house of God. This appears to me to be intended to convey that such persons set up their own images in the Scriptures in which the Word of God dwells, and which therefore are tropically called Bethel. The other image is said in the word to have been set up in Dan. Now the borders of Dan are at the extremities and are contiguous to the country of the heathens, as is plainly recorded in the Book of Jesus, son of Nave. Some of these images, then, are close to the borders of the heathen, which the brothers, as we showed, of Ader have devised.

3. Personal Appeal.

Do you then, sir, my son, study first of all the divine Scriptures. Study them I say. For we require to study the divine writings deeply, lest we should speak of them faster than we think; and while you study these divine works with a believing and God-pleasing intention, knock at that which is closed in them, and it shall be opened to thee by the porter, of whom Jesus says, "To him the porter opened." While you attend to this divine reading seek aright and with unwavering faith in God the hidden sense which is present in most passages of the divine Scriptures. And do not be content with knocking and seeking, for what is most necessary for understanding divine things is prayer, and in urging us to this the Savior says not only, "Knock, and it shall be opened to you," and "Seek, and ye shall find," but also "Ask, and it shall be given you." So much I have ventured on account of my fatherly love to you. Whether I have ventured well or not, God knows, and His Christ, and he who has part of the Spirit of God and the Spirit of Christ. May you partake in these; may you have an always increasing share of them, so that you may be able to say not only, "We are partakers of Christ," but also "We are partakers of God."

Origen's Commentary on the Gospel of John.

Book I.

1. How Christians are the Spiritual Israel.

That people which was called of old the people of God was divided into twelve tribes, and over and above the other tribes it had the Levitical order, which itself again carried on the service of God in various priestly and Levitical suborders. In the same manner, it appears to me that the whole people of Christ, when we regard it in the aspect of the hidden man of the heart, that people which is called "Jew inwardly," and is circumcised in the spirit, has in a more mystic way the characteristics of the tribes. This may be more plainly gathered from John in his Apocalyse, though the other prophets also do not by any means conceal the state of matters from those who have the faculty of hearing them. John speaks as follows: "And I saw another angel ascending from the sunrising, having the seal of the living God, and he cried with a loud voice to the four angels to whom it was given to hurt the earth and the sea, saying, Hurt not either the earth, or the sea, or the trees, till we have sealed the servants of our God on their foreheads. And I heard the number of them that were sealed, a hundred and forty-four thousand who were sealed, out of every tribe of the children of Israel; of the tribe of Juda were sealed twelve thousand, of the tribe of Roubem twelve thousand." And he mentioned each of the tribes singly, with the exception of Dan. Then, some way further on, he continues: "And I saw, and behold the Lamb standing on Mount Zion, and with Him a hundred and forty-four thousand, having His name and the name of His Father written on their foreheads. And I heard a voice from heaven as the voice of many waters, and as the voice of a great thunder. And the voice which I heard was as the voice of harpers harping with their harps; and they sing a new song before the throne and before the four beasts and the elders, and no one could learn the song but the hundred and forty-four thousand who had been purchased from the earth. These are they which were not defiled with women, for they are virgins. These are they who follow the Lamb whithersover He goes. These were purchased from among men, a first fruits to God and to the Lamb; and in their mouth was found no lie, for they are without blemish." Now this is said in John with reference to those who have believed in Christ, for they also, even if their bodily descent cannot be traced to the seed of the Patriarchs, are yet gathered out of the tribes. That this is so we may conclude from what is further said about them: "Hurt not," he says, "the earth, nor the sea, nor the trees, till we have sealed the servants of our God on their foreheads. And I heard the number of them that were sealed, a hundred and forty-four thousand, sealed from every tribe of the children of Israel."

2. The 144,000 Sealed in the Apocalypse are Converts to Christ from the Gentile World.

These, then, who are sealed on their foreheads from every tribe of the children of Israel, are a hundred and forty-four thousand in number; and these hundred and forty-four thousand are afterwards said in John to have the name of the Lamb and of His Father written on their foreheads, and to be virgins, not having defiled themselves with women. What else could the seal be which is on their foreheads but the name of the Lamb and the name of His Father? In both passages their foreheads are said to have the seal; in one the seal is spoken of, in the other it appears to contain the letters forming the name of the Lamb, and the name of His Father. Now these taken from the tribes are, as we showed before, the same persons as the virgins. But the number of believers is small who belong to Israel according to the flesh; one might venture to assert that they would not nearly make up the number of a hundred and forty-four thousand. It is clear, therefore, that the hundred and forty-four thousand who have not defiled themselves with women must be made up of those who have come to the divine word out of the Gentile world. In this way the truth of the statement may be upheld that the first fruits of each tribe are its virgins. For the passage goes on: "These were brought from among men to be a first fruits to God and to the Lamb; and in their mouth was found no guile, for they are without blemish." The statement about the hundred and forty-four thousand no doubt admits of mystical interpretation; but it is unnecessary at this point, and would divert us from our purpose, to compare with it those passages of the prophets in which the same lesson is taught regarding those who are called from among the Gentiles.

3. In the Spiritual Israel the High-Priests are Those Who Devote Themselves to the Study of Scripture.

But what is the bearing of all this for us? So you will ask when you read these words, Ambrosius, thou who art truly a man of God, a man in Christ, and who seeks to be not a man only, but a spiritual man. The bearing is this. Those of the tribes offer to God, through the Levites and priests, tithes and first fruits; not everything which they possess do they regard as tithe or first fruit. The Levites and priests, on the other hand, have no possessions but tithes and first fruits; yet they also in turn offer tithes to God through the high priests, and, I believe, first fruits too. The same is the case with those who approach Christian studies. Most of us devote most of our time to the things of this life, and dedicate to God only a few special acts, thus resembling those members of the tribes who had but few transactions with the priest, and discharged their religious duties with no great expense of time. But those who devote themselves to the divine word and have no other employment but the service of God may not unnaturally, allowing for the difference of occupation in the two cases, be called our Levites and priests. And those who fulfil a more distinguished office than their kinsmen will perhaps be high-priests, according to the order of Aaron, not that of Melchisedek. Here someone may object that it is somewhat too bold to apply the name of high-priests to men, when Jesus Himself is spoken of in many a prophetic passage as the one great priest, as "We have a great high-priest who has passed through the heavens, Jesus, the Son of God." But to this we reply that the Apostle clearly defined his meaning, and declared the prophet to have said about the Christ, "Thou art a priest forever, according to the order of Melchisedek," and not according to the order of Aaron. We say accordingly that men can be high-priests according to the order of Aaron, but according to the order of Melchisedek only the Christ of God.

4. The Study of the Gospels is the First Fruits Offered by These Priests of Christianity.

Now our whole activity is devoted to God, and our whole life, since we are bent on progress in divine things. If, then, it be our desire to have the whole of those first fruits spoken of above which are made up of the many first fruits, if we are not mistaken in this view, in what must our first fruits consist, after the bodily separation we have undergone from each other, but in the study of the Gospel? For we may venture to say that the Gospel is the first fruits of all the Scriptures. Where, then, could be the first fruits of our activity, since the time when we came to Alexandria, but in the first fruits of the Scriptures? It must not be forgotten, however, that the first fruits are not the same as the first growth. For the first fruits are offered after all the fruits (are ripe), but the first growth before them all. Now of the Scriptures which are current and are believed to be divine in all the churches, one would not be wrong in saying that the first growth is the law of Moses, but the first fruits the Gospel. For it was after all the fruits of the prophets who prophesied till the Lord Jesus, that the perfect word shot forth.

5. All Scripture is Gospel; but the Gospels are Distinguished above Other Scriptures. Here, however, someone may object, appealing to the notion just put forward of the unfolding of the first fruits last, and may say that the Acts and the letters of the Apostles came after the Gospels, and that this destroys our argument to the effect that the Gospel is the first fruits of all Scripture. To this we must reply that it is the conviction of men who are wise in Christ, who have profited by those epistles which are current, and who see them to be vouched for by the testimonies deposited in the law and the prophets, that the apostolic writings are to be pronounced wise and worthy

of belief, and that they have great authority, but that they are not on the same level with that "Thus sayeth the Lord Almighty." Consider on this point the language of St. Paul. When he declares that "Every Scripture is inspired of God and profitable," does he include his own writings? Or does he not include his dictum, "I say, and not the Lord," and "So I ordain in all the churches," and "What things I suffered at Antioch, at Iconium, at Lystra," and similar things which he writes in virtue of his own authority, and which do not quite possess the character of words flowing from divine inspiration. Must we also show that the old Scripture is not Gospel, since it does not point out the Coming One, but only foretells Him and heralds His coming at a future time; but that all the new Scripture is the Gospel. It not only says as in the beginning of the Gospel, "Behold the Lamb of God, which taketh away the sin of the world;" it also contains many praises of Him, and many of His teachings, on whose account the Gospel is a Gospel. Again, if God set in the Church apostles and prophets and evangelists (gospellers), pastors and teachers, we must first enquire what was the office of the evangelist, and mark that it is not only to narrate how the Savior cured a man who was blind from his birth, or raised up a dead man who was already stinking, or to state what extraordinary works he wrought; and the office of the evangelist being thus defined, we shall not hesitate to find Gospel in such discourse also as is not narrative but hortatory and intended to strengthen belief in the mission of Jesus; and thus we shall arrive at the position that whatever was written by the Apostles is Gospel. As to this second definition, it might be objected that the Epistles are not entitled "Gospel," and that we are wrong in applying the name of Gospel to the whole of the New Testament. But to this we answer that it happens not unfrequently in Scripture when two or more persons or things are named by the same name, the name attaches itself most significantly to one of those things or persons. Thus the Savior says, "Call no man Master upon the earth;" while the Apostle says that Masters have been appointed in the Church. These latter accordingly will not be Masters in the strict sense of the dictum of the Gospel. In the same way the Gospel in the Epistles will not extend to every word of them, when it is compared with the narrative of Jesus' actions and sufferings and discourses. No: the Gospel is the first fruits of all Scripture, and to these first fruits of the Scriptures we devote the first fruits of all those actions of ours which we trust to see turn out as we desire.

6. The Fourfold Gospel. John's the First Fruits of the Four. Qualifications Necessary for Interpreting It.

Now the Gospels are four. These four are, as it were, the elements of the faith of the Church, out of which elements the whole world which is reconciled to God in Christ is put together; as Paul says, "God was in Christ, reconciling the world to Himself;" of which world Jesus bore the sin; for it is of the world of the Church that the word is written, "Behold the Lamb of God which taketh away the sin of the world." The Gospels then being four, I deem the first fruits of the Gospels to be that which you have enjoined me to search into according to my powers, the Gospel of John, that which speaks of him whose genealogy had already been set forth, but which begins to speak of him at a point before he had any genealogy. For Matthew, writing for the Hebrews who looked for Him who was to come of the line of Abraham and of David, says: "The book of the generation of Jesus Christ, the son of David, the son of Abraham." And Mark, knowing what he writes, narrates the beginning of the Gospel; we may perhaps find what he aims at in John; in the beginning the Word, God the Word. But Luke, though he says at the beginning of Acts, "The former treatise did I make about all that Jesus began to do and to teach," yet leaves to him who lay on Jesus' breast the greatest and completest discourses about Jesus. For none of these plainly declared His Godhead, as John does when he makes Him say, "I am the light of the world,"

"I am the way and the truth and the life," "I am the resurrection," "I am the door," "I am the good shepherd;" and in the Apocalypse, "I am the Alpha and the Omega, the beginning and the end, the first and the last." We may therefore make bold to say that the Gospels are the first fruits of all the Scriptures, but that of the Gospels that of John is the first fruits. No one can apprehend the meaning of it except he have lain on Jesus' breast and received from Jesus Mary to be his mother also. Such a one must he become who is to be another John, and to have shown to him, like John, by Jesus Himself Jesus as He is. For if Mary, as those declare who with sound mind extol her, had no other son but Jesus, and yet Jesus says to His mother, "Woman, behold thy son," and not "Behold you have this son also," then He virtually said to her, "Lo, this is Jesus, whom thou didst bear." Is it not the case that everyone who is perfect lives himself no longer, but Christ lives in him; and if Christ lives in him, then it is said of him to Mary, "Behold thy son Christ." What a mind, then, must we have to enable us to interpret in a worthy manner this work, though it be committed to the earthly treasure-house of common speech, of writing which any passer-by can read, and which can be heard when read aloud by anyone who lends to it his bodily ears? What shall we say of this work? He who is accurately to apprehend what it contains should be able to say with truth, "We have the mind of Christ, that we may know those things which are bestowed on us by God." It is possible to quote one of Paul's sayings in support of the contention that the whole of the New Testament is Gospel. He writes in a certain place: "According to my Gospel." Now we have no written work of Paul which is commonly called a Gospel. But all that he preached and said was the Gospel; and what he preached and said he was also in the habit of writing, and what he wrote was therefore Gospel. But if what Paul wrote was Gospel, it follows that what Peter wrote was also Gospel, and in a word all that was said or written to perpetuate the knowledge of Christ's sojourn on earth, and to prepare for His second coming, or to bring it about as a present reality in those souls which were willing to receive the Word of God as He stood at the door and knocked and sought to come into them.

7. What Good Things are Announced in the Gospels.

But it is time we should inquire what is the meaning of the designation "Gospel," and why these books have this title. Now the Gospel is a discourse containing a promise of things which naturally, and on account of the benefits they bring, rejoice the hearer as soon as the promise is heard and believed. Nor is such a discourse any the less a Gospel that we define it with reference to the position of the hearer. A Gospel is either a word which implies the actual presence to the believer of something that is good, or a word promising the arrival of a good which is expected. Now all these definitions apply to those books which are named Gospels. For each of the Gospels is a collection of announcements which are useful to him who believes them and does not misinterpret them; it brings him a benefit and naturally makes him glad because it tells of the sojourn with men, on account of men, and for their salvation, of the first-born of all creation, Christ Jesus. And again each Gospel tells of the sojourn of the good Father in the Son with those minded to receive Him, as is plain to every believer; and moreover by these books a good is announced which had been formerly expected, as is by no means hard to see. For John the Baptist spoke in the name almost of the whole people when he sent to Jesus and asked, "Art thou He that should come or do we look for another?" For to the people the Messiah was an expected good, which the prophets had foretold, and they all alike, though under the law and the prophets, fixed their hopes on Him, as the Samaritan woman bears witness when she says: "I know that the Messiah comes, who is called Christ; when He comes He will tell us all things." Simon and Cleopas too, when talking to each other about all that had happened to Jesus Christ Himself, then risen, though they did not know that He had risen from the dead, speak thus, "Do you sojourn alone in Jerusalem, and knows not the things which have taken place there in these days? And when he said what things? they answered, The things concerning Jesus of Nazareth, which was a prophet, mighty in deed and in word before God and all the people, and how the chief priests and our rulers delivered Him up to be sentenced to death and crucified Him. But we hoped that it was He which should redeem Israel." Again, Andrew the brother of Simon Peter found his own brother Simon and said to him, "We have found the Messiah, which is, being interpreted, Christ." And a little further on Philip finds Nathanael and says to him, "We have found Him of whom Moses in the law, and the prophets, wrote, Jesus the son of Joseph, from Nazareth."


8. How the Gospels Cause the Other Books of Scripture Also to Be Gospel.

Now an objection might be raised to our first definition, because it would embrace books which are not entitled Gospels. For the law and the prophets also are to our eyes books containing the promise of things which, from the benefit they will confer on him, naturally rejoice the hearer as soon as he takes in the message. To this it may be said that before the sojourn of Christ, the law and the prophets, since He had not come who interpreted the mysteries they contained, did not convey such a promise as belongs to our definition of the Gospel; but the Savior, when He sojourned with men and caused the Gospel to appear in bodily form, by the Gospel caused all things to appear as Gospel. Here I would not think it beside the purpose to quote the example of Him who…a few things…and yet all. For when he had taken away the veil which was present in the law and the prophets, and by His divinity had proved the sons of men that the Godhead was at work, He opened the way for all those who desired it to be disciples of His wisdom, and to understand what things were true and real in the law of Moses, of which things those of old worshipped the type and the shadow, and what things were real of the things narrated in the histories which "happened to them in the way of type," but these things "were written for our sakes, upon whom the ends of the ages have come." With whomsoever, then, Christ has sojourned, he worships God neither at Jerusalem nor on the mountain of the Samaritans; he knows that God is a spirit, and worships Him spiritually, in spirit and in truth; no longer by type does he worship the Father and Maker of all. Before that Gospel, therefore, which came into being by the sojourning of Christ, none of the older works was a Gospel. But the Gospel, which is the new covenant, having delivered us from the oldness of the letter, lights up for us, by the light of knowledge, the newness of the spirit, a thing which never grows old, which has its home in the New Testament, but is also present in all the Scriptures. It was fitting, therefore, that that Gospel, which enables us to find the Gospel present, even in the Old Testament, should itself receive, in a special sense, the name of Gospel.

9. The Somatic and the Spiritual Gospel.

We must not, however, forget that the sojourning of Christ with men took place before His bodily sojourn, in an intellectual fashion, to those who were more perfect and not children, and were not under pedagogues and governors. In their minds they saw the fullness of the time to be at hand—the patriarchs, and Moses the servant, and the prophets who beheld the glory of Christ. And as before His manifest and bodily coming He came to those who were perfect, so also, after His coming has been announced to all, to those who are still children, since they are under pedagogues and governors and have not yet arrived at the fullness of the time, forerunners of Christ have come to sojourn, discourses (*logoi*) suited for minds still in their childhood, and rightly, therefore, termed pedagogues. But the Son Himself, the glorified God, the Word, has not yet come; He waits for the preparation which must take place on the part of men of God who are to admit His deity. And this, too, we must bear in mind, that as the law contains a shadow of good things to come, which are indicated by that law which is announced according to truth, so the Gospel also teaches a shadow of the mysteries of Christ, the Gospel which is thought to be capable of being understood by anyone. What John calls the eternal Gospel, and what may properly be called the spiritual Gospel, presents clearly to those who have the will to understand, all matters concerning the very Son of God, both the mysteries presented by His discourses and those matters of which His acts were the enigmas. In accordance with this we may conclude that, as it is with Him who is a Jew outwardly and circumcised in the flesh, so it is with the Christian and with baptism. Paul and Peter were, at an earlier period, Jews outwardly and circumcised, but later they received from Christ that they should be so in secret, too; so that outwardly they were Jews for the sake of the salvation of many, and by an economy they not only confessed in words that they were Jews, but showed it by their actions. And the same is to be said about their Christianity. As Paul could not benefit those who were Jews according to the flesh, without, when reason shows it to be necessary, circumcising Timothy, and when it appears the natural course getting himself shaved and making a vow, and, in a word, being to the Jews a Jew that he might gain the Jews—so also it is not possible for one who is responsible for the good of many to operate as he should by means of that Christianity only which is in secret. That will never enable him to improve those who are following the external Christianity, or to lead them on to better and higher things. We must, therefore, be Christians both somatically and spiritually, and where there is a call for the somatic (bodily) Gospel, in which a man says to those who are carnal that he knows nothing but Jesus Christ and Him crucified, so we must do. But should we find those who are perfected in the spirit, and bear fruit in it, and are enamored of the heavenly wisdom, these must be made to partake of that Word which, after it was made flesh, rose again to what it was in the beginning, with God.

10. How Jesus Himself is the Gospel.

The foregoing inquiry into the nature of the Gospel cannot be regarded as useless; it has enabled us to see what distinction there is between a sensible Gospel and an intellectual and spiritual one. What we have now to do is to transform the sensible Gospel into a spiritual one.

For what would the narrative of the sensible Gospel amount to if it were not developed to a spiritual one? It would be of little account or none; anyone can read it and assure himself of the facts it tells—no more. But our whole energy is now to be directed to the effort to penetrate to the deep things of the meaning of the Gospel and to search out the truth that is in it when divested of types. Now what the Gospels say is to be regarded in the light of promises of good things; and we must say that the good things the Apostles announce in this Gospel are simply Jesus. One good thing which they are said to announce is the resurrection; but the resurrection is in a manner Jesus, for Jesus says: "I am the resurrection."

Jesus preaches to the poor those things which are laid up for the saints, calling them to the divine promises. And the Holy Scriptures bear witness to the Gospel announcements made by the Apostles and to that made by our Savior. David says of the Apostles, perhaps also of the evangelists: "The Lord shall give the word to those that preach with great power; the King of the powers of the beloved;" teaching at the same time that it is not skillfully composed discourse, nor the mode of delivery, nor well practiced eloquence that produces conviction, but the communication of divine power. Hence also Paul says: "I will know not the word that is puffed up, but the power; for the kingdom of God is not in word but in power." And in another passage: "And my word and my preaching were not persuasive words of wisdom, but in demonstration of the spirit and of power." To this power Simon and Cleophas bear witness when they say: "Was not our heart burning within us by the way, as he opened to us the Scriptures?" And the Apostles, since the quantity of the power is great which God supplies to the speakers, had great power, according to the word of David: "The Lord will give the word to the preachers with great power." Isaiah too says: "How beautiful are the feet of them that proclaim good tidings;" he sees how beautiful and how opportune was the announcement of the Apostles who walked in Him who said, "I am the way," and praises the feet of those who walk in the intellectual way of Christ Jesus, and through that door go in to God. They announce good tidings, those whose feet are beautiful, namely, Jesus.

11. Jesus is All Good Things; Hence the Gospel is Manifold.

Let no one wonder if we have understood Jesus to be announced in the Gospel under a plurality of names of good things. If we look at the things by the names of which the Son of God is called, we shall understand how many good things Jesus is, whom those preach whose feet are beautiful. One good thing is life; but Jesus is the life. Another good thing is the light of the world, when it is true light, and the light of men; and all these things the Son of God is said to be. And another good thing which one may conceive to be in addition to life or light is the truth. And a fourth in addition to time is the way which leads to the truth. And all these things our Savior teaches that He is, when He says: "I am the way and the truth and the life." Ah, is not that good, to shake off earth and mortality, and to rise again, obtaining this boon from the Lord, since He is the resurrection, as He says: "I am the resurrection." But the door also is a good, through which one enters into the highest blessedness. Now Christ says: "I am the door." And what need is there to speak of wisdom, which "the Lord created the first principle of His ways, for His works," in whom the father of her rejoiced, delighting in her manifold intellectual beauty, seen by the eyes of the mind alone, and provoking him to love who discerns her divine and heavenly charm? A good indeed is the wisdom of God, proclaimed along with the other good foresaid by those whose feet are beautiful. And the power of God is the eighth good we enumerate, which is Christ. Nor must we omit to mention the Word, who is God after the Father of all. For this also is a good, less than no other. Happy, then, are those who accept these goods and receive them from those who announce the good tidings of them, those whose feet are beautiful. Indeed even one of the Corinthians to whom Paul declared that he knew nothing but Jesus Christ and Him crucified, should he learn Him who for our sakes became man, and so receive Him, he would become identified with the beginning of the good things we have spoken of; by the man Jesus he would be made a man of God, and by His death he would die to sin. For "Christ, in that He died, died unto sin once." But from His life, since "in that He lived, He lived unto God," everyone who is conformed to His resurrection receives that living to God. But who will deny that righteousness, essential righteousness, is a good, and essential sanctification, and essential redemption? And these things those preach who preach Jesus, saying that He is made to be of God righteousness and sanctification and redemption. Hence we shall have writings about Him without number, showing that Jesus is a multitude of goods; for from the things which can scarcely be numbered and which have been written we may make some conjecture of those things which actually exist in Him in whom "it pleased God that the whole fullness of the Godhead should dwell bodily," and which are not contained in writings. Why should I say, "are not contained in writings"? For John speaks of the whole world in this connection, and says: "I suppose that not even the world itself would contain the books which would be written." Now to say that the Apostles preach the Savior is to say that they preach these good things. For this is He who received from the good Father that He Himself should be these good things, so that each man receiving from Jesus the thing or things he is capable of receiving may enjoy good things. But the Apostles, whose feet were beautiful, and those imitators of them who sought to preach the good tidings, could not have done so had not Jesus Himself first preached the good tidings to them, as Isaiah says: "I myself that speak am here, as the opportunity on the mountains, as the feet of one preaching tidings of peace, as one preaching good things; for I will make My salvation to be heard, saying, God shall reign over thee, O Zion!" For what are the mountains on which the speaker declares that He Himself is present, but those who are less than none of the highest and the greatest of the earth? And these must be sought by the able ministers of the New Covenant, in order that they may observe the injunction which says: Go up into a high mountain, thou that preaches good tidings to Zion; thou that preaches good tidings to Jerusalem, lift up thy voice with strength!" Now it is not wonderful if to those who are to preach good tidings Jesus Himself preaches good tidings of good things, which are no other than Himself; for the Son of God preaches the good tidings of Himself to those who cannot come to know Him through others. And He who goes up into the mountains and preaches good things to them, being Himself instructed by His good Father, who "makes His sun to rise on the evil and on the good, and sends rain on the just and on the unjust," He does not despise those who are poor in soul. To them He preaches good tidings, as He Himself bears witness to us when He takes Isaiah and reads: "The spirit of the Lord is upon me, for the Lord hath anointed me to preach good tidings to the poor, He hath sent me to proclaim liberty to the captives, and sight to the blind. For closing the book He handed it to the minister and sat down. And when the eyes of all were fastened upon Him, He said, This day is this Scripture fulfilled in your ears."

12. The Gospel Contains the Ill Deeds Also Which Were Done to Jesus.

It ought not to be forgotten that in such a Gospel as this there is embraced every good deed which was done to Jesus; as, for example, the story of the woman who had been a sinner and had repented, and who, having experienced a genuine recovery from her evil state, had grace to pour her ointment over Jesus so that everyone in the house smelt the sweet savor. Hence, too, the words, "Wherever this Gospel shall be preached among all the nations, there also this that she has done shall be spoken of, for a memorial of her." And it is clear that whatever is done to the disciples of Jesus is done to Him. Pointing to those of them who met with kind treatment, He says to those who were kind to them, "What ye did to these, ye did to Me." So that every good deed we do to our neighbors is entered in the Gospel, that Gospel which is written on the heavenly tablets and read by all who are worthy of the knowledge of the whole of things. But on the other side, too, there is a part of the Gospel which is for the condemnation of the doers of the ill deeds which have been done to Jesus. The treachery of Judas and the shouts of the wicked crowd when it said, "Away with such a one from the earth," and "Crucify Him, crucify Him," the mocking of those who crowned Him with thorns, and everything of that kind, is included in the Gospels. And as a consequence of this we see that everyone who betrays the disciples of Jesus is reckoned as betraying Jesus Himself. To Saul, when still a persecutor it is said, "Saul Saul, why persecutes thou Me?" and, "I am Jesus whom thou persecutes." There are those who still have thorns with which they crown and dishonor Jesus, those, namely, who are choked by the cares, and riches, and pleasures of life, and though they have received the word of God, do not bring it to perfection.

We must beware, therefore, lest we also, as crowning Jesus with thorns of our own, should be entered in the Gospel and read of in this character by those who learn the Jesus, who is in all and is present in all rational and holy lives, learn how He is anointed with ointment, is entertained, is glorified, or how, on the other side, He is dishonored, and mocked, and beaten. All this had to be said; it is part of our demonstration that our good actions, and also the sins of those who stumble, are embodied in the Gospel, either to everlasting life or to reproach and everlasting shame.

### 13. The Angels also are Evangelists.

Now if there are those among men who are honored with the ministry of evangelists, and if Jesus Himself brings tidings of good things, and preaches the Gospel to the poor, surely those messengers who were made spirits by God, those who are a flame of fire, ministers of the Father of all, cannot have been excluded from being evangelists also. Hence an angel standing over the shepherds made a bright light to shine round about them, and said: "Fear not; behold I bring you good tidings of great joy, which shall be to all the people; for there is born to you, this day, a Savior, who is Christ the Lord, in the city of David." And at a time when there was no knowledge among men of the mystery of the Gospel, those who were greater than men and inhabitants of heaven, the army of God, praised God, saying, "Glory to God in the highest, and on earth peace, good will among men." And having said this, the angels go away from the shepherds into heaven, leaving us to gather how the joy preached to us through the birth of Jesus Christ is glory in the highest to God; they humbled themselves even to the ground, and then returned to their place of rest, to glorify God in the highest through Jesus Christ. But the angels also wonder at the peace which is to be brought about on account of Jesus on the earth, that seat of war, on which Lucifer, star of the morning, fell from heaven, to be warred against and destroyed by Jesus.

14. The Old Testament, Typified by John, is the Beginning of the Gospel.

In addition to what we have said, there is also this to be considered about the Gospel, that in the first instance it is that of Christ Jesus, the head of the whole body of the saved; as Mark says, "The beginning of the Gospel of Jesus Christ." Then also it is the Gospel of the Apostles; whence Paul says, "According to my Gospel." But the beginning of the Gospel—for in respect of its extent it has a beginning, a continuation, a middle, and an end—is nothing but the whole Old Testament. John is, in this respect, a type of the Old Testament, or, if we regard the connection of the New Testament with the Old, John represents the termination of the Old. For the same Mark says: "The beginning of the Gospel of Jesus Christ, as it is written in Isaiah the prophet, Behold I send my messenger before thy face, who shall prepare thy way. The voice of one crying in the wilderness, Prepare ye the way of the Lord, make His paths straight." And here I must wonder how the dissentients can connect the two Testaments with two different Gods. These words, were there no others, are enough to convict them of their error. For how can John be the beginning of the Gospel if they suppose he belongs to a different God, if he belongs to the demiurge, and, as they hold, is not acquainted with the new deity?

And the angels are not entrusted with but one evangelical ministry, and that a short one, not only with that addressed to the shepherds. For at the end an exalted and flying angel, having the Gospel, will preach it to every nation, for the good Father has not entirely deserted those who have fallen away from Him. John, son of Zebedee, says in his Apocalypse: "And I saw an angel flying in the midst of heaven, having the Eternal Gospel, to preach it to those who dwell upon the earth, and to every nation, and tribe, and tongue, and people, saying, with a loud voice, Fear God and give Him glory, for the hour of His judgment hath come, and worship Him that made the heaven, and the earth, and the sea, and the fountains of waters."

15. The Gospel is in the Old Testament, and Indeed in the Whole Universe. Prayer for Aid to Understand the Mystical Sense of the Work in Hand.

As, then, we have shown that the beginning of the Gospel, according to one interpretation, is the whole Old Testament, and is signified by the person of John, we shall add, lest this should be called a mere unsupported assertion, what is said in the Acts about the eunuch of the queen of the Ethiopians and Philip. Philip, it is said, began at the passage of Isaiah: "He was led as a lamb to the slaughter, and as a lamb before his shearer is dumb," and so preached to him the Lord Jesus. How can he begin with the prophet and preach Jesus, if Isaiah was not a part of the beginning of the Gospel? From this we may derive a proof of the assertion made at the outset, that every divine Scripture is Gospel. If he who preaches the Gospel preaches good things, and all those who spoke before the sojourn of Jesus in the flesh preach Christ, who is as we saw good things, then the words spoken by all of them alike are in a sense a part of the Gospel. And when the Gospel is said to be declared throughout the whole world, we infer that it is actually preached in the whole world, not, that is to say, in this earthly district only, but in the whole system of heaven and earth, or from heaven and earth. And why should we discuss any further what the Gospel is? What we have said is enough. Besides the passages we have adduced, passages by no means inept or unsuited for our purpose,—much to the same effect might be collected from the Scriptures, so that it is clearly seen what is the glory of the good things in Jesus Christ shed forth by the Gospel, the Gospel ministered by men and angels, and, I believe, also by authorities and powers, and thrones and dominions, and every name that is named, not only in this world, but also in the world to come, and indeed even by Christ Himself. Here, then, let us bring to a close what has to be said before proceeding to read the work itself. And now let us ask God to assist us through Jesus Christ by the Holy Spirit, so that we may be able to unfold the mystical sense which is treasured up in the words before us.

16. Meaning of "Beginning." (1) in Space.

"*In the beginning was the Word.*" It is not only the Greeks who consider the word "beginning" to have many meanings. Let anyone collect the Scripture passages in which the word occurs, and with a view to an accurate interpretation of it note what it stands for in each passage, and he will find that the word has many meanings in sacred discourse also. We speak of a beginning in reference to a transition. Here it has to do with a road and with length. This appears in the saying: "The beginning of a good way is to do justice." For since the good way is long, there have first to be considered in reference to it the question connected with action, and this side is presented in the words "to do justice;" the contemplative side comes up for consideration afterwards. In the latter the end of it comes to rest at last in the so-called restoration of all things, since no enemy is left them to fight against, if that be true which is said: "For He must reign until He have placed His enemies under His feet. But the last enemy to be destroyed is death." For then but one activity will be left for those who have come to God on account of His word which is with Him, that, namely, of knowing God, so that, being found by the knowledge of the Father, they may all be His Son, as now no one but the Son knows the Father. For should anyone enquire carefully at what time those are to know the Father to whom He who knows the Father reveals Him, and should he consider how a man now sees only through a glass and in a riddle, never having learned to know as he ought to know, he would be justified in saying that no one, no apostle even, and no prophet had known the Father, but when he became one with Him as a son and a father are one. And if anyone says that it is a digression which has led us to this point, our consideration of that one meaning of the word beginning, we must show that the digression is necessary and useful for the end we have in view. For if we speak of a beginning in the case of a transition, and of a way and its length, and if we are told that the beginning of a good way is to do justice, then it concerns us to know in what manner every good way has for its beginning to do justice, and how after such beginning it arrives at contemplation, and in what manner it thus arrives at contemplation.

17. (2) in Time. The Beginning of Creation.

Again, there is a beginning in a matter of origin, as might appear in the saying: "In the beginning God made the heaven and the earth." This meaning, however, appears more plainly in the Book of Job in the passage: "This is the beginning of God's creation, made for His angels to mock at." One would suppose that the heavens and the earth were made first, of all that was made at the creation of the world. But the second passage suggests a better view, namely, that as many beings were framed with a body, the first made of these was the creature called dragon, but called in another passage the great whale (leviathan) which the Lord tamed. We must ask about this; whether, when the saints were living a blessed life apart from matter and from anybody, the dragon, falling from the pure life, became fit to be bound in matter and in a body, so that the Lord could say, speaking through storm and clouds, "This is the beginning of the creation of God, made for His angels to mock at." It is possible, however, that the dragon is not positively the beginning of the creation of the Lord, but that there were many creatures made with a body for the angels to mock at, and that the dragon was the first of these, while others could subsist in a body without such reproach. But it is not so. For the soul of the sun is placed in a body, and the whole creation, of which the Apostle says: "The whole creation groaned and travailed in pain together until now," and perhaps the following is about the same: "The creation was made subject to vanity, not willingly, but on account of Him who subjected it for hope;" so that bodies might be in vanity, and doing the things of the body, as he who is in the body must....One who is in the body does the things of the body, though unwillingly. Wherefore the creation was made subject to vanity, not willingly, but he who does unwillingly the things of the body does what he does for the sake of hope, as if we should say that Paul desired to remain in the flesh, not willingly, but on account of hope. For though he thought it better to be dissolved and to be with Christ, it was not unreasonable that he should wish to remain in the flesh for the sake of the benefit to others and of advancement in the things hoped for, not only by him, but also by those benefited by him. This meaning of the term "beginning," as of origin, will serve us also in the passage in which Wisdom speaks in the Proverbs. "God," we read, "created me the beginning of His ways, for His works." Here the term could be interpreted as in the first application we spoke of, that of a way: "The Lord," it says, "created me the beginning of His ways." One might assert, and with reason, that God Himself is the beginning of all things, and might go on to say, as is plain, that the Father is the beginning of the Son; and the demiurge the beginning of the works of the demiurge, and that God in a word is the beginning of all that exists. This view is supported by our: "In the beginning was the Word." In the Word one may see the Son, and because He is in the Father He may be said to be in the beginning.

18. (3) of Substance.

In the third place a beginning may be that out of which a thing comes, the underlying matter from which things are formed. This, however, is the view of those who hold matter itself to be uncreated, a view which we believers cannot share, since we believe God to have made the things that are out of the things which are not, as the mother of the seven martyrs in the Maccabees teaches, and as the angel of repentance in the Shepherd inculcated.

19. (4) of Type and Copy.

In addition to these meanings there is that in which we speak of an arche, according to form; thus if the first-born of every creature is the image of the invisible God, then the Father is his arche. In the same way Christ is the arche of those who are made according to the image of God. For if men are according to the image, but the image according to the Father; in the first case the Father is the arche of Christ, and in the other Christ is the arche of men, and men are made, not according to that of which he is the image, but according to the image. With this example our passage will agree: "In the arche was the Word."

20. (5) of Elements and What is Formed from Them.

There is also an arche in a matter of learning, as when we say that the letters are the arche of grammar. The Apostle accordingly says: "When by reason of the time you ought to be teachers, you have need again that someone teach you what are the elements of the arche of the oracles of God." Now the arche spoken of in connection with learning is twofold; first in respect of its nature, secondly in its relation to us; as we might say of Christ, that by nature His arche is deity, but that in relation to us who cannot, for its very greatness, command the whole truth about Him, His arche is His manhood, as He is preached to babes, "Jesus Christ and

Him crucified." In this view, then, Christ is the arche of learning in His own nature, because He is the wisdom and power of God; but for us, the Word was made flesh, that He might tabernacle among us who could only thus at first receive Him. And perhaps this is the reason why He is not only the firstborn of all creation, but is also designated the man, Adam. For Paul says He is Adam: "The last Adam was made a life-giving spirit."

21. (6) of Design and Execution.

Again we speak of the arche of an action, in which there is a design which appears after the beginning. It may be considered whether wisdom is to be regarded as the arche of the works of God because it is in this way the principle of them.

22. The Word Was in the Beginning, I.e., in Wisdom, Which Contained All Things in Idea, Before They Existed. Christ's Character as Wisdom is Prior to His Other Characters.

So many meanings occur to us at once of the word arche. We have now to ask which of them we should adopt for our text, "In the beginning was the Word." It is plain that we may at once dismiss the meaning which connects it with transition or with a road and its length. Nor, it is pretty plain, will the meaning connected with an origin serve our purpose. One might, however, think of the sense in which it points to the author, to that which brings about the effect, if, as we read, "God commanded and they were created." For Christ is, in a manner, the demiurge, to whom the Father says, "Let there be light," and "Let there be a firmament." But Christ is demiurge as a beginning (arche), inasmuch as He is wisdom. It is in virtue of His being wisdom that He is called arche. For Wisdom says in Solomon: "God created me the beginning of His ways, for His works," so that the Word might be in an arche, namely, in wisdom. Considered in relation to the structure of contemplation and thoughts about the whole of things, it is regarded as wisdom; but in relation to that side of the objects of thought, in which reasonable beings apprehend them, it is considered as the Word. And there is no wonder, since, as we have said before, the Savior is many good things, if He comprises in Himself thoughts of the first order, and of the second, and of the third. This is what John suggested when he said about the Word: "That which was made was life in Him." Life then came in the Word. And on the one side the Word is no other than the Christ, the Word, He who was with the Father, by whom all things were made; while, on the other side, the Life is no other than the Son of God, who says: "I am the way and the truth and the life." As, then, life came into being in the Word, so the Word in the arche. Consider, however, if we are at liberty to take this meaning of arche for our text: "In the beginning was the Word," so as to obtain the meaning that all things came into being according to wisdom and according to the models of the system which are present in his thoughts. For I consider that as a house or a ship is built and fashioned in accordance with the sketches of the builder or designer, the house or the ship having their beginning (arche) in the sketches and reckonings in his mind, so all things came into being in accordance with the designs of what was to be, clearly laid down by God in wisdom. And we should add that having created, so to speak, ensouled wisdom, He left her to hand over, from the types which were in her, to things existing and to matter, the actual emergence of them, their molding and their forms. But I consider, if it be permitted to say this, that the beginning (arche) of real existence was the Son of God, saying: "I am the beginning and the end, the A and the $\Omega$, the first and the last." We must, however, remember that He is not the arche in respect of every name which is applied to Him. For how can He be the beginning in respect of His being life, when life came in the Word, and the Word is manifestly the arche of life? It is also tolerably evident that He cannot be the arche in respect of His being the first-born from the dead. And if we go through all His titles carefully we find that He is the arche only in respect of His being wisdom. Not even as the Word is He the arche, for the Word was in the arche. And so one might venture to say that wisdom is anterior to all the thoughts that are expressed in the titles of the first-born of every creature. Now God is altogether one and simple; but our Savior, for many reasons, since God set Him forth a propitiation and a first fruits of the whole creation, is made many things, or perhaps all these things; the whole creation, so far as capable of redemption, stands in need of Him. And, hence, He is made the light of men, because men, being darkened by wickedness, need the light that shines in darkness, and is not overtaken by the darkness; had not men been in darkness, He would not have become the light of men. The same thing may be observed in respect of His being the first-born of the dead. For supposing the woman had not been deceived, and Adam had not fallen, and man created for incorruption had obtained it, then He would not have descended into the grave, nor would He have died, there being no sin, nor would His love of men have required that He should die, and if He had not died, He could not have been the first-born of the dead. We may also ask whether He would ever have become a shepherd, had man not been thrown together with the beasts which are devoid of reason, and made like to them. For if God saves man and beasts, He saves those beasts which He does save, by giving them a shepherd, since they cannot have a king. Thus if we collect the titles of Jesus, the question arises which of them were conferred on Him later, and would never have assumed such importance if the saints had begun and had also persevered in blessedness. Perhaps Wisdom would be the only remaining one, or perhaps the Word would remain too, or perhaps the Life, or perhaps the Truth, not the others, which He took for our sake. And happy indeed are those who in their need for the Son of God have yet become such persons as not to need Him in His character as a physician healing the sick, nor in that of a shepherd, nor in that of redemption, but only in His characters as wisdom, as the word and righteousness, or if there be any other title suitable for those who are so perfect as to receive Him in His fairest characters. So much for the phrase "In the beginning."

23. The Title "Word" Is to Be Interpreted by the Same Method as the Other Titles of Christ. The Word of God is Not a Mere Attribute of God, But a Separate Person. What is Meant When He is Called the Word.

Let us consider, however, a little more carefully what is the Word which is in the beginning. I am often led to wonder when I consider the things that are said about Christ, even by those who are in earnest in their belief in Him. Though there is a countless number of names which can be applied to our Savior, they omit the most of them, and if they should remember them, they declare that these titles are not to be understood in their proper sense, but tropically. But when they come to the title Logos (Word), and repeat that Christ alone is the Word of God, they are not consistent, and do not, as in the case of the other titles, search out what is behind the meaning of the term "Word." I wonder at the stupidity of the general run of Christians in this matter. I do not mince matters; it is nothing but stupidity. The Son of God says in one passage, "I am the light of the world," and in another, "I am the resurrection," and again, "I am the way and the truth and the life." It is also written, "I am the door," and we have the saying, "I am the good shepherd," and when the woman of Samaria says, "We know the Messiah is coming, who is called Christ; when He comes, He will tell us all things," Jesus answers, "I that speak unto thee am He." Again, when He washed the disciples' feet, He declared Himself in these words to be their Master and Lord: "You call Me Master and Lord, and you say well, for so I am." He also distinctly announces Himself as the Son of God, when He says, "He whom the Father sanctified and sent unto the world, to Him do you say, Thou blasphemes, because I said, I am the Son of God?" and "Father, the hour is come; glorify Thy Son, that the Son also may glorify Thee." We also find Him declaring Himself to be a king, as when He answers Pilate's question, "Art Thou the King of the Jews?" by saying, "My kingdom is not of this world; if My kingdom were of this world, then would My servants fight, that I should not be delivered to the Jews, but now is My kingdom not from hence." We have also read the words, "I am the true vine and My Father is the husbandman," and again, "I am the vine, ye are the branches." Add to these testimonies also the saying, "I am the bread of life, that came down from heaven and giveth life to the world." These texts will suffice for the present, which we have picked up out of the storehouse of the Gospels, and in all of which He claims to be the Son of God. But in the Apocalypse of John, too, He says, "I am the first and the last, and the living One, and I was dead. Behold, I am alive for evermore." And again, "I am the A and the Ω, and the first and the last, the beginning and the end." The careful student of the sacred books, moreover, may gather not a few similar passages from the prophets, as where He calls Himself a chosen shaft, and a servant of God, and a light of the Gentiles. Isaiah also says, "From my mother's womb hath He called me by my name, and He made my mouth as a sharp sword, and under the shadow of His hand did He hide me, and He said to me, Thou art My servant, O Israel, and in thee will I be glorified." And a little farther on: "And my God shall be my strength, and He said to me, this is a great thing for thee to be called My servant, to set up the tribes of Jacob and to turn again the diaspora of Israel. Behold I have set thee for a light of the Gentiles, that you should be for salvation to the end of the earth." And in Jeremiah too He likens Himself to a lamb, as thus: "I was as a gentle lamb that is led to the slaughter." These and other similar sayings He applies to Himself. In addition to these one might collect in the Gospels and the Apostles and in the prophets a countless number of titles which are applied to the Son of God, as the writers of the Gospels set forth their own views of what He is, or the Apostles extol Him out of what they had learned, or the prophets proclaim in advance His coming advent and announce the things concerning Him under various names. Thus John calls Him the Lamb of God, saying, "Behold the Lamb of God which taketh away the sins of the world," and in these words he declares Him as a man, "This is He about whom I said, that there cometh after me a man who is there before me; for He was before me." And in his Catholic Epistle John says that He is a Paraclete for our souls with the Father, as thus: "And if anyone sin, we have a Paraclete with the Father, Jesus Christ the righteous," and he adds that He is a propitiation for our sins, and similarly Paul says He is a propitiation: "Whom God set forth as a propitiation through faith in His blood, on account of forgiveness of the forepast sins, in the forbearance of God." According to Paul, too, He is declared to be the wisdom and the power of God, as in the Epistle to the Corinthians: "Christ the power of God and the wisdom of God." It is added that He is also sanctification and redemption: "He was made to us of God," he says, "wisdom and righteousness and sanctification and redemption." But he also teaches us, writing to the Hebrews, that Christ is a High-Priest: "Having, therefore, a great High-Priest, who has passed through the heavens, Jesus the Son of God, let us hold fast our profession." And the prophets have other names for Him besides these. Jacob in his blessing of his sons says, "Judah, thy brethren shall extol thee; thy hands are on the necks of thine enemies. A lion's whelp is Judah, from a shoot, my son, art thou sprung up; thou hast lain down and slept as a lion; who shall awaken him?" We cannot now linger over these phrases, to show that what is said of Judah applies to Christ. What may be quoted against this view, viz., "A ruler shall not part from Judah nor a leader from his loins, until He come for whom it is reserved;" this can better be cleared up on another occasion. But

Isaiah knows Christ to be spoken of under the names of Jacob and Israel, when he says, "Jacob is my servant, I will help Him; Israel is my elect, my soul hath accepted Him. He shall declare judgment to the Gentiles. He shall not strive nor cry, neither shall any one hear His voice on the streets. A bruised rod shall He not break, and smoking flax shall He not quench, till He bring forth judgment from victory, and in His name shall the nations hope." That it is Christ about whom such prophecies are made, Matthew shows in his Gospel, where he quotes from memory and says: "That the saying might be fulfilled, He shall not strive nor cry," etc. David also is called Christ, as where Ezekiel in his prophecy to the shepherds adds as from the mouth of God: "I will raise up David my servant, who shall be their shepherd." For it is not the patriarch David who is to rise and be the shepherd of the saints, but Christ. Isaiah also called Christ the rod and the flower: "There shall come forth a rod out of the root of Jesse, and a flower shall spring out of this root, and the spirit of God shall rest upon Him, the spirit of wisdom and understanding, the spirit of counsel and of might, the spirit of knowledge and of godliness, and He shall be full of the spirit of the fear of the Lord." And in the Psalms our Lord is called the stone, as follows: "The stone which the builders rejected is made the head of the corner. It is from the Lord, and it is wonderful in our eyes." And the Gospel shows, as also does Luke in the Acts, that the stone is no other than Christ; the Gospel as follows: "Have ye never read, the stone which the builders rejected is made the head of the corner. Whosoever falls on this stone shall be broken, but on whomsoever it shall fall, it will scatter him as dust." And Luke writes in Acts: "This is the stone, which was set at naught of you the builders, which has become the head of the corner." And one of the names applied to the Savior is that which He Himself does not utter, but which John records;—the Word who was in the beginning with God, God the Word. And it is worth our while to fix our attention for a moment on those scholars who omit consideration of most of the great names we have mentioned and regard this as the most important one. As to the former titles, they look for any account of them that anyone may offer, but in the case of this one they proceed differently and ask, What is the Son of God when called the Word? The passage they employ most is that in the Psalms, "My heart hath produced a good Word;" and they imagine the Son of God to be the utterance of the Father deposited, as it were, in syllables, and accordingly they do not allow Him, if we examine them farther, any independent hypostasis, nor are they clear about His essence. I do not mean that they confuse its qualities, but the fact of His having an essence of His own. For no one can understand how that which is said to be "Word" can be a Son. And such an animated Word, not being a separate entity from the Father, and accordingly as it, having no subsistence. is not a Son, or if he is a Son, let them say that God the Word is a separate being and has an essence of His own. We insist, therefore, that as in the case of each of the titles spoken of above we turn from the title to the concept it suggests and apply it and demonstrate how the Son of God is suitably described by it, the same course must be followed when we find Him called the Word. What caprice it is, in all these cases, not to stand upon the term employed, but to enquire in what sense Christ is to be understood to be the door, and in what way the vine, and why He is the way; but in the one case of His being called the Word, to follow a different course. To add to the authority, therefore, of what we have to say on the question, how the Son of God is the Word, we must begin with those names of which we spoke first as being applied to Him. This, we cannot deny, will seem to some to be superfluous and a digression, but the thoughtful reader will not think it useless to ask as to the concepts for which the titles are used; to observe these matters will clear the way for what is coming. And once we have entered upon the theology concerning the Savior, as we seek with what diligence we can and find the various things that are taught about Him, we shall necessarily understand more about Him not only in His character as the Word, but in His other characters also.

24. Christ as Light; How He, and How His Disciples are the Light of the World.

He said, then, that He was the light of the world; and we have to examine, along with this title, those which are parallel to it; and, indeed, are thought by some to be not merely parallel, but identical with it. He is the true light, and the light of the Gentiles. In the opening of the Gospel now before us He is the light of men: "That which was made," it says, "was life in Him, and the life was the light of men; and the light shines in darkness, and the darkness did not overtake it." A little further on, in the same passage, He is called the true light: "The true light, which lightens every man, was coming into the world." In Isaiah, He is the light of the Gentiles, as we said before. "Behold, I have set Thee for a light of the Gentiles, that You should be for salvation to the end of the earth." Now the sensible light of the world is the sun, and after it comes very worthily the moon, and the same title may be applied to the stars; but those lights of the world are said in Moses to have come into existence on the fourth day, and as they shed light on the things on the earth, they are not the true light. But the Savior shines on creatures which have intellect and sovereign reason, that their minds may behold their proper objects of vision, and so he is the light of the intellectual world, that is to say, of the reasonable souls which are in the sensible world, and if there be any beings beyond these in the world from which He declares Himself to be our Savior. He is, indeed, the most determining and distinguished part of that world, and, as we may say, the sun who makes the great day of the Lord. In view of this day He says to those who partake of His light, "Work while it is day; the night cometh when no man can work. As long as I am in the world, I am the light of the world." Then He says to His disciples, "Ye are the light of the world," and "Let your light shine before men." Thus we see the Church, the bride, to present an analogy to the moon and stars, and the disciples have a light, which is their own or borrowed from the true sun, so that they are able to illuminate those who have no command of any spring of light in themselves. We may say that Paul and Peter are the light of the world, and that those of their disciples who are enlightened themselves, but are not able to enlighten others, are the world of which the Apostles were the light. But the Savior, being the light of the world, illuminates not bodies, but by His incorporeal power the incorporeal intellect, to the end that each of us, enlightened as by the sun, may be able to discern the rest of the things of the mind. And as when the sun is shining the moon and the stars lose their power of giving light, so those who are irradiated by Christ and receive His beams have no need of the ministering apostles and prophets—we must have courage to declare this truth—nor of the angels; I will add that they have no need even of the greater powers when they are disciples of that first-born light. To those who do not receive the solar beams of Christ, the ministering saints do afford an illumination much less than the former; this illumination is as much as those persons can receive, and it completely fills them. Christ, again, the light of the world, is the true light as distinguished from the light of sense; nothing that is sensible is true. Yet though the sensible is other than the true, it does not follow that the sensible is false, for the sensible may have an analogy with the intellectual, and not everything that is not true can correctly be called false. Now I ask whether the light of the world is the same thing with the light of men, and I conceive that a higher power of light is intended by the former phrase than by the latter, for the world in one sense is not only men. Paul shows that the world is something more than men when he writes to the Corinthians in his first Epistle: "We are made a spectacle unto the world, and to angels, and to men." In one sense, too, it may be considered, the world is the creation which is being delivered from the bondage of corruption into the liberty of the glory of the children of God, whose earnest expectation is waiting for the manifestation of the sons of God. We also draw attention to the comparison which may be drawn between the statement, "I am the light of the world," and the words addressed to the disciples, "Ye are the light of the world." Some suppose that the genuine disciples of Jesus are greater than other creatures, some seeking the reason of this in the natural growth of these disciples, others inferring it from their harder struggle. For those beings which are in flesh and blood have greater labors and a life more full of dangers than those which are in an ethereal body, and the lights of heaven might not, if they had put on bodies of earth, have accomplished this life of ours free from danger and from error. Those who incline to this argument may appeal to those texts of Scripture which say the most exalted things about men, and to the fact that the Gospel is addressed directly to men; not so much is said about the creation, or, as we understand it, about the world. We read, "As I and Thou are one, that they also may be one in Us," and "Where I am, there will also My servant be." These sayings, plainly, are about men; while about the creation it is said that it is delivered from the bondage of corruption into the liberty of the glory of the children of God. It might be added that not even when it is delivered will it take part in the glory of the sons of God. Nor will those who hold this view forget that the first-born of every creature, honoring man above all else, became man, and that it was not any of the constellations existing in the sky, but one of another order, appointed for this purpose and in the service of the knowledge of Jesus, that was made to be the Star of the East, whether it was like the other stars or perchance better than they, to be the sign of Him who is the most excellent of all. And if the boasting of the saints is in their tribulations, since "tribulation worked patience, and patience probation, and probation hope, and hope makes not ashamed," then the afflicted creation cannot have the like patience with man, nor the like probation, nor the like hope, but another degree of these, since "the creation was made subject to vanity, not willingly, but on account of Him who subjected it, for hope." Now he who shrinks from conferring such great attributes on man will turn to another direction and say that the creature being subjected to vanity groans and suffers greater affliction than those who groan in this tabernacle, for has she not suffered for the utmost extent of time in her service of vanity—nay, many times as long as man? For why does she do this not willingly, but that it is against her nature to be subject to vanity, and not to have the best arrangement of her life, that which she shall receive when she is set free, when the world is destroyed and released even from the vanity of bodies. Here, however, we may appear to be stretching too far, and aiming at more than the question now before us requires. We may return, therefore, to the point from which we set out, and ask for what reason the Savior is called the light of the world, the true light, and the light of men. Now we saw that He is called the true light with reference to the sensible light of the world, and that the light of the world is the same thing as the light of men, or that we may at least enquire whether they are the same. This discussion is not superfluous. Some students do not take anything at all out of the statement that the Savior is the Word; and it is important for us to assure ourselves that we are not chargeable with caprice in fixing our attention on that notion. If it admits of being taken in a metaphorical sense we ought not to take it literally. When we apply the mystical and allegorical method to the expression "light of the world" and the many analogous terms mentioned above, we should surely do so with this expression also.

### 25. Christ as the Resurrection.

Now He is called the light of men and the true light and the light of the word, because He brightens and irradiates the higher parts of men, or, in a word, of all reasonable beings. And similarly it is from and because of the energy with which He causes the old deadness to be put aside and that which is *par excellence* life to be put on, so that those who have truly received Him rise again from the dead, that He is called the resurrection. And this He does not only at the moment at which a man says, "We are buried with Christ through baptism and have risen again with Him," but much rather when a man, having laid off all about him that belongs to death, walks in the newness of life which belongs to Him, the Son, while here. We always "carry about in our body the dying of the Lord Jesus," and thus we reap the vast advantage, "that the life of the Lord Jesus might be made manifest in our bodies."

26. Christ as the Way.

But that progress too, which is in wisdom and which is found by those who seek their salvation in it to do for them what they require both in respect of exposition of truth in the divine word and in respect of conduct according to true righteousness, it lets us understand how Christ is the way. In this way we have to take nothing with us, neither wallet nor coat; we must travel without even a stick, nor must we have shoes on our feet. For this road is itself sufficient for all the supplies of our journey; and everyone who walks on it wants nothing. He is clad with a garment which is fit for one who is setting out in response to an invitation to a wedding; and on this road he cannot meet anything that can annoy him. "No one," Solomon says, "can find out the way of a serpent upon a rock." I would add, or that of any other beast. Hence there is no need of a staff on this road, on which there is no trace of any hostile creature, and the hardness of which, whence also it is called rock (*petra*), makes it incapable of harboring anything hurtful.

## 27. Christ as the Truth.

Further, the Only-begotten is the truth, because He embraces in Himself according to the Father's will the whole reason of all things, and that with perfect clearness, and being the truth communicates to each creature in proportion to its worthiness. And should anyone enquire whether all that the Father knows, according to the depth of His riches and His wisdom and His knowledge, is known to our Savior also, and should he, imagining that he will thereby glorify the Father, show that some things known to the Father are unknown to the Son, although He might have had an equal share of the apprehensions of the unbegotten God, we must remind him that it is from His being the truth that He is Savior, and add that if He is the truth complete, then there is nothing true which He does not know; truth must not limp for the want of the things which, according to those persons, are known to the Father only. Or else let it be shown that some things are known to which the name of truth does not apply, but which are above the truth.

## 28. Christ as Life.

It is clear also that the principle of that life which is pure and unmixed with any other element, resides in Him who is the first-born of all creation, taking from which those who have a share in Christ live the life which is true life, while all those who are thought to live apart from this, as they have not the true light, have not the true life either.

29. Christ as the Door and as the Shepherd.

But as one cannot be in the Father or with the Father except by ascending from below upwards and coming first to the divinity of the Son, through which one may be led by the hand and brought to the blessedness of the Father Himself, so the Savior has the inscription "The Door." And as He is a lover of men, and approves the impulse of human souls to better things, even of those who do not hasten to reason (the Logos), but like sheep have a weakness and gentleness apart from all accuracy and reason, so He is the Shepherd. For the Lord saves men and beasts, and Israel and Juda are sowed with the seed not of men only but also of beasts.

30. Christ as Anointed (Christ) and as King.

In addition to these titles we must consider at the outset of our work that of Christ, and we must also consider that of King, and compare these two so as to find out the difference between them. Now it is said in the forty-fourth Psalm, "Thou hast loved righteousness and hated iniquity, whence Thou art anointed (Christ) above Thy fellows." His loving righteousness and hating iniquity were thus added claims in Him; His anointing was not contemporary with His being nor inherited by Him from the first. Anointing is a symbol of entering on the kingship, and sometimes also on the priesthood; and must we therefore conclude that the kingship of the Son of God is not inherited nor congenital to Him? But how is it conceivable that the First-born of all creation was not a king and became a king afterwards because He loved righteousness, when, moreover, He Himself was righteousness? We cannot fail to see that it is as a man that He is Christ, in respect of His soul, which was human and liable to be troubled and sore vexed, but that He is conceived as king in respect of the divine in Him. I find support for this in the seventy-first Psalm, which says, "Give the king Thy judgment, O God, and Thy righteousness to the king's Son, to judge Thy people in righteousness and Thy poor in judgment." This Psalm, though addressed to Solomon, is evidently a prophecy of Christ, and it is worthwhile to ask to what king the prophecy desires judgment to be given by God, and to what king's Son, and what king's righteousness is spoken of. I conceive, then, that what is called the King is the leading nature of the Firstborn of all creation, to which judgment is given on account of its eminence; and that the man whom He assumed, formed and molded by that nature, according to righteousness, is the King's Son. I am the more led to think that this is so, because the two beings are here brought together in one sentence, and are spoken of as if they were not two but one. For the Savior made both one, that is, He made them according to the prototype of the two which had been made one in Himself before all things. The two I refer to human nature, since each man's soul is mixed with the Holy Spirit, and each of those who are saved is thus made spiritual. Now as there are some to whom Christ is a shepherd, as we said before, because of their meek and composed nature, though they are less guided by reason; so there are those to whom He is a king, those, namely, who are led in their approach to religion rather by the reasonable part of their nature. And among those who are under a king there are differences; some experience his rule in a more mystic and hidden and more divine way, others in a less perfect fashion. I should say that those who, led by reason, apart from all agencies of sense, have beheld incorporeal things, the things which Paul speaks of as "invisible," or "not seen," that they are ruled by the leading nature of the Only-begotten, but that those who have only advanced as far as the reason which is conversant with sensible things, and on account of these glorify their Maker, that these also are governed by the Word, by Christ. No offence need be taken at our distinguishing these notions in the Savior; we draw the same distinctions in His substance.

31. Christ as Teacher and Master.

It is plain to all how our Lord is a teacher and an interpreter for those who are striving towards godliness, and on the other hand a master of those servants who have the spirit of bondage to fear, who make progress and hasten towards wisdom, and are found worthy to possess it. For "the servant knows not what the master wills," since he is no longer his master, but has become his friend. The Lord Himself teaches this, for He says to hearers who were still servants: "You call Me Master and Lord, and you say well, for so I am," but in another passage, "I call you no longer servants, for the servant knows not what is the will of his master, but I call you friends," because "you have continued with Me in all My temptations." They, then, who live according to fear, which God exacts from those who are not good servants, as we read in Malachi, "If I am a Master, where is My fear?" are servants of a master who is called their Savior.

32. Christ as Son.

None of these testimonies, however, sets forth distinctly the Savior's exalted birth; but when the words are addressed to Him, "Thou art My Son, this day have I begotten Thee," this is spoken to Him by God, with whom all time is to-day, for there is no evening with God, as I consider, and there is no morning, nothing but time that stretches out, along with His unbeginning and unseen life. The day is today with Him in which the Son was begotten, and thus the beginning of His birth is not found, as neither is the day of it.

33. Christ the True Vine, and as Bread.

To what we have said must be added how the Son is the true vine. Those will have no difficulty in apprehending this who understand, in a manner worthy of the prophetic grace, the saying: "Wine makes glad the heart of man." For if the heart be the intellectual part, and what rejoices it is the Word most pleasant of all to drink which takes us off human things, makes us feel ourselves inspired, and intoxicates us with an intoxication which is not irrational but divine, that, I conceive, with which Joseph made his brethren merry, then it is very clear how He who brings wine thus to rejoice the heart of man is the *true* vine. He is the true vine, because the grapes He bears are the truth, the disciples are His branches, and they, also, bring forth the truth as their fruit. It is somewhat difficult to show the difference between the vine and bread, for He says, not only that He is the vine, but that He is the bread of life. May it be that as bread nourishes and makes strong, and is said to strengthen the heart of man, but wine, on the contrary, pleases and rejoices and melts him, so ethical studies, bringing life to him who learns them and reduces them to practice, are the bread of life, but cannot properly be called the fruit of the vine, while secret and mystical speculations, rejoicing the heart and causing those to feel inspired who take them in, delighting in the Lord, and who desire not only to be nourished but to be made happy, are called the juice of the true vine, because they flow from it.

### 34. Christ as the First and the Last; He is Also What Lies between These.

Further, we have to ask in what sense He is called in the Apocalypse the First and the Last, and how, in His character as the First, He is not the same as the Alpha and the beginning, while in His character as the Last He is not the same as the Omega and the end. It appears to me, then, that the reasonable beings which exist are characterized by many forms, and that some of them are the first, some the second, some the third, and so on to the last. To pronounce exactly, however, which is the first, what kind of a being the second is, which may truly be designated third, and to carry this out to the end of the series, this is not a task for man, but transcends our nature. We shall yet venture, such as we are, to stand still a little at this point, and to make some observations on the matter. There are some gods of whom God is god, as we hear in prophecy, "Thank ye the God of gods," and "The God of gods hath spoken, and called the earth." Now God, according to the Gospel, "is not the God of the dead but of the living." Those gods, then, are living of whom God is god. The Apostle, too, writing to the Corinthians, says: "As there are gods many and lords many," and so we have spoken of these gods as really existing. Now there are, besides the gods of whom God is god, certain others, who are called thrones, and others called dominions, lordships, also, and powers in addition to these. The phrase, "above every name that is named, not only in this world, but also in that which is to come," leads us to believe that there are yet others besides these which are less familiar to us; one kind of these the Hebrews called Sabai, from which Sabaoth was formed, who is their ruler, and is none other than God. Add to all these the reasonable being who is mortal, man. Now the God of all things made first in honor some race of reasonable beings; this I consider to be those who are called gods, and the second order, let us say, for the present, are the thrones, and the third, undoubtedly, the dominions. And thus we come down in order to the last reasonable race, which, perhaps, cannot be any other than man. The Savior accordingly became, in a diviner way than Paul, all things to all, that He might either gain all or perfect them; it is clear that to men He became a man, and to the angels an angel. As for His becoming man no believer has any doubt, but as to His becoming an angel, we shall find reason for believing it was so, if we observe carefully the appearances and the words of the angels, in some of which the powers of the angels seem to belong to Him. In several passages angels speak in such a way as to suggest this, as when "the angel of the Lord appeared in a flame of fire. And he said, I am the God of Abraham and of Isaac and of Jacob." But Isaiah also says: "His name is called Angel of Great Counsel." The Savior, then, is the first and the last, not that He is not what lies between, but the extremities are named to show that He became all things. Consider, however, whether the last is man, or the things said to be under the earth, of which are the demons, all of them or some. We must ask, too, about those things which the Savior became which He speaks of through the prophet David, "And I became as a man without any to help him, free among the dead." His birth from the Virgin and His life so admirably lived showed Him to be more than man, and it was the same among the dead. He was the only free person there, and His soul was not left in hell. Thus, then, He is the first and the last. Again, if there be letters of God, as such there are, by reading which the saints may say they have read what is written on the tablets of heaven, these letters, by which heavenly things are to be read, are the notions, divided into small parts, into A and so on to Ω, the Son of God. Again, He is the beginning and the end, but He is this not in all His aspects equally. For He is the beginning, as the Proverbs teach us, inasmuch as He is wisdom; it is written: "The Lord founded Me in the beginning of His ways, for His works." In the respect of His being the Logos He is not the beginning. "The Word was in the beginning." Thus in His aspects one comes first and is the beginning, and there is a second after the beginning, and a third, and so on to the end, as if He had said, I am the beginning. Inasmuch as I am wisdom, and the second, perhaps, inasmuch as I am invisible, and the third in that I am life, for "what was made was life in Him." One who was qualified to examine and to discern the sense of Scripture might, no doubt, find many members of the series; I cannot say if he could find them all. "The beginning and the end" is a phrase we usually apply to a thing that is a completed unity; the beginning of a house is its foundation and the end the parapet. We cannot but think of this figure, since Christ is the stone which is the head of the corner, to the great unity of the body of the saved. For Christ the only begotten Son is all and in all, He is as the beginning in the man He assumed, He is present as the end in the last of the saints, and He is also in those between, or else He is present as the beginning in Adam, as the end in His life on earth, according to the saying: "The last Adam was made a quickening spirit." This saying harmonizes well with the interpretation we have given of the first and the last.

### 35. Christ as the Living and the Dead.

In what has been said about the first and the last, and about the beginning and the end, we have referred these words at one point to the different forms of reasonable beings, at another to the different conceptions of the Son of God. Thus we have gained a distinction between the first and the beginning, and between the last and the end, and also the distinctive meaning of A and Ω. It is not hard to see why he is called "the Living and the Dead," and after being dead He that is alive for evermore. For since we were not helped by His original life, sunk as we were in sin, He came down into our deadness in order that, He having died to sin, we, bearing about in our body the dying of Jesus. Might then receive that life of His which is for evermore. For those who always carry about in their body the dying of Jesus shall obtain the life of Jesus also, manifested in their bodies.

### 36. Christ as a Sword.

The texts of the New Testament, which we have discussed, are things said by Himself about Himself. Isaiah, however, He said that His mouth had been set by His Father as a sharp sword, and that He was hidden under the shadow of His hand, made like to a chosen shaft and kept close in the Father's quiver, called His servant by the God of all things, and Israel, and Light of the Gentiles. The mouth of the Son of God is a sharp sword, for "The word of God is living, and active, and sharper than any two-edged sword, and piercing to the dividing of soul and spirit, of both joints and marrow, and quick to discern the thoughts and intents of the heart." And indeed He came not to bring peace on the earth, that is, to corporeal and sensible things, but a sword, and to cut through, if I may say so, the disastrous friendship of soul and body, so that the soul, committing herself to the spirit which was against the flesh, may enter into friendship with God. Hence, according to the prophetic word, He made His mouth as a sword, as a sharp sword. Can anyone behold so many wounded by the divine love, like her in the Song of Songs, who complained that she was wounded: "I am wounded with love," and find the dart that wounded so many souls for the love of God, in any but Him who said, "He hath made Me as a chosen shaft."

37. Christ as a Servant, as the Lamb of God, and as the Man Whom John Did Not Know.

Again, let anyone consider how Jesus was to His disciples, not as He who sits at meat, but as He who serves, and how though the Son of God He took on Him the form of a servant for the sake of the freedom of those who were enslaved in sin, and he will be at no loss to account for the Father's saying to Him: "Thou art My servant," and a little further on: "It is a great thing that you should be called My servant." For we do not hesitate to say that the goodness of Christ appears in a greater and more divine light, and more according to the image of the Father, because "He humbled Himself, becoming obedient unto death, even the death of the cross," than if He had judged it a thing to be grasped to be equal with God, and had shrunk from becoming a servant for the salvation of the world. Hence He says, desiring to teach us that in accepting this state of servitude He had received a great gift from His Father: "And My God shall be My strength. And He said to Me, It is a great thing for Thee to be called My servant." For if He had not become a servant, He would not have raised up the tribes of Jacob, nor have turned the heart of the diaspora of Israel, and neither would He have become a light of the Gentiles to be for salvation to the ends of the earth. And it is no great thing for Him to become a servant, even if it is called a great thing by His Father, for this is in comparison with His being called with an innocent sheep and with a lamb. For the Lamb of God became like an innocent sheep being led to the slaughter, that He may take away the sin of the world. He who supplies reason (λογος) to all is made like a lamb which is dumb before her shearer, that we might be purified by His death, which is given as a sort of medicine against the opposing power, and also against the sin of those who open their minds to the truth. For the death of Christ reduced to impotence those powers which war against the human race, and it set free from sin by a power beyond our words the life of each believer. Since, then, He takes away sin until every enemy shall be destroyed and death last of all, in order that the whole world may be free from sin, therefore John points to Him and says: "Behold the Lamb of God which taketh away the sin of the world." It is not said that He will take it away in the future, nor that He is at present taking it, nor that He has taken it, but is not taking it away now. His taking away sin is still going on, He is taking it away from every individual in the world, till sin be taken away from the whole world, and the Savior deliver the kingdom prepared and completed to the Father, a kingdom in which no sin is left at all, and which, therefore, is ready to accept the Father as its king, and which on the other hand is waiting to receive all God has to bestow, fully, and in every part, at that time when the saying is fulfilled, "That God may be all in all." Further, we hear of a man who is said to be coming after John, who was made before him and was before him. This is to teach us that the man also of the Son of God, the man who was mixed with His divinity, was older than His birth from Mary. John says he does not know this man, but must he not have known Him when he leapt for joy when yet a babe unborn in Elisabeth's womb, as soon as the voice of Mary's salutation sounded in the ears of the wife of Zacharias? Consider, therefore, if the words "I know Him not" may have reference to the period before the bodily existence. Though he did not know Him before He assumed His body, yet he knew Him when yet in his mother's womb, and perhaps he is here learning something new about Him beyond what was known to him before, namely, that on whomsoever the Holy Spirit shall descend and abide on him, that is he who is to baptize with the Holy Spirit and with fire. He knew him from his mother's womb, but not all about Him. He did not know perhaps that this is He who baptizes with the Holy Spirit and with fire, when he saw the Spirit descending and abiding on Him. Yet that He was indeed a man, and the first man, John did not know.

38. Christ as Paraclete, as Propitiation, and as the Power of God.

But none of the names we have mentioned expresses His representation of us with the Father, as He pleads for human nature, and makes atonement for it; the Paraclete, and the propitiation, and the atonement. He has the name Paraclete in the Epistle of John: "If any man sin, we have a Paraclete with the Father, Jesus Christ the righteous." And He is said in the same epistle to be the atonement for our sins. Similarly, in the Epistle to the Romans, He is called a propitiation: "Whom God set forth to be a propitiation through faith." Of this proportion there was a type in the inmost part of the temple, the Holy of Holies, namely, the golden mercy-seat placed upon the two cherubim. But how could He ever be the Paraclete, and the atonement, and the propitiation without the power of God, which makes an end of our weakness, flows over the souls of believers, and is administered by Jesus, who indeed is prior to it and Himself the power of God, who enables a man to say: "I can do all things through Jesus Christ who strengthened me." Whence we know that Simon Magus, who gave himself the title of "The power of God, which is called great," was consigned to perdition and destruction, he and his money with him. We, on the contrary, who confess Christ as the true power of God, believe that we share with Him, inasmuch as He is that power, all things in which any energy resides.

39. Christ as Wisdom and Sanctification and Redemption.

We must not, however, pass over in silence that He is of right the wisdom of God, and hence is called by that name. For the wisdom of the God and Father of all things does not apprehend His substance in mere visions, like the phantasms of human thoughts. Whoever is able to conceive a bodiless existence of manifold speculations which extend to the rationale of existing things, living and, as it were, ensouled, he will see how well the Wisdom of God which is above every creature speaks of herself, when she says: "God created me the beginning of His ways, for His works." By this creating act the whole creation was enabled to exist, not being unreceptive of that divine wisdom according to which it was brought into being; for God, according to the prophet David, made all things in wisdom. But many things came into being by the help of wisdom, which do not lay hold of that by which they were created: and few things indeed there are which lay hold not only of that wisdom which concerns themselves, but of that which has to do with many things besides, namely, of Christ who is the whole of wisdom. But each of the sages, in proportion as he embraces wisdom, partakes to that extent of Christ, in that He is wisdom; just as everyone who is greatly gifted with power, in proportion as he has power, in that proportion also has a share in Christ, inasmuch as He is power. The same is to be thought about sanctification and redemption; for Jesus Himself is made sanctification to us and redemption. Each of us is sanctified with that sanctification, and redeemed with that redemption. Consider, moreover, if the words "to us," added by the Apostle, have any special force. Christ, he says, "was made to us of God, wisdom, and righteousness, and sanctification, and redemption." In other passages, he speaks about Christ as being wisdom, without any such qualification, and of His being power, saying that Christ is the power of God and the wisdom of God, though we might have conceived that He was not the wisdom of God or the power of God, absolutely, but only for us. Now, in respect of wisdom and power, we have both forms of the statement, the relative and the absolute; but in respect of sanctification and redemption, this is not the case. Consider, therefore, since "He that sanctifies and they that are sanctified are all of one," whether the Father is the sanctification of Him who is our sanctification, as, Christ being our head, God is His head. But Christ is our redemption because we had become prisoners and needed ransoming. I do not enquire as to His own redemption, for though He was tempted in all things as we are, He was without sin, and His enemies never reduced Him to captivity.

40. Christ as Righteousness; As the Demiurge, the Agent of the Good God, and as High-Priest.

Having expiscated the "to us" and the "absolutely"—sanctification and redemption being "to us" and not absolute, wisdom and redemption both to us and absolute—we must not omit to enquire into the position of righteousness in the same passage. That Christ is righteousness relatively to us appears clearly from the words: "Who was made to us of God wisdom and righteousness and sanctification and redemption." And if we do not find Him to be righteousness absolutely as He is the wisdom and the power of God absolutely, then we must enquire whether to Christ Himself, as the Father is sanctification, so the Father is also righteousness. There is, we know, no unrighteousness with God; He is a righteous and holy Lord, and His judgments are in righteousness, and being righteous, He orders all things righteously.

The heretics drew a distinction for purposes of their own between the just and the good. They did not make the matter very clear, but they considered that the demiurge was just, while the Father of Christ was good. That distinction may, I think, if carefully examined, be applied to the Father and the Son; the Son being righteousness, and having received power to execute judgment, because He is the Son of Man and will judge the world in righteousness, but the Father doing good to those who have been disciplined by the righteousness of the Son. This is after the kingdom of the Son; then the Father will manifest in His works His name the Good, when God becomes all in all. And perhaps by His righteousness the Savior prepares everything at the fit times, and by His word, by His ordering, by His chastisements, and, if I may use such an expression, by His spiritual healing aids, disposes all things to receive at the end the goodness of the Father. It was from His sense of that goodness that He answered him who addressed the Only-begotten with the words "Good Master," and said, "Why call Me good? None is good but one, God, the Father." This we have treated of elsewhere, especially in dealing with the question of the greater than the demiurge; Christ we have taken to be the demiurge, and the Father the greater than He. Such great things, then, He is, the Paraclete, the atonement, the propitiation, the sympathizer with our weaknesses, who was tempted in all human things, as we are, without sin; and in consequence He is a great High-Priest, having offered Himself as the sacrifice which is offered once for all, and not for men only but for every rational creature. For without God He tasted death for everyone. In some copies of the Epistle to the Hebrews the words are "by the grace of God." Now, whether He tasted death for everyone without God, He died not for men only but for all other intellectual beings too, or whether He tasted death for everyone by the grace of God, He died for all without God, for by the grace of God He tasted death for everyone. It would surely be absurd to say that He tasted death for human sins and not for any other being besides man which had fallen into sin, as for example for the stars. For not even the stars are clean in the eyes of God, as we read in Job, "The stars are not clean in His sight," unless this is to be regarded as a hyperbole. Hence he is a great High-Priest, since He restores all things to His Father's kingdom, and arranges that whatever defects exist in each part of creation shall be filled up so as to be full of the glory of the Father. This High-Priest is called, from some other notion of him than those we have noticed, Judas, that those who are Jews secretly may take the name of Jew not from Judah, son of Jacob, but from Him, since they are His brethren, and praise Him for the freedom they have attained. For it is He who sets them free, saving them from their enemies on whose backs He lays His hand to subdue them. When He has put under His feet the opposing power, and is alone in presence of His Father, then He is Jacob and Israel; and thus as we are made light by Him, since He is the light of the world, so we are made Jacob since He is called Jacob, and Israel since He is called Israel.

41. Christ as the Rod, the Flower, the Stone.

Now He receives the kingdom from the king whom the children of Israel appointed, beginning the monarchy not at the divine command and without even consulting God. He therefore fights the battles of the Lord and so prepares peace for His Son, His people, and this perhaps is the reason why He is called David. Then He is called a rod; such He is to those who need a harder and severer discipline, and have not submitted to the love and gentleness of God. On this account, if He is a rod, He has to "go forth;" He does not remain in Himself, but appears to go beyond His earlier state. Going forth, then, and becoming a rod, He does not remain a rod, but after the rod He becomes a flower that rises up, and after being a rod He is made known as a flower to those who, by His being a rod, have met with visitation. For "God will visit their iniquities with a rod," that is, Christ. But "His mercy He will not take from him," for He will have mercy on him, for on whom the Son has mercy the Father has mercy also. An interpretation may be given which makes Him a rod and a flower in respect of different persons, a rod to those who have need of chastisement, a flower to those who are being saved; but I prefer the account of the matter given above. We must add here, however, that, perhaps, looking to the end, if Christ is a rod to any man He is also a flower to him, while it is not the case that he who receives Him as a flower must also know Him as a rod. And yet as one flower is more perfect than another and plants are said to flower, even though they bring forth no perfect fruit, so the perfect receive that of Christ which transcends the flower. Those, on the other hand, who have known Him as a rod will partake along with it, not in His perfection, but in the flower which comes before the fruit. Last of all, before we come to the word Logos, Christ was a stone, set at naught by the builders but placed on the head of the corner, for the living stones are built up as on a foundation on the other stones of the Apostles and prophets, Christ Jesus Himself our Lord being the chief corner-stone, because He is a part of the building made of living stones in the land of the living; therefore He is called a stone. All this we have said to show how capricious and baseless is the procedure of those who, when so many names are given to Christ, take the mere appellation "the Word," without enquiring, as in the case of His other titles, in what sense it is used; surely they ought to ask what is meant when it is said of the Son of God that He was the Word, and God, and that He was in the beginning with the Father, and that all things were made by Him.

42. Of the Various Ways in Which Christ is the Logos.

As, then, from His activity in enlightening the world whose light He is, Christ is named the Light of the World, and as from His making those who sincerely attach themselves to Him put away their deadness and rise again and put on newness of life, He is called the Resurrection, so from an activity of another kind He is called Shepherd and Teacher, King and Chosen Shaft, and Servant, and in addition to these Paraclete and Atonement and Propitiation. And after the same fashion He is also called the Logos, because He takes away from us all that is irrational, and makes us truly reasonable, so that we do all things, even to eating and drinking, to the glory of God, and discharge by the Logos to the glory of God both the commoner functions of life and those which belong to a more advanced stage. For if, by having part in Him, we are raised up and enlightened, herded also it may be and ruled over, then it is clear that we become in a divine manner reasonable, when He drives away from us what in us is irrational and dead, since He is the Logos (reason) and the Resurrection. Consider, however, whether all men have in some way part in Him in His character as Logos. On this point the Apostle teaches us that He is to be sought not outside the seeker, and that those find Him in themselves who set their heart on doing so; "Say not in thy heart, Who shall ascend into heaven? That is to bring Christ down; or, Who shall descend into the abyss? That is to bring Christ up from the dead. But what says the Scripture? The Word is very nigh thee, in thy mouth and in thy heart," as if Christ Himself were the same thing as the Word said to be sought after. But when the Lord Himself says "If I had not come and spoken unto them, they had not had sin; but now they have no cloak for their sin," the only sense we can find in His words is that the Logos Himself says that those are not chargeable with sin to whom He (reason) has not fully come, but that those, if they sin, are guilty who, having had part in Him, act contrary to the ideas by which He declares His full presence in us. Only when thus read is the saying true: "If I had not come and spoken to them, they had not had sin." Should the words be applied, as many are of opinion that they should, to the visible Christ, then how is it true that those had no sin to whom He did not come? In that case all who lived before the advent of the Savior will be free from sin, since Jesus, as seen in flesh, had not yet come. And more—all those to whom He has never been preached will have no sin, and if they have no sin, then it is clear they are not liable to judgment. But the Logos in man, in which we have said that our whole race had part, is spoken of in two senses; first, in that of the filling up of ideas which takes place, prodigies excepted, in everyone who passes beyond the age of boyhood, but secondly, in that of the consummation, which takes place only in the perfect. The words, therefore, "If I had not come and spoken to them, they would not have had sin, but now they have no cloak for their sin," are to be understood in the former sense; but the words, "All that ever came before me are thieves and robbers, and the sheep did not hear them," in the latter. For before the consummation of reason comes, there is nothing in man but what is blameworthy; all is imperfect and defective, and can by no means command the obedience of those irrational elements in us which are tropically spoken of as sheep. And perhaps the former meaning is to be recognized in the words "The Logos was made flesh," but the second in "The Logos was God." We must accordingly look at what there is to be seen in human affairs between the saying, "The Word (reason) was made flesh" and "The Word was God." When the Word was made flesh can we say that it was to some extent broken up and thinned out, and can we say that it recovered from that point onward till it became again what it was at first, God the Word, the Word with the Father; the Word whose glory John saw, the verily only begotten, as from the Father. But the Son may also be the Logos (Word), because He reports the secret things of His Father who is intellect in the same way as the Son who is called the Word. For as with us the word is a messenger of those things which the mind perceives, so the Word of God, knowing the Father, since no created being can approach Him without a guide, reveals the Father whom He knows. For no one knows the Father save the Son, and he to whomsoever the Son reveals Him, and inasmuch as He is the Word He is the Messenger of Great Counsel, who has the government upon His shoulders; for He entered on His kingdom by enduring the cross. In the Apocalypse, moreover, the Faithful and True (the Word), is said to sit on a white horse, the epithets indicating, I consider, the clearness of the voice with which the Word of truth speaks to us when He sojourns among us. This is scarcely the place to show how the word "horse" is often used in passages spoken for our encouragement in sacred learning. I only cite two of these: "A horse is deceitful for safety," and "Some trust in chariots and some in horses, but we will rejoice in the name of the Lord our God." Nor must we leave unnoticed a passage in the forty-fourth Psalm, frequently quoted by many writers as if they understood it: "My heart hath belched forth a good word, I speak my works to the King." Suppose it is God the Father who speaks thus; what is His heart, that the good word should appear in accordance with His heart? If, as these writers suppose, the Word (Logos) needs no interpretation, then the heart is to be taken in the natural sense too. But it is quite absurd to suppose God's heart to be a part of Him as ours is of our body. We must remind such writers that as when the hand of God is spoken of, and His arm and His finger, we do not read the words literally but enquire in what sound sense we may take them so as to be worthy of God, so His heart is to be understood of His rational power, by which He disposes all things, and His word of that which announces what is in this heart of His. But who is it that announces the counsel of the Father to those of His creatures who are worthy and who have risen above themselves, who but the Savior? That "belched forth" is not, perhaps, without significance; a hundred other terms might have been employed; "My heart has produced a good word," it might have been said, or "My heart has spoken a good word." But in belching, some wind that was hidden makes its way out to the world, and so it may be that the Father gives out views of truth not continuously, but as it were after the fashion of belching, and the word has the character of the things thus produced, and is called, therefore, the image of the invisible God. We may enter our agreement, therefore, with the ordinary acceptation of these words, and take them to be spoken by the Father. It is not, however, a matter of course, that it is God Himself who announces these things. Why should it not be a prophet? Filled with the Spirit and unable to contain himself, he brings forth a word about his prophecy concerning Christ: "My heart hath belched forth a good word, I speak my works to the King, my pen is the tongue of a ready writer. Excellent in beauty is He beyond the sons of men." Then to the Christ Himself: "Grace is poured out on Thy lips." If the Father were the speaker, how could He go on after the words, "Grace is poured out on thy lips," to say, "Therefore God hath blessed thee forever," and a little further on, "Therefore God, thy God, hath anointed thee with the oil of gladness above thy fellows." Some of those who wish to make the Father the speaker may appeal to the words, "Hear, O daughter, and behold and incline thine ear, and forget thy people and thy father." The prophet, it may be said, could not address the Church in the words, "Hear, O daughter." It is not difficult, however, to show that changes of person occur frequently in the Psalms, so that these words, "Hear, O daughter," might be from the Father, in this passage, though the Psalm as a whole is not. To our discussion of the Word we may here add the passage, "By the word of the Lord were the heavens founded, and all the power of them by the breath of His mouth." Some refer this to the Savior and the Holy Spirit. The passage, however, does not necessarily imply any more than that the heavens were founded by the reason (logos) of God, as when we say that a house is built by the plan (logos) of the architect, or a ship by the plan (logos) of the shipbuilder. In the same way the heavens were founded (made solid) by the Word of God, for they are of a more divine substance, which on this account is called solid; it has little fluidity for the most part, nor is it easily melted like other parts of the world, and specially the lower parts. On account of this difference the heavens are said in a special manner to be constituted by the Word of God.

The saying then stands, first, "In the beginning was the Logos;" we are to place that full in our view; but the testimonies we cited from the Proverbs led us to place wisdom first, and to think of wisdom as preceding the Word which announces her. We must observe, then, that the Logos is in the beginning, that is, in wisdom, always. Its being in wisdom, which is called the beginning, does not prevent it from being with God and from being God, and it is not simply with God, but is in the beginning, in wisdom, with God. For he goes on: "He was in the beginning with God." He might have said, "He was with God;" but as He was in the beginning, so He was with God in the beginning, and "All things were made by Him," being in the beginning, for God made all things, as David tells us, in wisdom. And to let us understand that the Word has His own definite place and sphere as one who has life in Himself (and is a distinct person), we must also speak about powers, not about power. "Thus says the Lord of powers, (A.V. hosts)" we frequently read; there are certain creatures, rational and divine, which are called powers: and of these Christ was the highest and best, and is called not only the wisdom of God but also His power. As, then, there are several powers of God, each of them in its own form, and the Savior is different from these, so also Christ, even if that which is Logos in us is not in respect of form outside of us, will be understood from our discussion up to this point to be the Logos, who has His being in the beginning, in wisdom. This for the present may suffice, on the word: "In the beginning was the Logos."

## Book II.

1. *"And the Word was with God, and the Word was God."* In the preceding section, my revered brother Ambrosius, brother formed according to the Gospel, we have discussed, as far as is at present in our power, what the Gospel is, and what is the beginning in which the Word was, and what the Word is which was in the beginning. We now come to consider the next point in the work before us, How the Word was with God. To this end it will be of service to remember that what is called the Word came to certain persons; as "The Word of the Lord which came to Hosea, the son of Beeri," and "The Word which came to Isaiah, the son of Amos, concerning Judah and concerning Jerusalem," and "The Word which came to Jeremiah concerning the drought." We must enquire how this Word came to Hosea, and how it came also to Isaiah the son of Amos, and again to Jeremiah concerning the drought; the comparison may enable us to find out how the Word was with God. The generality will simply look at what the prophets said, as if that were the Word of the Lord or the Word, that came to them. May it not be, however, that as we say that this person comes to that, so the Son, the Word, of whom we are now theologizing, came to Hosea, sent to him by the Father; historically, that

is to say, to the son of Beeri, the prophet Hosea, but mystically to him who is saved, for Hosea means, etymologically, *Saved*; and to the son of Beeri, which etymologically means wells, since everyone who is saved becomes a son of that spring which gushes forth out of the depths, the wisdom of God. And it is nowise marvelous that the saint should be a son of wells. From his brave deeds he is often called a son, whether, from his works shining before men, of light, or from his possessing the peace of God which passes all understanding, of peace, or, once more, from the help which wisdom brings him, a child of wisdom; for wisdom, it says, is justified of her children. Thus he who by the divine spirit searches all things, and even the deep things of God, so that he can exclaim, "O the depth of the riches both of the wisdom and the knowledge of God!" he can be a son of wells, to whom the Word of the Lord comes. Similarly the Word comes also to Isaiah, teaching the things which are coming upon Judæa and Jerusalem in the last days; and so also it comes to Jeremiah lifted up by a divine elation. For Iao means etymologically lifting up, elation. Now the Word comes to men who formerly could not receive the advent of the Son of God who is the Word; but to God it does not come, as if it had not been with Him before. The Word was always with the Father; and so it is said, "And the Word was with God." He did not come to God, and this same word "was" is used of the Word because He was in the beginning at the same time when He was with God, neither being separated from the beginning nor being bereft of His Father. And again, neither did He come to be in the beginning after He had not been in it, nor did He come to be with God after not having been with Him. For before all time and the remotest age the

Word was in the beginning, and the Word was with God. Thus to find out what is meant by the phrase, "The Word was with God," we have adduced the words used about the prophets, how He came to Hosea, to Isaiah, to Jeremiah, and we have noticed the difference, by no means accidental, between "became" and "was." We have to add that in His coming to the prophets He illuminates the prophets with the light of knowledge, causing them to see things which had been before them, but which they had not understood till then. With God, however, He is God, just because He is with Him. And perhaps it was because he saw some such order in the Logos, that John did not place the clause "The Word was God" before the clause "The Word was with God." The series in which he places his different sentences does not prevent the force of each axiom from being separately and fully seen. One axiom is, "In the beginning was the Word," a second, "The Word was with God," and then comes, "And the Word was God." The arrangement of the sentences might be thought to indicate an order; we have first "In the beginning was the Word," then, "And the Word was with God," and thirdly, "And the Word was God," so that it might be seen that the Word being with God makes Him God.

2. In What Way the Logos is God. Errors to Be Avoided on This Question. We next notice John's use of the article in these sentences. He does not write without care in this respect, nor is he unfamiliar with the niceties of the Greek tongue. In some cases he uses the article, and in some he omits it. He adds the article to the Logos, but to the name of God he adds it sometimes only. He uses the article, when the name of God refers to the uncreated

cause of all things, and omits it when the Logos is named God. Does the same difference which we observe between God with the article and God without it prevail also between the Logos with it and without it? We must enquire into this. As the God who is over all is God with the article not without it, so "the Logos" is the source of that reason (Logos) which dwells in every reasonable creature; the reason which is in each creature is not, like the former called *par excellence* The Logos. Now there are many who are sincerely concerned about religion, and who fall here into great perplexity. They are afraid that they may be proclaiming two Gods, and their fear drives them into doctrines which are false and wicked. Either they deny that the Son has a distinct nature of His own besides that of the Father, and make Him whom they call the Son to be God all but the name, or they deny the divinity of the Son, giving Him a separate existence of His own, and making His sphere of essence fall outside that of the Father, so that they are separable from each other. To such persons we have to say that God on the one hand is Very God (Autotheos, God of Himself); and so the Savior says in His prayer to the Father, "That they may know Thee the only true God;" but that all beyond the Very God is made God by participation in His divinity, and is not to be called simply God (with the article), but rather God (without article). And thus the first-born of all creation, who is the first to be with God, and to attract to Himself divinity, is a being of more exalted rank than the other gods beside Him, of whom God is the God, as it is written, "The God of gods, the Lord, hath spoken and called the earth." It was by the offices of the first-born that they became gods, for He drew from God in generous measure that they should be made gods, and He communicated it to them according to His own bounty. The true God, then, is "The God," and those who are formed after Him are gods, images, as it were, of Him the prototype. But the archetypal image, again, of all these images is the Word of God, who was in the beginning, and who by being with God is at all times God, not possessing that of Himself, but by His being with the Father, and not continuing to be God, if we should think of this, except by remaining always in uninterrupted contemplation of the depths of the Father.

### 3. Various Relations of the Logos to Men.

Now it is possible that some may dislike what we have said representing the Father as the one true God, but admitting other beings besides the true God, who have become gods by having a share of God. They may fear that the glory of Him who surpasses all creation may be lowered to the level of those other beings called gods. We drew this distinction between Him and them that we showed God the Word to be to all the other gods the minister of their divinity. To this we must add, in order to obviate objections, that the reason which is in every reasonable creature occupied the same relation to the reason who was in the beginning with God, and is God the Word, as God the Word occupies to God. As the Father who is Very God and the True God is to His image and to the images of His image— men are said to be according to the image, not to be images of God—so He, the Word, is to the reason (word) in every man. Each fills the place of a fountain—the Father is the fountain of divinity, the Son of reason. As, then, there are many gods, but to us there is but one God the Father, and many Lords, but to us there is one Lord, Jesus Christ, so there are many

Λόγοι, but we, for our part, pray that that one Λόγος may be with us who was in the beginning and was with God, God the Logos. For whoever does not receive this Logos who was in the beginning with God, or attach himself to Him as He appeared in flesh, or take part in some of those who had part in this Logos, or whoever having had part in Him falls away from Him again, he will have his portion in what is called most opposite to reason. What we have drawn out from the truths with which we started will now be clear enough. First, we spoke about God and the Word of God, and of Gods, either, that is, beings who partake in deity or beings who are called Gods and are not. And again of the Logos of God and of the Logos of God made flesh, and of logoi, or beings which partake in some way of the Logos, of second logoi or of third, thought to be logoi, in addition to that Logos that was before them all, but not really so. Irrational Reasons these may be styled; beings are spoken of who are said to be Gods but are not, and one might place beside these Gods who are no Gods, Reasons which are no Reasons. Now the God of the universe is the God of the elect, and in a much greater degree of the Saviors of the elect; then He is the God of these beings who are truly Gods, and then He is the God, in a word, of the living and not of the dead. But God the Logos is the God, perhaps, of those who attribute everything to Him and who consider Him to be their Father. Now the sun and the moon and the stars were connected, according to the accounts of men of old times, with beings who were not worthy to have the God of gods counted their God. To this opinion they were led by a passage in Deuteronomy which is somewhat on this wise: "Lest when thou lifts up thine eyes to heaven, and sees the sun and the moon and the whole host of heaven, thou wander away and worship them and serve them which the Lord thy God hath appointed to all the peoples. But to you the Lord thy God hath not so given them." But how did God appoint the sun and the moon and all the host of heaven to all the nations, if He did not give them in the same way to Israel also, to the end that those who could not rise to the realm of intellect, might be inclined by gods of sense to consider about the Godhead, and might of their own free will connect themselves with these and so be kept from falling away to idols and demons? Is it not the case that some have for their God the God of the universe, while a second class, after these, attach themselves to the Son of God, His Christ, and a third class worship the sun and the moon and all the host of heaven, wandering, it is true, from God, but with a far different and a better wandering than that of those who invoke as gods the works of men's hands, silver and gold,—works of human skill. Last of all are those who devote themselves to the beings which are called gods but are no gods. In the same way, now, some have faith in that Reason which was in the beginning and was with God and was God; so did Hosea and Isaiah and Jeremiah and others who declared that the Word of the Lord, or the Logos, had come to them. A second class are those who know nothing but Jesus Christ and Him crucified, considering that the Word made flesh is the whole Word, and knowing only Christ after the flesh. Such is the great multitude of those who are counted believers. A third class give themselves to logoi (discourses) having some part in the Logos which they consider superior to all other reason: these are they who follow the honorable and distinguished philosophical schools among the Greeks. A fourth class besides these are they who put their trust in corrupt and godless discourses, doing away with Providence, which is so manifest and almost visible, and who recognize another end for man to follow than the good. It may appear to some that we have wandered from our theme, but to my thinking the view we have reached of four things connected with the name of God and four things connected with the Logos comes in very well at this point. There was God with the article and God without the article, then there were gods in two orders, at the summit of the higher order of whom is God the Word, transcended Himself by the God of the universe. And, again, there was the Logos with the article and the Logos without the article, corresponding to God absolutely and a god; and the Logoi in two ranks. And some men are connected with the Father, being part of Him, and next to these, those whom our argument now brings into clearer light, those who have come to the Savior and take their stand entirely in Him. And third are those of whom we spoke before, who reckon the sun and the moon and the stars to be gods, and take their stand by them. And in the fourth and last place those who submit to soulless and dead idols. To all this we find analogies in what concerns the Logos. Some are adorned with the Word Himself; some with what is next to Him and appears to be the very original Logos Himself, those, namely, who know nothing but Jesus Christ and Him crucified, and who behold the Word as flesh. And the third class, as we described them a little before. Why should I speak of those who are thought to be in the Logos, but have fallen away, not only from the good itself, but from the very traces of it and from those who have a part in it?

4. That the Logos is One, Not Many. Of the Word, Faithful and True, and of His White Horse.

*"He was in the beginning with God."* By his three foregoing propositions the Evangelist has made us acquainted with three orders, and he now sums up the three in one, saying, "This (Logos) was in the beginning with God." In the first premise we learned where the Logos was: He was in the beginning; then we learned with whom He was, with God; and then who He was, that He was God. He now points out by this word "He," the Word who is God, and gathers up into a fourth proposition the three which went before, "In the beginning was the Word," "The Word was with God," and "The Word was God." Now he says, He, this (Word) was in the beginning with God. The term beginning may be taken of the beginning of the world, so that we may learn from what is said that the Word was older than the things which were made from the beginning. For if "in the beginning God created heaven and earth," but "He" was in the beginning, then the Logos is manifestly older than those things which were made at the beginning, older not only than the firmament and the dry land, but than the heavens and earth. Now someone might ask, and not unreasonably, why it is not said, "In the beginning was the Word of God, and the Word of God was with God, and the Word of God was God." But he who asked such a question could be shown to be taking for granted that there are a plurality of logoi, differing perhaps from each other in kind, one being the word of God, another perhaps the word of angels, a third of men, and so on with the other logoi. Now, if this were so with the Logos, the case would be the same with wisdom and with righteousness. But it would be absurd that there should be a number of

things equally to be called "The Word;" and the same would apply to wisdom and to righteousness. We shall be driven to confess that we ought not to look for a plurality of logoi, or of wisdom, or of righteousness, if we look at the case of truth. Anyone will confess that there is only one truth; it could never be said in this case that there is one truth of God, and another of the angels, and another of man,—it lies in the nature of things that the truth about anything is one. Now, if truth be one, it is clear that the preparation of it and its demonstration, which is wisdom, must in reason be conceived as one, since what is regarded as wisdom cannot justly claim that title where truth, which is one, is absent from its grasp. But if truth is one and wisdom one, then Reason (Logos) also, which announces truth and makes truth simple and manifest to those who are fitted to receive it, will be one. This we say, by no means denying that truth and wisdom and reason are of God, but we wish to indicate the purpose of the omission in this passage of the words "of God," and of the form of the statement, "In the beginning the Logos was with God." The same John in the Apocalypse gives Him His name with the addition "of God," where he says: "And I saw heaven opened, and behold a white horse, and He that sat thereon called Faithful and True; and in righteousness doth He judge and make war. And His eyes are as a flame of fire, and on His head are many diadems, and He hath a name written which no one knows but He Himself. And He is arrayed in a garment sprinkled with blood, and His name is called Word of God. And His armies in heaven followed Him on white horses, clothed in pure fine linen. And out of His mouth proceeded a sharp sword, that with it He should smite the nations, and He shall rule them with a rod of iron, and He treaded the winepress of the fierceness of the wrath of Almighty God. And He hath on His garment and on His thigh a name written: King of kings, and Lord of lords." In this passage Logos is necessarily spoken of absolutely without the article, and also with the addition Logos of God; had the first not been the case (i.e., had the article been given) we might have been led to take up the meaning wrongly, and so to depart from the truth about the Logos. For if it had been called simply Logos, and had not been said to be the Logos of God, then we would not be clearly informed that the Logos is the Logos of God. And, again, had it been called Logos of God but not said to be Logos absolutely, then we might imagine many logoi, according to the constitution of each of the rational beings which exist; then we might assume a number of logoi properly so called. Again, in his description in the Apocalypse of the Logos of God, the Apostle and Evangelist (and the Apocalypse entitles him to be styled a prophet, too) says he saw the Word of God in the opened heaven, and that He was riding on a white horse. Now we must consider what he means to convey when he speaks of heaven being opened and of the white horse, and of the Word of God riding on the white horse, and also what is meant by saying that the Word of God is Faithful and True, and that in righteousness He judges and makes war. All this will greatly advance our study on the subject of the Word of God. Now I conceive heaven to have been shut against the ungodly, and those who bear the image of the earthly, and to have been opened to the righteous and those adorned with the image of the heavenly. For to the former, being below and still dwelling in the flesh, the better things are closed, since they cannot understand them and have neither power nor will to see their beauty, looking down as they do and not striving to look up. But to the excellent, or those who have their commonwealth in heaven, he opens, with the key of David, the things in heavenly places and discloses them to their view, and makes all clear to them by riding on his horse. These words also have their meaning; the horse is white because it is the nature of higher knowledge (γνῶσις) to be clear and white and full of light. And on the white horse sits He who is called Faithful, seated more firmly, and so to speak more royally, on words which cannot be set aside, words which run sharply and more swiftly than any horse, and overhear in their rushing course every so-called word that simulates the Word, and every so-called truth that simulates the Truth. He who sits on the white horse is called Faithful, not because of the faith He cherishes, but of that which He inspires, because He is worthy of faith. Now the Lord Jehovah, according to Moses, is Faithful and True. He is true also in respect of His relation to shadow, type, and image; for such is the Word who is in the opened heaven, for He is not on earth as He is in heaven; on earth He is made flesh and speaks through shadow, type, and image. The multitude, therefore, of those who are reputed to believe are disciples of the shadow of the Word, not of the true Word of God which is in the opened heaven. Hence Jeremiah says, "The Spirit of our face is Christ the Lord, of whom we said, In His shadow shall we live among the nations." Thus the Word of God who is called Faithful is also called True, and in righteousness He judges and makes war; since He has received from God the faculty of judging in very righteousness and very judgment, and of apportioning its due to every existing creature. For none of those who have some portion of righteousness and of the faculty of judgment can receive on his soul such copies and impressions of righteousness and judgment as to come short in no point of absolute righteousness and absolute justice, just as no painter of a picture can communicate to the representation all the qualities of the original. This, I conceive, is the reason why David says, "Before Thee shall no living being be justified." He does not say, no man, or no angel, but no living being, since even if any being partakes of life and has altogether put off mortality, not even then can it be justified in comparison of Thee, who art, as it were, Life itself. Nor is it possible that one who partakes of life and is therefore called living, should become life itself, or that one who partakes of righteousness and, therefore, is called righteous should become equal to righteousness itself. Now it is the function of the Word of God, not only to judge in righteousness, but also to make war in righteousness, that by making war on His enemies by reason and righteousness, so that what is irrational and wicked is destroyed, He may dwell in the soul of him who, for his salvation, so to speak, has become captive to Christ, and may justify that soul and cast out from her all adversaries. We shall, however, obtain a better view of this war which the Word carries on if we remember that He is an ambassador for the truth, while there is another who pretends to be the Word and is not, and one who calls herself the truth and is not, but a lie. Then the Word, arming Himself against the lie, slays it with the breath of His mouth and brings it to naught by the manifestation of His coming. And consider whether these words of the Apostle to the Thessalonians may be understood in an intellectual sense. For what is that which is destroyed by the breath of the mouth of Christ, Christ being the Word and Truth and Wisdom, but the lie? And what is that which is brought to naught by the manifestation of Christ's coming, Christ being conceived as wisdom and reason, what but that which announces itself as wisdom, when in reality it is one of those things with which God deals as the Apostle describes, "He taketh the wise, those who are not wise with the true wisdom, in their own craftiness"? To what he says of the rider on the white horse, John adds the wonderful statement: "His eyes are like a flame of fire." For as the flame of fire is bright and illuminating, but at the same time fiery and destructive of material things, so, if I may so say, are the eyes of the Logos with which He sees, and everyone who has part in Him; they have not only the inherent quality of laying hold of the things of the mind, but also that of consuming and putting away those conceptions which are more material and gross, since whatever is in any way false flees from the directness and lightness of truth. It is in a very natural order that after speaking of Him who judges in righteousness and makes war in accordance with His righteous judgments, and then after His warring of His giving light, the writer goes on to say, "On His head are many diadems." For had the lie been one, and of one form only, against which the True and Faithful Word contended, and for conquering which, He was crowned, then one crown alone would naturally have been given Him for the victory. As it is, however, as the lies are many which profess the truth and for warring against which the Word is crowned, the diadems are many which surround the head of the conqueror of them all. As He has overcome every revolting power many diadems mark His victory. Then after the diadems He is said to have a name written which no one knows but He Himself. For there are some things which are known to the Word alone; for the beings which come into existence after Him have a poorer nature than His, and none of them is able to behold all that He apprehends. And perhaps it is the case that only those who have part in that Word know the things which are kept from the knowledge of those who do not partake of Him. Now, in John's vision, the Word of God as He rides on the white horse is not naked: He is clothed with a garment sprinkled with blood, for the Word who was made flesh and therefore died is surrounded with marks of the fact that His blood was poured out upon the earth, when the soldier pierced His side. For of that passion, even should it be our lot someday to come to that highest and supreme contemplation of the Logos, we shall not lose all memory, nor shall we forget the truth that our admission was brought about by His sojourning in our body. This Word of God is followed by the heavenly armies one and all; they follow the Word as their leader, and imitate Him in all things, and chiefly in having mounted, they also, white horses. To him that understands, this secret is open. And as sorrow and grief and wailing fled away at the end of things, so also, I suppose, did obscurity and doubt, all the mysteries of God's wisdom being precisely and clearly opened. Look also at the white horses of the followers of the Word and at the white and pure linen with which they were clothed. As linen comes out of the earth, may not those linen garments stand for the dialects on the earth in which those voices are clothed which make clear announcements of things? We have dealt at some length with the statements found in the Apocalypse about the Word of God; it is important for us to know clearly about Him.

5. He (This One) Was in the Beginning with God.

To those who fail to distinguish with care the different propositions of the context the Evangelist may appear to be repeating himself. "He was in the beginning with God" may seem to add nothing to "And the Word was with God." We must observe more carefully. In the statement "The Word was with God" we are not told anything of the when or the where; that is added in the fourth axiom. There are four axioms, or, as some call them, propositions, the fourth being "He was in the beginning with God." Now "The Word was with God" is not the same thing as "He was," etc.; for here we are told, not only that He was with God, but when and where He was so: "He was in the beginning with God." The "He," too, used as it is for a demonstration, will be considered to refer to the Word, or by a less careful enquirer, to God. What was noted before is now summed up in this designation "He," the notion of the Logos and that of God; and as the argument proceeds the different notions are collected in one; for the notion God is not included in the notion Logos, nor the notion Logos in that of God. And perhaps the proposition before us is a summing up in one of the three which have preceded. Taking the statement that the Word was in the beginning, we have not yet learned that He was with God, and taking the statement that the Word was with God it is not yet clear to us that He was with God in the beginning; and taking the statement that the Word was God, it has neither been shown that He was in the beginning, nor that He was with God.

Now when the Evangelist says, "He was in the beginning with God," if we apply the pronoun "He" to the Word and to God (as He is God) and consider that "in the beginning" is conjoined with it, and "with God" added to it, then there is nothing left of the three propositions that is not summed up and brought together in this one. And as "in the beginning" has been said twice, we may consider if there are not two lessons we may learn. First, that the Word was in the beginning, as if He was by Himself and not with anyone, and secondly, that He was in the beginning with God. And I consider that there is nothing untrue in saying of Him both that He was in the beginning, and in the beginning with God, for neither was He with God alone, since He was also in the beginning, nor was He in the beginning alone and not with God, since "He was in the beginning with God."

6. How the Word is the Maker of All Things, and Even the Holy Spirit Was Made through Him.

*"All things were made through Him."* The "through whom" is never found in the first place but always in the second, as in the Epistle to the Romans, "Paul a servant of Christ Jesus, a called Apostle, separated to the Gospel of God which He promised before by His prophets in Holy Scriptures, concerning His Son, who was born of the seed of David according to the flesh, determined the Son of God in power according to the Spirit of holiness, by the resurrection of the dead, Jesus Christ our Lord, through whom we received grace and apostleship, for obedience of the faith among all the nations, for His name's sake." For God promised aforehand by the prophets His own Gospel, the prophets being His ministers, and having their word to speak about Him "through whom." And again God gave grace and apostleship to Paul and to the others for the obedience of the faith among all the nations, and this He gave them

through Jesus Christ the Savior, for the "through whom" belonged to Him. And the Apostle Paul says in the Epistle to the Hebrews: "At the end of the days He spoke to us in His Son, whom He made the heir of all things, 'through whom' also He made the ages," showing us that God made the ages through His Son, the "through whom" belonging, when the ages were being made, to the Only-begotten. Thus, if all things were made, as in this passage also, *through* the Logos, then they were not made *by* the Logos, but by a stronger and greater than He. And who else could this be but the Father? Now if, as we have seen, all things were made through Him, we have to enquire if the Holy Spirit also was made through Him. It appears to me that those who hold the Holy Spirit to be created, and who also admit that "all things were made through Him," must necessarily assume that the Holy Spirit was made through the Logos, the Logos accordingly being older than He. And he who shrinks from allowing the Holy Spirit to have been made through Christ must, if he admits the truth of the statements of this Gospel, assume the Spirit to be uncreated. There is a third resource besides these two (that of allowing the Spirit to have been made by the Word, and that of regarding it as uncreated), namely, to assert that the Holy Spirit has no essence of His own beyond the Father and the Son. But on further thought one may perhaps see reason to consider that the Son is second beside the Father, He being the same as the Father, while manifestly a distinction is drawn between the Spirit and the Son in the passage, "Whosoever shall speak a word against the Son of Man, it shall be forgiven him, but whosoever shall blaspheme against the Holy Spirit, he shall not have forgiveness, either in this world or in the world to come." We consider, therefore, that there are three hypostases, the Father and the Son and the Holy Spirit; and at the same time we believe nothing to be uncreated but the Father. We therefore, as the more pious and the truer course, admit that all things were made by the Logos, and that the Holy Spirit is the most excellent and the first in order of all that was made by the Father through Christ. And this, perhaps, is the reason why the Spirit is not said to be God's own Son. The Only begotten only is by nature and from the beginning a Son, and the Holy Spirit seems to have need of the Son, to minister to Him His essence, so as to enable Him not only to exist, but to be wise and reasonable and just, and all that we must think of Him as being. All this He has by participation of the character of Christ, of which we have spoken above. And I consider that the Holy Spirit supplies to those who, through Him and through participation in Him, are called saints, the material of the gifts, which come from God; so that the said material of the gifts is made powerful by God, is ministered by Christ, and owes its actual existence in men to the Holy Spirit. I am led to this view of the charisms by the words of Paul which he writes somewhere, "There are diversities of gifts but the same Spirit, and diversities of ministrations, and the same Lord. And there are diversities of workings, but it is the same God that worked all in all." The statement that all things were made by Him, and its seeming corollary, that the Spirit must have been called into being by the Word, may certainly raise some difficulty. There are some passages in which the Spirit is placed above Christ; in Isaiah, for example, Christ declares that He is sent, not by the Father only, but also by the Holy Spirit. "Now the Lord hath sent Me," He says, "and His Spirit," and in the Gospel He declares that there is forgiveness for the sin committed against Himself, but that for blasphemy against the Holy Spirit there is no forgiveness, either in this age or in the age to come. What is the reason of this? Is it because the Holy Spirit is of more value than Christ that the sin against Him cannot be forgiven? May it not rather be that all rational beings have part in Christ, and that forgiveness is extended to them when they repent of their sins, while only those have part in the Holy Spirit who have been found worthy of it, and that there cannot well be any forgiveness for those who fall away to evil in spite of such great and powerful cooperation, and who defeat the counsels of the Spirit who is in them. When we find the Lord saying, as He does in Isaiah, that He is sent by the Father and by His Spirit, we have to point out here also that the Spirit is not originally superior to the Savior, but that the Savior takes a lower place than He in order to carry out the plan which has been made that the Son of God should become man. Should anyone stumble at our saying that the Savior in becoming man was made lower than the Holy Spirit, we ask him to consider the words used in the Epistle to the Hebrews, where Jesus is shown by Paul to have been made less than the angels on account of the suffering of death. "We behold Him," he says, "who hath been made a little lower than the angels, Jesus, because of the suffering of death, crowned with glory and honor." And this, too, has doubtless to be added, that the creation, in order to be delivered from the bondage of corruption, and not least of all the human race, required the introduction into human nature of a happy and divine power, which should set right what was wrong upon the earth, and that this action fell to the share, as it were, of the Holy Spirit; but the Spirit, unable to support such a task, puts forward the Savior as the only one able to endure such a conflict. The Father therefore, the principal, sends the Son, but the Holy Spirit also sends Him and directs Him to go before, promising to descend, when the time comes, to the Son of God, and to work with Him for the salvation of men. This He did, when, in a bodily shape like a dove, He flew to Him after the baptism. He remained on Him, and did not pass Him by, as He might have done with men not able continuously to bear His glory. Thus John, when explaining how he knew who Christ was, spoke not only of the descent of the Spirit on Jesus, but also of its remaining upon him. For it is written that John said: "He who sent me to baptize said, On whomsoever thou shalt see the Spirit descending and abiding upon Him, the same is He that baptizes with the Holy Spirit and with fire." It is not said only, "On whomsoever thou shalt see the Spirit descending," for the Spirit no doubt descended on others too, but "descending and abiding on Him." Our examination of this point has been somewhat extended, since we were anxious to make it clear that if all things were made by Him, then the Spirit also was made through the Word, and is seen to be one of the "all things" which are inferior to their Maker. This view is too firmly settled to be disturbed by a few words which may be adduced to the opposite effect. If anyone should lend credence to the Gospel according to the Hebrews, where the Savior Himself says, "My mother, the Holy Spirit took me just now by one of my hairs and carried me off to the great mount Tabor," he will have to face the difficulty of explaining how the Holy Spirit can be the mother of Christ when it was itself brought into existence through the Word. But neither the passage nor this difficulty is hard to explain. For if he who does the will of the Father in heaven is Christ's brother and sister and mother, and if the name of brother of Christ may be applied, not only to the race of men, but to beings of diviner rank than they, then there is nothing absurd in the Holy Spirit's being His mother, everyone being His mother who does the will of the Father in heaven.

On the words, "All things were made by Him," there is still one point to be examined. The "word" is, as a notion, from "life," and yet we read, "What was made in the Word was life, and the life was the light of men." Now as all things were made through Him, was the life made through Him, which is the light of men, and the other notions under which the Savior is presented to us? Or must we take the "all things were made by Him" subject to the exception of the things which are in Himself? The latter course appears to be the preferable one. For supposing we should concede that the life which is the light of men was made through Him, since it said that the life "was made" the light of men, what are we to say about wisdom, which is conceived as being prior to the Word? That, therefore, which is about the Word (His relations or conditions) was not made by the Word, and the result is that, with the exception of the notions under which Christ is presented, all things were made through the Word of God, the Father making them in wisdom. "In wisdom hast Thou made them all," it says, not *through*, but *in* wisdom.

7. Of Things Not Made Through the Logos.

Let us see, however, why the words are added, "And without Him was not anything (Gr. even one thing) made." Some might think it superfluous to add to the words "All things were made through Him," the phrase "Without Him was not anything made." For if everything whatsoever was made through the Logos, then nothing was made without Him. Yet it does not follow from the proposition that without the Logos nothing was made, that all things were made through the Logos. It is possible that though nothing was made without the Logos, all things were made, not through the Logos only, but some things by Him. We must, therefore, make ourselves sure in what sense the "all things" is to be understood, and in what sense the "nothing." For, without a clear preliminary definition of these terms, it might be maintained that, if all things were made through the Logos, and evil is a part of all things, then the whole matter of sin, and everything that is wicked, that these also were made through the Logos. But this we must regard as false. There is nothing absurd in thinking that creatures were made through the Logos, and also that men's brave deeds have been done through Him, and all the useful acts of those who are now in bliss; but with the sins and misfortunes of men it is otherwise. Now some have held that since evil is not based in the constitution of things—for it did not exist at the beginning and at the end it will have ceased—that, therefore, the evils of which we spoke are the Nothing; and as some of the Greeks say that genera and forms, such as the (general) animal and the man, belong to the category of Nothings, so it has been supposed that all that is not of God is Nothing, and has not even obtained through the Word the subsistence it appears to have. We ask whether it is possible to show from Scripture in any convincing way that this is so. As for the meanings of the word "Nothing" and "Not-being," they would appear to be synonymous, for Nothing can be spoken of as Not-being, and the Not-being can be described as Nothing. The Apostle, however, appears to count the things which are not, not among those which have no existence whatever, but rather among things which are evil. To him the Not-being is evil; "God," he says, "called the things that are not as things that are." And Mardochæus, too, in the Esther of the Septuagint, calls the enemies of Israel "those that are not," saying, "Deliver not Thy scepter, O Lord, to those that are not." We may also notice how evil men, on account of their wickedness, are said not to be, from the name ascribed to God in Exodus: "For the Lord said to Moses, I am, that is My name." The good God says this with respect of us also who pray that we may be part of His congregation. The Savior praises him, saying, "None is good but one, God the Father." The good, then, is the same as He who is. Over against good is evil or wickedness, and over against Him who is that which is not, whence it follows that evil and wickedness are that which is not. This, perhaps, is what has led some to affirm that the devil is not created by God. In respect that he is the devil he is not the work of God, but he who is the devil is a created being, and as there is no other creator but our God, he is a work of God. It is as if we should say that a murderer is not a work of God, while we may say that in respect he is a man, God made him. His being as a man he received from God; we do not assert that he received from God his being as a murderer. All, then, who have part in Him who is, and the saints have part in Him, may properly be called Beings; but those who have given up their part in the Being, by depriving themselves of Being, have become Not-beings. But we said when entering on this discussion, that Not-being and Nothing are synonymous, and hence those who are not beings are Nothing, and all evil is nothing, since it is Not-being, and thus since they are called Not-being came into existence without the Logos, not being numbered among the all things which were made through Him. Thus we have shown, so far as our powers admit, what are the "all things" which were made through the Logos, and what came into existence without Him, since at no time is it Being, and it is, therefore, called "Nothing."

## 8. Heracleon's View that the Logos is Not the Agent of Creation.

It was, I consider, a violent and unwarranted procedure which was adopted by Heracleon, the friend, as it is said, of Valentinus, in discussing this sentence: "All things were made through Him." He excepted the whole world and all that it contains, excluding, as far as his hypothesis goes, from the "all things" what is best in the world and its contents. For he says that the æon (age), and the things in it, were not made by the Logos; he considers them to have come into existence before the Logos. He deals with the statement, "Without Him was nothing made," with some degree of audacity, nor is he afraid of the warning: "Add not to His words, lest He find thee out and thou prove a liar," for to the "Nothing" he adds: "Of what is in the world and the creation." And as his statements on the passage are obviously very much forced and in the face of the evidence, for what he considers divine is excluded from the all, and what he regards as purely evil is, that and nothing else, the all things, we need not waste our time in rebutting what is, on the face of it, absurd, when, without any warrant from Scripture, he adds to the words, "Without Him was nothing made," the further words, "Of what is in the earth and the creation." In this proposal, which has no inner probability to recommend it, he is asking us, in fact, to trust him as we do the prophets, or the Apostles, who had authority and were not responsible to men for the writings belonging to man's salvation, which they handed to those about them and to those who should come after. He had, also, a private interpretation of his own of the words: "All things were made through Him," when he said that it was the Logos who caused the demiurge to make the world, not, however, the Logos from whom or by whom, but Him through whom, taking the written words in a different sense from that of common parlance. For, if the truth of the matter was as he considers, then the writer ought to have said that all things were made through the demiurge by the Word, and not through the Word by the demiurge. We accept the "through whom," as it is usually understood, and have brought evidence in support of our interpretation, while he not only puts forward a new rendering of his own, unsupported by the divine Scripture, but appears even to scorn the truth and shamelessly and openly oppose it. For he says: "It was not the Logos who made all things, as under another who was the operating agent," taking the "through whom" in this sense, "but another made them, the Logos Himself being the operating agent." This is not a suitable occasion for the proof that it was not the demiurge who became the servant of the Logos and made the world; but that the Logos became the servant of the demiurge and formed the world. For, according to the prophet David, "God spoke and they came into being, He commanded and they were created." For the unbegotten God commanded the first-born of all creation, and they were created, not only the world and what is therein, but also all other things, whether thrones or dominions or principalities or powers, for all things were made through Him and unto Him, and He is before all things."

9. That the Logos Present in Us is Not Responsible for Our Sins.

One point more on the words: "Without Him was not anything made." The question about evil must receive adequate discussion; what was said of it has not, it is true, a very likely appearance, and yet it appears to me that it ought not to be simply overlooked. The question is whether evil, also, was made through the Logos, taking the Logos, now be it well noted, in the sense of that reason which is in everyone, as thus brought into being by the reason which was from the beginning. The Apostle says: "Without the law sin was dead," and adds, "But when the commandment came sin revived," and so teaches generally about sin that it has no power before the law and the commandment (but the Logos is, in a sense, law and commandment), and there would be no sin were there no law, for, "sin is not imputed where there is no law." And, again, there would be no sin but for the Logos, for "if I had not come and spoken unto them," Christ says, "they had not had sin." For every excuse is taken away from one who wants to make excuse for his sin, if, though the Word is in him and shows him what he ought to do, he does not obey it. It seems, then, that all things, the worse things not excepted, were made by the Logos, and without Him, taking the nothing here in its simpler sense, was nothing made. Nor must we blame the Logos if all things were made by Him, and without Him nothing was made, any more than we blame the master who has showed the pupil his duty, when the instruction has been such as to leave the pupil, should he sin, no excuse or room to say that he erred through ignorance. This appears the more plainly when we consider that master and pupil are inseparable. For as master and pupil are correlatives, and belong together, so the Logos is present in the nature of reasonable beings as such, always suggesting what they ought to do, even should we pay no heed to his commands, but devote ourselves to pleasure and allow his best counsels to pass by us unregarded. As the eye is a servant given us for the best purposes, and yet we use it to see things on which it is wrong for us to look, and as we make a wrong use of our hearing when we spend our time in listening to singing competitions and to other forbidden sounds, so we outrage the Logos who is in us, and use Him otherwise than as we ought, when we make Him assist in our transgressions. For He is present with those who sin, for their condemnation, and He condemns the man who does not prefer Him to everything else. Hence we find it written: "The word which I have spoken unto you, the same shall judge you." That is as if He should say: "I, the Word, who am always lifting up my voice in you, I, myself, will judge you, and no refuge or excuse will then be left you." This interpretation, however, may appear somewhat strained, as we have taken the Word in one sense to be the Word in the beginning, who was with God, God the Word, and have now taken it in another sense, speaking of it, not only in reference to the principal works of creation, as in the words, "All things were made through Him," but as related to all the acts of reasonable beings, this last being the Logos (reason), without whose presence none of our sins are committed. The question arises whether the Logos in us is to be pronounced the same being as that which was in the beginning and was with God, God the Word. The Apostle, certainly, does not appear to make the Logos in us a different being from the Logos who was in the beginning with God. "Say not in thine heart," he says, "who shall go up into heaven; that is to bring Christ down, or who shall go down into the abyss; that is to bring Christ up from the dead. But what says the Scripture? The Logos is very nigh thee, in thy mouth and in thy heart."

10. "That Which Was Made Was Life in Him, and the Life Was the Light of Men."

This Involves the Paradox that What Does Not Derive Life from the Logos Does Not Live at All.

The Greeks have certain apothegms, called paradoxes, in which the wisdom of their sages is presented at its highest, and some proof, or what appears to be proof, is given. Thus it is said that the wise man alone, and that every wise man, is a priest, because the wise man alone and every wise man possesses knowledge as to the service of God. Again, that the wise man alone and that every wise man is free and has received from the divine law authority to do what he himself is minded to do, and this authority they call lawful power of decision. Why should we say more about these so-called paradoxes? Much discussion is devoted to them, and they call for a comparison of the sense of Scripture with the doctrine thus conveyed. So that we may be in a position to determine where religious doctrine agrees with them and where it differs from them. This has been suggested to us by our study of the words, "That which was made was life in Him;" for it appears possible to follow the words of Scripture here and to make out a number of things which partake of the character of the paradoxes and are even more paradoxical than these sentences of the Greeks. If we consider the Logos in the beginning, who was with God, God the Word, we shall perhaps be able to declare that only he who partakes of this being, considered in this character, is to be pronounced reasonable ("logical"), and thus we should demonstrate that the saint alone is reasonable. Again, if we apprehend that life has come in the Logos, he, namely, who said, "I am the life," then we shall say that no one is alive who is outside the faith of Christ, that all are dead who are not living to God, that their life is life to sin, and therefore, if I may so express myself, a life of death. Consider however, whether the divine Scriptures do not in many places teach this; as where the Savior says, "Or have ye not read that which was spoken at the bush, I am the God of Abraham and the God of Isaac and the God of Jacob. He is not God of the dead but of the living." And "Before Thee shall no living being be justified." But why need we speak about God Himself or the Savior? For it is disputed to which of them the voice belongs which says in the prophets, "As I live, says the Lord."

11. How No One is Righteous or Can Truly Be Said to Live in Comparison with God.

First let us look at the words, "He is not the God of the dead but of the living." That is equivalent to saying that He is not the God of sinners but of saints. For it was a great gift to the Patriarchs that God in place of His own name should add their name to His own designation as God, as Paul says, "Therefore God is not ashamed to be called their God." He is the God, therefore, of the fathers and of all the saints; it might be hard to find a passage to the effect that God is the God of any of the wicked. If, then, He is the God of the saints, and is said to be the God of the living, then the saints are the living and the living are saints; neither is there any saint outside the living, nor when any one is called living is the further implication absent that in addition to his having life he is a holy one. Near akin to this is the lesson to be drawn from the saying, "I shall be well pleasing to the Lord in the land of the living." The good pleasure of the Lord, he appears to say, is in the ranks of the saints, or in the place of the saints, and it is there that he hopes to be. No one pleases God well who has not entered the rank of the saints, or the place of the saints; and to that place everyone must come who has assumed beforehand, as it were in this life, the shadow and image of true God-pleasing. The passage which declares that before God no living being shall be justified shows that in comparison with God and the righteousness that is in Him none, even of the most finished saints, will be justified. We might take a parable from another quarter and say that no candle can give light before the sun, not that the candle will not give light, only it will not when the sun outshines it. In the same way every "living" will be justified, only not before God, when it is compared with those who are below and who are in the power of darkness. To them the light of the saints will shine. Here, perhaps, we have the key to the meaning of that verse: "Let your light shine before men." He does not say, let your light shine before God; had he said so he would have given a commandment impossible of fulfilment, as if he had bidden those lights which have souls to let their light shine before the sun. It is not only, therefore, the ordinary mass of the living who will not be justified before God, but even those among the living who are distinguished above the rest, or, to put it more truly, the whole righteousness of the living will not be justified before God, as compared with the righteousness of God, as if I were to call together all the lights which shine on the earth by night, and to say that they could not give light in comparison with the rays of the sun. We rise from these considerations to a higher level when we take the words before our minds, "I live, says the Lord." Life, in the full sense of the word, especially after what we have been saying on the subject, belongs perhaps to God and none but Him. Is this the reason why the Apostle, after speaking of the supreme excellency of the life of God and being led to the highest expression about it, says about God (showing in this a true understanding of that saying, "I live, says the Lord"); "who only hath immortality." No living being besides God has life free from change and variation. Why should we be in further doubt? Even Christ did not share the Father's immortality; for He "tasted death for every man."

12. Is the Savior All that He Is, to All?

We have thus enquired as to the life of God, and the life which is Christ, and the living who are in a place by themselves, and have seen how the living are not justified before God, and we have noticed the cognate statement, "Who alone hath immortality." We may now take up the assumption which may appear to be involved in this, namely, that whatever being is gifted with reason does not possess blessedness as a part of its essence, or as an inseparable part of its nature. For if blessedness and the highest life were an inseparable characteristic of reasonable being, how could it be truly said of God that He only has immortality? We should therefore remark, that the Savior is some things, not to Himself but to others, and some things both to Himself and others, and we must enquire if there are some things which He is to

Himself and to no other. Clearly it is to others that He is a Shepherd, not a shepherd like those among men who make gain out of their occupation; unless the benefit conferred on the sheep might be regarded, on account of His love to men, as a benefit to Himself also. Similarly it is to others that He is the Way and the Door, and, as all will admit, the Rod. To Himself and to others He is Wisdom and perhaps also Reason (Logos). It may be asked whether, as He has in Himself a system of speculations, inasmuch as He is wisdom, there are some of those speculations which cannot be received by any nature that is begotten, but His own, and which He knows for Himself only. Nor should the reverence we owe to the Holy Spirit keep us from seeking to answer this question. For the Holy Spirit Himself receives instruction, as is clear from what is said about the Paraclete and the Holy Spirit, "He shall take of mine and shall declare it to you." Does He, then, from these instructions, take in everything that the Son, gazing at the Father from the first, Himself knows? That would require further consideration. And if the Savior is some things to others, and some things it may be to Himself, and to no other, or to one only, or to few, then we ask, in so far as He is the life which came in the Logos, whether he is life to Himself and to others, or to others, and if to others, to what others. And are life and the light of men the same thing, for the text says, "That which was made was life in Him and the life was the light of men." But the light of men is the light only of some, not of all, rational creatures; the word "men" which is added shows this. But He is the light of men, and so He is the life of those whose light he is also. And inasmuch as He is life He may be called the Savior, not for Himself but to be life to others, whose light also He is. And this life comes to the Logos and is inseparable from Him, once it has come to Him. But the Logos, who cleanses the soul, must have been in the soul first; it is after Him and the cleansing that proceeds from Him, when all that is dead or weak in her has been taken away, that pure life comes to everyone who has made himself a fit dwelling for the Logos, considered as God.

13. How the Life in the Logos Comes After the Beginning.

Here, we must carefully observe, we have two things which are one, and we have to define the difference between them. First, what is before us in *The Word in the beginning,* then what is implied in *The Life in the Word.* The Word was not *made* in the beginning; there was no time when the beginning was devoid of the Word, and hence it is said, "In the beginning was the Word." Of life, on the other hand, we read, not that it was as the Word, but that it was made; if at least it be the case that the life is the light of men. For when man was not yet, there was no light of men; for the light of men is conceived only in relation to men. And let no one annoy us with the objection that we have put this under the category of time, though it be the order of the things themselves, that make them first and second and so on, and even though there should have been no time when the things placed by the Logos third and fourth were not in existence. As, then, all things *were made* by Him, not all things *were* by Him, and as without Him *was* nothing *made,* not, without Him nothing *was,* so what *was made* in Him, not what *was* in Him, was life. And, again, not what *was made* in the beginning was the Word, but what *was* in the beginning was the Word. Some of the copies, it is true, have a reading which is not devoid of probability, "What was made is life in Him." But if life is the same thing as the light of men, then no one who is in darkness is living, and none of the living is in darkness; but everyone who is alive is also in light, and everyone who is in light is living, so that not he only who is living, but everyone who is living, is a son of light; and he who is a son of light is he whose work shines before men.

14. How the Natures of Men are Not So Fixed from the First, But that They May Pass from Darkness to Light.

We have been discussing certain things which are opposite, and what has been said of them may serve to suggest what has been omitted. We are speaking of life and the light of men, and the opposite to life is death; the opposite to the light of men, the darkness of men. It is therefore plain that he who is in the darkness of men is in death, and that he who works the works of death is nowhere but in darkness. But he who is mindful of God, if we consider what it is to be mindful of Him, is not in death, according to the saying, "In death there is no one who remembers Thee." Are the darkness of men, and death, such as they are by nature? On this point we have another passage, "We were once darkness, but now light in the Lord," even if we be now in the fullest sense saints and spiritual persons. Thus he who was once darkness has become, like Paul, capable of being light in the Lord. Some consider that some natures are spiritual from the first, such as those of Paul and the holy Apostles; but I scarcely see how to reconcile with such a view, what the above text tells us, that the spiritual person was once darkness and afterwards became light. For if the spiritual was once darkness what can the earthy have been? But if it is true that darkness became light, as in the text, how is it unreasonable to suppose that all darkness is capable of becoming light? Had not Paul said, "We were once in darkness, but now are we light in the Lord," and thus implied of those whom they consider to be naturally lost, that they were darkness, or are darkness still, the hypothesis about the different natures might have been admissible. But Paul distinctly says that he had once been darkness but was now light in the Lord, which implies the possibility that darkness should turn into light. But he who perceives the possibility of a change on each side for the better or for the worse, will not find it hard to gain an insight into every darkness of men, or into that death which consists in the darkness of men.

15. Heracleon's View that the Lord Brought Life Only to the Spiritual. Refutation of This.

Heracleon adopts a somewhat violent course when he arrives at this passage, "What was made in Him was life." Instead of the "In Him" of the text he understands "to those men who are spiritual," as if he considered the Logos and the spiritual to be identical, though this he does not plainly say; and then he proceeds to give, as it were, an account of the origin of the matter and says, "He (the Logos) provided them with their first form at their birth, carrying further and making manifest what had been sown by another, into form and into illumination and into an outline of its own." He did not observe how Paul speaks of the spiritual, and how he refrains from saying that they are men. "A natural man receives not the things of the spirit of God, for they are foolishness to him; but the spiritual judges all things." We maintain that it was not without a meaning that he did not add the word *men* to the word *spiritual*. Spiritual is something better than man, for man receives his form either in soul, or in body, or in both together, not in what is more divine than these, namely, in spirit; and it is after he has come to have a prevailing share of this that he is called "spiritual." Moreover, in bringing forward such a hypothesis as this, he furnishes not even the presence of a proof, and shows himself unable to reach even a moderate degree of plausibility for his argument on the subject. So much, then, for him.

16. The Life May Be the Light of Others Besides.

Let us suggest another question, namely, whether the life was the light of men only, and not of every being as well that is in blessedness. For if the life were the same thing as the light of men, and if the light of Christ were for men alone, then the life also would be only for men. But such a view is both foolish and impious, since the other Scriptures testify against this interpretation and declare that, when we are somewhat more advanced, we shall be equal to the angels. The question is to be solved on the principle that when a predicate is applied to certain persons, it is not to be at once taken to apply to them alone. Thus, when the light of men is spoken of, it is not the light of men only; had that been the meaning, a word would have been added to express it; the life, it would have read, was the light of men only. For it is possible for the light of men to be the light of others besides men, just as it is possible that certain animals and certain plants may form the food of men, and that the same animals and plants should be the food of other creatures too. That is an example from common life; it is fitting that another analogy should be adduced from the inspired books. Now the question here before us, is why the light of men should not be the light of other creatures also, and we have seen that to speak of the light of men by no means excludes the possibility that the light may be that of other beings besides man, whether inferior to him or like him. Now a name is given to God; He is said to be the God of Abraham and of Isaac and of Jacob. He, then, who infers from the saying, "The life was the light of men," that the light is for no other than for men, ought also to conclude that the God of Abraham and the God of Isaac and the God of Jacob is the God of no one else but these three patriarchs. But He is also the God of Elijah, and, as Judith says, of her father Simeon, and the God of the Hebrews. By analogy of reasoning, then, if nothing prevents Him from being the God of others, nothing prevents the light of men from being the light of others besides men.

17. The Higher Powers are Men; And Christ is Their Light Also.

Another, again, appeals to the text, "Let us make man according to our image and likeness," and maintains that whatever is made according to God's image and likeness is man. To support this, numberless instances are adduced to show that in Scripture "man" and "angel" are used indifferently, and that the same subject is entitled both angel and man. This is true of the three who were entertained by Abraham, and of the two who came to Sodom; in the whole course of Scripture, persons are styled sometimes men, sometimes angels. Those who hold this view will say that since persons are styled angels who are manifestly men, as when Zechariah says, "The messenger of the Lord, I am with you, says the Lord Almighty," and as it is written of John the Baptist,

"Behold I send My messenger before thy face," the angels (messengers) of God are so called on account of their office, and are not here called men on account of their nature. It confirms this view that the names applied to the higher powers are not those of species of living beings, but those of the orders, assigned by God to this and to that reasonable being. "Throne" is not a species of living being, nor "dominion," nor "principality," nor "power"; these are names of the businesses to which those clothed with the names have been appointed; the subjects themselves are nothing but men, but the subject has come to be a throne, or a dominion, or a principality, or a power. In Joshua, the son of Nun, we read that in Jericho there appeared to Joshua a man who said, "I am captain of the Lord's host, now am I come." The outcome of this is that the light of men must be held to be the same as the light of every being endowed with reason; for every reasonable being is man, since it is according to the image and likeness of God. It is spoken of in three different ways, "the light of men," and simply "the light," and "the true light." It is the light of men either, as we showed before, because there is nothing to prevent us from regarding it as the light of other beings besides men, or because all beings endowed with reason are called men because they are made in the image of God.

18. How God also is Light, but in a Different Way; And How Life Came before Light.

The Savior is here called simply light. But in the Catholic Epistle of this same John we read that God is light. This, it has been maintained, furnishes a proof that the Son is not in substance different from the Father. Another student, however, looking into the matter more closely and with a sounder judgment, will say that the light which shines in darkness and is not overtaken by it, is not the same as the light in which there is no darkness at all. The light which shines in darkness comes upon this darkness, as it were, and is pursued by it, and, in spite of attempts made upon it, is not overtaken. But the light in which there is no darkness at all neither shines on darkness, nor is at first pursued by it, so as to prove victor and to have it recorded that it was not overtaken by its pursuer. The third designation was "the true light." But in proportion as God, since He is the Father of truth, is more and greater than truth, and since He is the Father of wisdom is greater and more excellent than wisdom, in the same proportion He is more than the true light. We may learn, perhaps, in a more suggestive manner, how the Father and the Son are two lights, from David, who says in the thirty-fifth Psalm, "In Thy light we shall see light." This same light of men which shines in darkness, the true light, is called, further on in the Gospel, the light of the world; Jesus says, "I am the light of the world." Nor must we omit to notice that whereas the passage might very well have run, "That which was made was in Him the light of men, and the light of men was life," he chose the opposite order. He puts life before the light of men, even if life and the light of men are the same thing; in thinking of those who have part in life, though that life is also the light of men, we are to come first to the fact that they are living the divine life spoken of before; then we come to their enlightenment. For life must come first if the living person is to be enlightened; it would not be a good arrangement to speak of the illumination of one not yet conceived as living, and to make life come after the illumination. For though "life" and "the light" of men are the same thing, the notions are taken separately. This light of men is also called, by Isaiah, "the light of the Gentiles," where he says, "Behold I have set Thee for a covenant of the generation, for a light of the Gentiles;" and David, placing his confidence in this light, says in the twenty-sixth Psalm, "The Lord is my illumination and my Savior; whom shall I fear?"

19. The Life Here Spoken of is the Higher Life, that of Reason.

As for those who make up a mythology about the æons and arrange them in syzygies (yokes or pairs), and who consider the Logos and Life to have been emitted by Intellect and Truth, it may not be beside the point to state the following difficulties. How can life, in their system, the yokefellow of the Word, derive his origin from his yokefellow? For "what was made in Him," he says, evidently referring to the Word, mentioned immediately before, "was life." Will they tell us how life, the yokefellow, as they say, of the Word, came into being in the Word, and how life rather than the Word is the light of men. It would be quite natural if men of reasonable minds, who are perplexed with such questions and find the point we have raised hard to dispose of, should turn round upon us and invite us to discuss the reason why it is not the Word that is said to be the light of men, but life which originated in the Word. To such an enquiry we shall reply that the life here spoken of is not that which is common to rational beings and to beings without reason, but that life which is added to us upon the completion of reason in us, our share in that life, being derived from the first reason (Logos). It is when we turn away from the life which is life in appearance only, not in truth, and when we yearn to be filled with the true life, that we are made partakers of it, and when it has arisen in us it becomes the foundation of the light of the higher knowledge (gnosis). With some it may be that this life is only potentially and not actually light, with those who do not strive to search out the things of the higher knowledge, while with others it is actually light. With these it clearly is so who act on Paul's injunction, "Seek earnestly the best gifts;" and among the greatest gifts is that which all are enjoined to seek, namely, the word of wisdom, and it is followed by the word of knowledge. This wisdom and this knowledge lie side by side; into the difference between them this is not a fitting occasion to enquire.

### 20. Different Kinds of Light; And of Darkness.

"And the light shines in darkness and the darkness hath not overtaken it." We are still enquiring about the light of men, since it is what was spoken of in the preceding verse, and also, I consider, about darkness, which is named as its adversary, the darkness also being, if the definition of it is correct, that of men. The light of men is a generic notion covering two special things; and with the darkness of men it is the same. He who has gained the light of men and shares its beams will do the work of light and know in the higher sense, being illuminated by the light of the higher knowledge. And we must recognize the analogous case of those on the other side, and of their evil actions, and of that which is thought to be but is not really knowledge, since those who exercise it have the reason (Logos) not of light but of darkness. And because the sacred word knows the things which produce light, Isaiah says: "Because Thy commandments are a light upon the earth," and David says in the Psalm, "The precept of the Lord is clear, enlightening the eyes." But since in addition to the commandments and the precepts there is a light of higher knowledge, we read in one of the twelve (prophets), "Sow to yourselves for righteousness, reap to yourselves for the fruit of life, make light for yourselves the light of knowledge." There is a further light of knowledge in addition to the commandments, and so we read, "Make light for yourselves," not simply light, but what light?—the light of knowledge. For if any light that a man kindles for himself were a light of knowledge, then the added words, "Make light for yourselves, the light of knowledge," would have no meaning. And again that darkness is brought upon men by their evil deeds, we learn from John himself, when he says in his epistle, "If we say that we have fellowship with Him and walk in darkness, we lie and do not the truth," and again, "He that says he is in the light, and hates his brother, is in darkness even until now," and again, "He that hates his brother is in darkness, and walks in darkness, and knows not whither he goes, because darkness hath blinded his eyes." Walking in darkness signifies evil conduct, and to hate one's brother, is not that to fall away from that which is properly called knowledge? But he also who is ignorant of divine things walks in darkness, just because of that ignorance; as David says, "They knew not, they understood not, they walk in darkness." Consider, however, this passage, "God is light and in Him is no darkness," and see if the reason for this saying is not that darkness is not one, being either two, because there are two kinds of it, or many, because it is taken distributively, individually with reference to the many evil actions and the many false doctrines; so that there are many darknesses, not one of which is in God. The saying of the Savior could not be spoken of the Holy One, "Ye are the light of the world;" for the Holy One is light of the world (absolute, not particular), and there is not in Him any darkness.

21. Christ is Not, Like God, Quite Free from Darkness: Since He Bore Our Sins.

Now someone will ask how this statement that there is no darkness in Him can be regarded as a thing peculiar to Him, when we consider that the Savior also was quite without sin. Could it not be said of Him also that "He is light, and that there is no darkness in Him"? The difference between the two cases has been partly set forth above. We will now, however, go a step further than we did before, and add, that if God made Christ who knew no sin to be sin for us, then it could not be said of Him that there was no darkness in Him. For if Jesus was in the likeness of the flesh of sin and for sin, and condemned sin by taking upon Him the likeness of the flesh of sin, then it cannot be said of Him, absolutely and directly, that there was no darkness in Him. We may add that "He took our infirmities and bare our sicknesses," both infirmities of the soul and sicknesses of the hidden man of our heart. On account of these infirmities and sicknesses which He bore away from us, He declares His soul to be sorrowful and sore troubled, and He is said in Zechariah to have put on filthy garments, which, when He was about to take them off, are said to be sins. "Behold, it is said, I have taken away thy sins." Because He had taken on Himself the sins of the people of those who believed in Him, he uses many such expressions as these: "Far from my salvation are the words of my transgressions," and "Thou knows my foolishness, and my sins were not hid from Thee." And let no one suppose that we say this from any lack of piety towards the Christ of God; for as the Father alone has immortality and our Lord took upon Himself, for His love to men, the death He died for us, so to the Father alone the words apply, "In Him is no darkness," since Christ took upon Himself, for His goodwill towards men, our darknesses. This He did, that by His power He might destroy our death and remove the darkness which is in our soul, so that the saying in Isaiah might be fulfilled, "The people that sat in darkness saw a great light." This light, which came into being in the Logos, and is also life, shines in the darkness of our souls, and it has come where the rulers of this darkness carry on their struggle with the race of men and strive to subdue to darkness those who do not stand firm with all their power; that they might be enlightened the light has come so far, and that they might be called sons of light. And shining in darkness this light is pursued by the darkness, but not overtaken.

22. How the Darkness Failed to Overtake the Light.

Should anyone consider that we are adding something that is not written, namely, the pursuit of the light by the darkness, let him reflect that unless the darkness had pursued the light the words, "The darkness did not overtake it," would have no meaning. John writes for those who have wit to see what is omitted and to supply it as the context requires, and so he wrote, "The darkness did not overtake it." If it did not overtake it, it must first have pursued it, and that the darkness did pursue the light is clear from what the Savior suffered, and those also who received His teachings, His own children, when darkness was doing what it could against the sons of light and was minded to drive light away from men. But since, if God be for us, no one, however that way minded, can be against us, the more they humbled themselves the more they grew, and they prevailed exceedingly. In two ways the darkness did not overtake the light. Either it was left far behind and was itself so slow, while the light was in its course so sharp and swift, that it was not even able to keep following it, or if the light sought to lay a snare for the darkness, and waited for it in pursuance of the plan it had formed, then darkness, coming near the light, was brought to an end. In either case the darkness did not overtake the light.

23. There is a Divine Darkness which is Not Evil, and Which Ultimately Becomes Light.

In connection with this subject it is necessary for us to point out that darkness is not to be understood, every time it is mentioned, in a bad sense; Scripture speaks of it sometimes in a good sense. The heterodox have failed to observe this distinction, and have accordingly adopted most shameful doctrines about the Maker of the world, and have indeed revolted from Him, and addicted themselves to fictions and myths. We must, therefore, show how and when the name of darkness is taken in a good sense. Darkness and clouds and tempest are said in Exodus to be round about God, and in the seventeenth Psalm, "He made darkness His secret place, His tent round about Him, dark water in clouds of the air." Indeed, if one considers the multitude of speculation and knowledge about God, beyond the power of human nature to take in, beyond the power, perhaps, of all originated beings except Christ and the Holy Spirit, then one may know how God is surrounded with darkness, because the discourse is hid in ignorance which would be required to tell in what darkness He has made His hiding-place when He arranged that the things concerning Him should be unknown and beyond the grasp of knowledge. Should anyone be staggered by these expositions, he may be reconciled to them both by the "dark sayings" and by the "treasures of darkness," hidden, invisible, which are given to Christ by God. In nowise different, I consider, are the treasures of darkness which are hid in Christ, from what is spoken of in the text, "God made darkness His secret place," and (the saint) "shall understand parable and dark saying." And consider if we have here the reason of the Savior's saying to His disciples, "What ye have heard in darkness, speak ye in the light." The mysteries committed to them in secret and where few could hear, hard to be known and obscure, He bids them, when enlightened and therefore said to be in the light, to make known to everyone who is made light. I might add a still stranger feature of this darkness which is praised, namely, that it hastens to the light and overtakes it, and so at last, after having been unknown as darkness, undergoes for him who does not see its power such a change that he comes to know it and to declare that what was formerly known to him as darkness has now become light.

24. John the Baptist Was Sent. From Where? His Soul Was Sent from a Higher Region.

"There was a man sent from God, whose name was John." He who is sent is sent from somewhere to somewhere; and the careful student will, therefore, enquire from what quarter John was sent, and whither. The "whither" is quite plain on the face of the story; he was sent to Israel, and to those who were willing to hear him when he was staying in the wilderness of Judæa and baptizing by the banks of the Jordan. According to the deeper sense, however, he was sent into the world, the world being understood as this earthly place where men are; and the careful student will have this in view in enquiring from where John was sent. Examining the words more closely, he will perhaps declare that as it is written of Adam, "And the Lord sent him forth out of the Paradise of pleasure to till the earth, out of which he was taken," so also John was sent, either from heaven or from Paradise, or from some other quarter to this place on the earth. He was sent that he might bear witness of the light. There is, however, an objection to this interpretation, which is not to be lightly dismissed. It is written in Isaiah: "Whom shall I send, and who will go to the people?" The prophet answers: "Here am I,—send me." He, then, who objects to that rendering of our passage which appears to be the deeper may say that Isaiah was sent not to this world from another place, but after having seen "the Lord sitting on a throne high and lifted up," was sent to the people, to say, "Hearing, ye shall hear and shall not understand," and so on; and that in the same manner John, the beginning of his mission not being narrated, is sent after the analogy of the mission of Isaiah, to baptize, and to make ready for the Lord a people prepared for Him, and to bear witness of the light. So much we have said of the first sense; and now we adduce certain solutions which help to confirm the deeper meaning about John. In the same passage it is added, "He came for witness, to bear witness of the light." Now, if he came, where did he come from? To those who find it difficult to follow us, we point to what John says afterwards of having seen the Holy Spirit as a dove descending on the Savior. "He that sent me," he says, "to baptize with water, He said unto me, upon whomsoever thou shalt see the Holy Spirit descending and abiding upon Him, the same is He that baptizes with the Holy Spirit and with fire." When did He send him and give him this injunction? The answer to this question will probably be that when He sent him to begin to baptize, then He who was dealing with him uttered this word. But a more convincing argument for the view that John was sent from another region when he entered into the body, the one object of his entry into this life being that he should bear witness of the truth, may be drawn from the narrative of his birth. Gabriel, when announcing to Zacharias the birth of John, and to Mary the advent of our Savior among men, says: That John is to be "filled with the Holy Spirit even from his mother's womb." And we have also the saying, "For behold, when the voice of thy salutation came into mine ears, the babe leaped in my womb for joy." He who sedulously guards himself in his dealings with Scripture against forced, or casual, or capricious procedure, must necessarily assume that John's soul was older than his body, and subsisted by itself before it was sent on the ministry of the witness of the light. Nor must we overlook the text, "This is Elijah which is to come." For if that general doctrine of the soul is to be received, namely, that it is not sown at the same time with the body, but is before it, and is then, for various causes, clothed with flesh and blood; then the words "sent from God" will not appear to be applicable to John alone. The most evil of all, the man of sin, the son of perdition, is said by Paul to be sent by God: "God sends them a working of error that they should believe a lie; that they all might be judged who believed not the truth, but had pleasure in unrighteousness." But our present question may, perhaps, be solved in this way, that as every man is a man of God, simply because God created him, but not every man is called a man of God, but only he who has devoted himself to God, such as Elijah and those who are called men of God in the Scriptures, thus every man might be said in ordinary language to be sent from God, but in the absolute sense no one is to be spoken of in this way who has not entered this life for a divine ministry and in the service of the salvation of mankind. We do not find it said of anyone but the saints that he is sent by God. It is said of Isaiah as we showed before; it is also said of Jeremiah, "To whomsoever I shall send thee thou shalt go"; and it is said of Ezekiel, "I send thee to nations that are rebellious and have not believed in Me." The examples, however, do not expressly speak of a mission from the region outside life into life, and as it is a mission into life that we are enquiring about, they may seem to have little bearing on our subject. But there is nothing absurd in our transferring the argument derived from them to our question. They tell us that it is only the saints, and we were speaking of them, whom God is said to send, and in this sense they may be applied to the case of those who are sent into this life.

25. Argument from the Prayer of Joseph, to Show that the Baptist May Have Been an Angel Who Became a Man.

As we are now engaged with what is said of John, and are asking about his mission, I may take the opportunity to state the view which I entertain about him.

We have read this prophecy about him, "Behold, I send My messenger (angel) before Thy face, who shall prepare Thy way before Thee;" and at this we ask if it can be one of the holy angels who is sent down on this ministry as forerunner of our Savior. No wonder if, when the first-born of all creation was assuming a human body, some of them should have been filled with love to man and become admirers and followers of Christ, and thought it good to minister to his kindness towards man by having a body like that of men. And who would not be moved at the thought of his leaping for joy when yet in the belly, surpassing as he did the common nature of man? Should the piece entitled "The prayer of Joseph," one of the apocryphal works current among the Hebrews, be thought worthy of credence, this dogma will be found in it clearly expressed. Those at the beginning, it is represented, having some marked distinction beyond men, and being much greater than other souls, because they were angels, they have come down to human nature. Thus Jacob says: "I, Jacob, who speak to you, and Israel, I am an angel of God, a ruling spirit, and Abraham and Isaac were created before every work of God; and I am Jacob, called Jacob by men, but my name is Israel, called Israel by God, a man seeing God, because I am the first-born of every creature which God caused to live." And he adds: "When I was coming from Mesopotamia of Syria, Uriel, the angel of God, came forth, and said, I have come down to the earth and made my dwelling among men, and I am called Jacob by name. He was wroth with me and fought with me and wrestled against me, saying that his name and the name of Him who is before every angel should be before my name. And I told him his name and how great he was among the sons of God; Art not thou Uriel my eighth, and I am Israel and archangel of the power of the Lord and a chief captain among the sons of God? Am not I Israel, the first minister in the sight of God, and I invoked my God by the inextinguishable name?" It is likely that this was really said by Jacob, and was therefore written down, and that there is also a deeper meaning in what we are told, "He supplanted his brother in the womb." Consider whether the celebrated question about Jacob and Esau has a solution. We read, "The children being not yet born, neither having done anything good or bad, that the purpose of God according to election might stand, not of works but of him that called, it was said, "The elder shall serve the younger." Even as it is written: "Jacob I loved, but Esau I hated." What shall we say, then? Is there unrighteousness with God? God forbid." If, then, when they were not yet born, and had not done anything either good or evil, in order that God's purpose according to election might stand, not of works, but of him that called, if at such a period this was said, how if we do not go back to the works done before this life, can it be said that there is no unrighteousness with God when the elder serves the younger and is hated (by God) before he has done anything worthy of slavery or of hatred? We have made something of a digression in introducing this story about Jacob and appealing to a writing which we cannot well treat with contempt; but it certainly adds weight to our argument about John, to the effect that as Isaiah's voice declares he is an angel who assumed a body for the sake of bearing witness to the light. So much about John considered as a man.

26. John is Voice, Jesus is Speech. Relation of These Two to Each Other. Now we know voice and

speech to be different things. The voice can be produced without any meaning and with no speech in it, and similarly speech can be reported to the mind without voice, as when we make mental excursions, within ourselves. And thus the Savior is, in one view of Him, speech, and John differs from Him; for as the Savior is speech, John is voice. John himself invites me to take this view of him, for to those who asked who he was, he answered, "I am the voice of one crying in the wilderness, Prepare the way of the Lord! Make His paths straight!" This explains, perhaps, how it was that Zacharias lost his voice at the birth of the voice which points out the Word of God, and only recovered it when the voice, forerunner of the Word, was born. A voice must be perceived with the ears if the mind is afterwards to receive the speech which the voice indicates. Hence, John is, in point of his birth, a little older than Christ, for our voice comes to us before our speech. But John also points to Christ; for speech is brought forward by the voice. And Christ is baptized by John, though John declares himself to have need to be baptized by Christ; for with men speech is purified by voice, though the natural way is that speech should purify the voice which indicates it. In a word, when John points out Christ, it is man pointing out God, the Savior incorporeal, the voice pointing out the Word.

27. Significance of the Names of John and of His Parents.

The force that is in names may be applied in many matters, and it may be worth our while to ask at this point what is the significance of the names John and Zacharias. The relatives wish, as the giving of a name is a thing not to be lightly disposed of, to call the child Zacharias, and are surprised that Elisabeth should want him to be called John. Zacharias then writes, "His name is John," and is at once freed from his troublesome silence. On examining the names, then, we find "Joannes" to be "Joa" without the "nes." The New Testament gives Hebrew names a Greek form and treats them as Greek words; Jacob is changed into Jacobus, Symeon into Simon, and Joannes is the same as Joa. Zacharias is said to be memory, and Elisabeth "oath of my God," or "strength of my God." John then came into the world from grace of God (=Joa=Joannes), and his parents were Memory (about God) and the Oath of our God, about the fathers. Thus was he born to make ready for the Lord a people fit for Him, at the end of the Covenant now grown old, which is the end of the Sabbatic period. Hence it is not possible that the rest after the Sabbath should have come into existence from the seventh of our God; on the contrary, it is our Savior who, after the pattern of His own rest, caused us to be made in the likeness of His death, and hence also of His resurrection.

28. The Prophets Bore Witness to Christ and Foretold Many Things Concerning Him. "He came for a witness that He might bear witness of the light, that all through Him might believe." Some of the dissenters from the Church's doctrine, men who profess to believe in Christ, have desired another being, as indeed their system requires, besides the Creator, and hence cannot allow His coming to the world to have been foretold by the prophets. They therefore endeavor to get rid of the testimonies of the prophets about Christ, and say that the Son of God has no need of witnesses, but that He brings

with Him His own evidence, partly in the sound words full of power which He proclaimed and partly in the wonderful works He did, which were sufficient at once to convince anyone whatever. Then they say: If Moses is believed on account of his word and his works, and has no need of any witnesses to announce him beforehand, and if the prophets were received, every one of them, by these people, as messengers from God, how should not one who is much greater than Moses and the prophets accomplish His mission and benefit the human race, without prophets to bear witness about Him? They regard it as superfluous that He should have been foretold by the prophets, since the prophets were concerned, as these opponents would say, that those who believed in Christ should not receive Him as a new God, and therefore did what they could to bring them to that same God whom Moses and the prophets taught before Jesus. To this we must say that as there are many causes which may lead men to believe, since men who are not moved by one argument may be by another, so God is able to provide for men a number of occasions, any of which may cause their minds to open to the truth that God, who is over all, has taken on Himself human nature. It is manifest to all, how some are brought by the prophetic writings to the admiration of Christ. They are astounded at the voices of so many prophets before Him, which establish the place of His birth, the country of His upbringing, the power of His teaching, His working of wonderful works, and His human passion brought to a close by His resurrection. We must notice, too, that Christ's stupendous acts of power were able to bring to the faith those of Christ's own time, but that they lost their demonstrative force with the lapse of years and began to be regarded as mythical. Greater evidential value than that of the miracles then performed attaches to the comparison which we now make between these miracles and the prophecy of them; this makes it impossible for the student to cast any doubt on the former. The prophetic testimonies do not declare merely the advent of the Messiah; it is by no means the case that they teach this and nothing else. They teach a great deal of theology. The relation of the Father to the Son and of the Son to the Father may be learned not less from what the prophets announce about Christ, than from the Apostles narrating the splendors of the Son of God. A parallel case, which we may venture to adduce, is that of the martyrs, who were honored by the witness they bore Him, and by no means conferred any favor on Him by their witnessing for the Son of God. And how is it if, as many of Christ's true disciples were honored by having thus to witness for Him, so the prophets received from God as their special gift that of understanding about Christ and announcing Him before, and that they taught not only those living after Christ's advent how they should regard the Son of God, but those also who lived in the generations before Him? As he who in these times does not know the Son has not the Father either, so also we are to understand it was in these earlier times. Hence "Abraham rejoiced to see the day of Christ, and he saw it and was glad." He, therefore, who declares that they are not to testify about Christ is seeking to deprive the chorus of the prophets of the greatest gift they have; for what office of equal importance would be left to prophecy, inspired as it is by the Holy Spirit, if all connection with the economy of our Lord and Master were taken away from it? For as these have their faith well-ordered who approach the God of the universe through Mediator and High-Priest and Paraclete, and as his religion is a halting one who does not go in through the door to the Father, so also in the case of men of old time. Their religion was sanctified and made acceptable to God by their knowledge and faith and expectation of Christ. For we have observed that God declares Himself to be a witness and exhorts them all to declare the same about Christ, and to be imitators of Him, bearing witness of Him to all who require it. For he says, "Be witnesses for Me, and I am witness, says the Lord God, and My servant whom I have chosen." Now everyone who bears witness to the truth, whether he support it by words or deeds, or in whatever way, may properly be called a witness (martyr); but it has come to be the custom of the brotherhood, since they are struck with admiration of those who have contended to the death for truth and valor, to keep the name of martyr more properly for those who have borne witness to the mystery of godliness by shedding their blood for it. The Savior gives the name of martyr to everyone who bears witness to the truth He declares; thus at the Ascension He says to His disciples: "You shall be my witnesses in Jerusalem and in Judæa and in Samaria and unto the uttermost parts of the earth." The leper who was cleansed had still to bring the gift which Moses commanded for a testimony to those who did not believe in the Christ. In the same way the martyrs bear witness for a testimony to the unbelieving, and so do all the saints whose deeds shine before men. They spend their life rejoicing in the cross of Christ and bearing witness to the true light.

29. The Six Testimonies of the Baptist Enumerated. Jesus' "Come and See." Significance of the Tenth Hour.

Accordingly John came to bear witness of the light, and in his witness-bearing he cried, saying, "He that cometh after me exists before me; for He was before me; for of His fullness we have all received and grace for grace, for the law was given by Moses, but grace and truth came through Jesus Christ. No one hath seen God at any time; the only-begotten God, who is in the bosom of the Father, He hath declared Him." This whole speech is from the mouth of the Baptist bearing witness to the Christ. Some take it otherwise, and consider that the words from "for of His fullness" to "He hath declared Him" are from the writer, John the Apostle. The true state of the case is that John's first testimony begins, as we said before, "He that cometh after me," and ends, "He hath declared Him," and his second testimony is that spoken to the priests and Levites sent from Jerusalem, whom the Jews had sent. To them he confesses and does not deny the truth, namely, that he is not the Christ, nor Elijah, nor the prophet, but "the voice of one crying in the wilderness, Make straight the way of the Lord, as says Isaiah the prophet." After this there is another testimony of the same Baptist to Christ, still teaching His superior nature, which goes forth into the whole world and enters into reasonable souls. He says, "There stands One among you whom you know not, even He that cometh after me, the latchet of whose shoe I am not worthy to unloose." Consider if, since the heart is in the middle of the whole body, and the ruling principle in the heart, the saying, "There stands One among you whom you know not," can be understood of the reason which is in every man. John's fourth testimony of Christ after these points to His human sufferings. He says, "Behold the Lamb of God, which taketh away the sin of the world. This is He of whom I said, After me cometh a man who exists before me, for He was before me. And I knew Him not, but that He should be made manifest to Israel, therefore am I come baptizing with water." And the fifth testimony is recorded in the words, "I beheld the Spirit descending as a dove out of heaven, and it abode upon Him, and I knew Him not, but He that sent me to baptize with water, He said unto me, Upon whomsoever thou shalt see the Spirit descending and abiding upon Him, the same is He that baptizes with the Holy Spirit. And I have seen and borne witness that this is the Son of God." In the sixth place John witnesses of Christ to the two disciples: "He looked on Jesus as He walked and says, Behold the Lamb of God." After this testimony the two disciples who heard it followed Jesus; and Jesus turned and beheld them following, and says unto them, "What seek ye?" Perhaps it is not without significance that after six testimonies John ceases from his witness-bearing and Jesus brings forward in the seventh place His "What seek ye?" Very becoming in those who have been helped by John's testimony is the speech in which they address Christ as their Master, and declare their wish to see the dwelling of the Son of God; for they say to Him, "Rabbi," which answers to "Master," in our language, "where dwells Thou?" And since everyone that seeks finds, when John's disciples seek Jesus' dwelling, Jesus shows it to them, saying, "Come and see." By the word "Come" He exhorts them perhaps to the practical part of life, while the "see" is to suggest to them that that speculation which comes in the train of right conduct will be vouchsafed to those who desire it; in Jesus' dwelling they will have it. After they had asked where Jesus dwells, and had followed the Master and had seen, they desired to stay with Him and to spend that day with the Son of God. Now the number ten is a sacred one, not a few mysteries being indicated by it; and so we are to understand that the mention of the tenth hour as that at which these disciples turned in with Jesus, is not without significance. Of these disciples, Andrew, the brother of Simon Peter, is one; and he having profited by this day with Jesus and having found his own brother Simon (perhaps he had not found him before), told him that he had found the Messiah, which is, being interpreted, Christ. It is written that "he that seeks finds." Now he had sought where Jesus dwelt, and had followed Him and looked upon His dwelling; he stays with the Lord "at the tenth hour," and finds the Son of God, the Word, and Wisdom, and is ruled by Him as King. That is why he says, "We have found the Messiah," and this a thing which everyone can say who has found this Word of God and is ruled as by a king, by His Divinity. As a fruit he at once brings his brother to Christ, and Christ deigned to look upon Simon, that is to say, by looking at him to visit and enlighten his ruling principle; and Simon by Jesus' looking at him was enabled to grow strong, so as to earn a new name from that work of firmness and strength, and to be called Peter.

### 30. How John Was a Witness of Christ, and Especially of "The Light."

It may be asked why we should have gone through all this when the verse before us is, "He came for witness, that he might bear witness of the light." But it was necessary to give John's testimonies to the light, and to show the order in which they took place, and also, in order to show how effective John's testimony proved, to set forth the help it afforded afterwards to those to whom he bore it. But before all these testimonies there was an earlier one when the Baptist leaped in the womb of Elisabeth at the greeting of Mary. That was a testimony to Christ and attested His divine conception and birth. And what more need I say? John is everywhere a witness and forerunner of Christ. He anticipates His birth and dies a little before the death of the Son of God, and thus witnesses not only for those at the time of the birth, but to those who were expecting the freedom which was to come for man through the death of Christ. Thus, in all his life, he is a little before Christ, and everywhere makes ready for the Lord a people prepared for Him. And John's testimony precedes also the second and diviner coming of Christ, for we read, "If ye will receive it, this is Elijah which is to come. He that hath ears to hear let him hear." Now, there was a beginning, in which the Word was,—and we saw from Proverbs that that beginning was wisdom,—and the Word was in existence, and in the Word life was made, and the life was the light of men; and all this being so, I ask why the man who came, sent from God, whose name was John, why he came for witness to bear witness especially of the light? Why did he not come to bear witness of the life, or of the Word, or about the beginning, or about any other of the many aspects in which Christ appears? Consider here the texts, "The people which sat in darkness saw a great light," and "The light shines in darkness, and the darkness overtook it not," and consider how those who are in darkness, that is, men, have need of light. For if the light of men shines in darkness, and there is no active power in darkness to attain to it, then we must partake of other aspects of

Christ; at present we have no real share of Him at all. For what share have we of life, we who are still in the body of death, and whose life is hid with Christ in God? "For when Christ who is our life shall appear, then shall we also appear with Him in glory." It was not possible, therefore, that he who came should bear witness about a life which is still hid with Christ in God. Nor did he come for witness to bear witness of the Word, for we know the Word who was in the beginning with God and who is God the Word; for the Word was made flesh on the earth. And though the witness had been, at least apparently, about the Word, it would in fact have been about the Word made flesh and not about the word of God. He did not come, therefore, to bear witness of the Word. And how could there be any witness-bearing about wisdom, to those who, even if they appear to know something, cannot understand pure truth, but behold it through a glass and in an enigma? It is likely, however, that before the second and diviner advent of Christ, John or Elias will come to bear witness about life a little before Christ our life is made manifest, and that then they will bear witness about the Word, and offer also their testimony about wisdom. Some inquiry is necessary whether a testimony such as that of John is to precede each of the aspects of Christ. So much for the words, "He came for witness, to bear witness of the light." What we are to understand by the further words, "That all might believe through Him," may be considered later.

Fragments of the Fourth Book.
(*Three Leaves from the Beginning.*)
1. He who distinguishes in himself voice and meaning and things for which the meaning stands, will

not be offended at rudeness of language if, on enquiry, he finds the things spoken of to be sound. The more may this be so when we remember how the holy men acknowledge their speech and their preaching to be not in persuasion of the wisdom of words, but in demonstration of the Spirit and of power....

[*Then, after speaking of the rudeness of style of the Gospel, he proceeds*: ]

2. The Apostles are not unaware that in some things they give offence, and that in some respects their culture is defective, and they confess themselves accordingly to be rude in speech but not in knowledge; for we must consider that the other Apostles would have said this, too, as well as Paul. As for the text, "But we have this treasure in earthen vessels, that the excellency of the power may be of God and not of us," we interpret it in this way. By "treasures" we understand here, as in other passages, the treasure of knowledge (gnosis) and of hidden wisdom. By "earthen vessels" we understand the humble diction of the Scriptures, which the Greek might so readily be led to despise, and in which the excellency of God's power appears so clearly. The mystery of the truth and the power of the things said were not hindered by the humble diction from travelling to the ends of the earth, nor from subduing to the word of Christ, not only the foolish things of the world, but sometimes its wise things, too. For we see our calling, not that no wise man according to the flesh, but that not many wise according to the flesh. But Paul, in his preaching of the Gospel, is a debtor to deliver the word not to Barbarians only, but also to Greeks, and not only to the unwise, who would easily agree with him, but also to the wise. For he was made sufficient by God to be a minister of the New Covenant,

wielding the demonstration of the spirit and of power, so that when the believers agreed with him their belief should not be in the wisdom of men, but in the power of God. For, perhaps, if the Scripture possessed, like the works the Greeks admire, elegance and command of diction, then it would be open to suppose that not the truth of them had laid hold of men, but that the apparent sequence and splendor of language had carried off the hearers, and had carried them off by guile.

From the Fifth Book.
*From the Preface.*
You are not content to fulfil the office, when I am present with you, of a taskmaster to drive me to labor at theology; even when I am absent you demand that I should spend most of my time on you and on the task I have to do for you. I, for my part, am inclined to shrink from toil, and to avoid that danger which threatens from God those who give themselves to writing on divinity; thus I would take shelter in Scripture in refraining from making many books. For Solomon says in Ecclesiastes, "My son, beware of making many books; there is no end of it, and much study is a weariness of the flesh." For we, except that text have some hidden meaning which we do not yet perceive, have directly transgressed the injunction, we have not guarded ourselves against making many books.

[*Then, after saying that this discussion of but a few sentences of the Gospel have run to four volumes, he goes on:*]

2. How Scripture Warns Us Against Making Many Books.

For, to judge by the words of the phrase, "My son, beware of making many books," two things appear to be indicated by it: first, that we ought not to possess many books, and then that we ought not to compose many books. If the first is not the meaning the second must be, and if the second is the meaning the first does not necessarily follow. In either case we appear to be told that we ought not to make many books. I might take my stand on this dictum which now confronts us, and send you the text as an excuse, and I might appeal in support of this position to the fact that not even the saints found leisure to compose many books; and thus I might cry off from the bargain we made with each other, and give up writing what I was to send to you. You, on your side, would no doubt feel the force of the text I have cited, and might, for the future, excuse me. But we must treat Scripture conscientiously, and must not congratulate ourselves because we see the primary meaning of a text, that we understand it altogether. I do not, therefore, shrink from bringing forward what excuse I think I am able to offer for myself, and to point out the arguments, which you would certainly use against me, if I acted contrary to our agreement. And in the first place, the Sacred History seems to agree with the text in question, inasmuch as none of the saints composed several works, or set forth his views in a number of books. I will take up this point: when I proceed to write a number of books, the critic will remind me that even such a one as Moses left behind him only five books.

3. The Apostles Wrote Little.

But he who was made fit to be a minister of the New Covenant, not of the letter, but of the spirit, Paul, who fulfilled the Gospel from Jerusalem round about to Illyricum, did not write epistles to all the churches he taught, and to those to whom he did write he sent no more than a few lines. And Peter, on whom the Church of Christ is built, against which the gates of hell shall not prevail left only one epistle of acknowledged genuineness. Suppose we allow that he left a second; for this is doubtful. What are we to say of him who leaned on Jesus' breast, namely, John, who left one Gospel, though confessing that he could make so many that the world would not contain them? But he wrote also the Apocalypse, being commanded to be silent and not to write the voices of the seven thunders. But he also left an epistle of very few lines. Suppose also a second and a third, since not all pronounce these to be genuine; but the two together do not amount to a hundred lines.

[*Then, after enumerating the prophets and Apostles, and showing how each wrote only a little, or not even a little, he goes on:*]

4. I feel myself growing dizzy with all this, and wonder whether, in obeying you, I have not been obeying God, nor walking in the footsteps of the saints, unless it be that my too great love to you, and my unwillingness to cause you any pain, has led me astray and caused me to think of all these excuses. We started from the words of the preacher, where he says: "My son, beware of making many books." With this I compare a saying from the Proverbs of the same Solomon, "In the multitude of words thou shalt not escape sin; but in sparing thy lips thou shalt be wise." Here I ask whether speaking many words of whatever kind is a multitude of words (in the sense of the preacher), even if the many words a man speaks are

sacred and connected with salvation. If this be the case, and if he who makes use of many salutary words is guilty of "multitude of words," then Solomon himself did not escape this sin, for "he spoke three thousand proverbs, and five thousand songs, and he spoke of trees from the cedar that is in Lebanon even unto the hyssop that springs out of the wall, he spoke also of beasts and of fowl, and of creeping things and of fishes." How, I may ask, can anyone give any course of instruction, without a multitude of words, using the phrase in its simplest sense? Does not Wisdom herself say to those who are perishing, "I stretched out my words, and ye heeded not"? Do we not find Paul, too, extending his discourse from morning to midnight, when Eutychus was borne down with sleep and fell down, to the dismay of the hearers, who thought he was killed? If, then, the words are true, "In much speaking thou wilt not escape sin," and if Solomon was yet not guilty of great sin when he discoursed on the subjects above mentioned, nor Paul when he prolonged his discourse till midnight, then the question arises, What is that much speaking which is referred to? And then we may pass on to consider what are the many books. Now the entire Word of God, who was in the beginning with God, is not much speaking, is not *words*; for the Word is one, being composed of the many speculations (theoremata), each of which is a part of the Word in its entirety. Whatever words there be outside of this one, which promise to give any description and exposition, even though they be words about truth, none of these, to put it in a somewhat paradoxical way, is Word or Reason, they are all words or reasons. They are not the monad, far from it; they are not that which agrees and is one in itself, by their inner divisions and conflicts unity has departed from them, they have become numbers, perhaps infinite numbers. We are obliged, therefore, to say that whoever speaks that which is foreign to religion is using many words, while he who speaks the words of truth, even should he go over the whole field and omit nothing, is always speaking the one word. Nor are the saints guilty of much speaking, since they always have the aim in view which is connected with the one word. It appears, then, that the much speaking which is condemned is judged to be so rather from the nature of the views propounded, than from the number of the words pronounced. Let us see if we cannot conclude in the same way that all the sacred books are one book, but that those outside are the "many books" of the preacher. The proof of this must be drawn from Holy Scripture, and it will be most satisfactorily established if I am able to show that it is not only one book, taking the word now in its commoner meaning, that we find to be written about Christ. Christ is written about even in the Pentateuch; He is spoken of in each of the Prophets, and in the Psalms, and, in a word, as the Savior Himself says, in all the Scriptures. He refers us to them all, when He says: "Search the Scriptures, for in them ye think ye have eternal life, and these are they which testify of Me." And if He refers us to the Scriptures as testifying of Him, it is not to one that He sends us, to the exclusion of another, but to all that speak of Him, those which, in the Psalms, He calls the chapter of the book, saying, "In the chapter of the book it is written of Me." If anyone proposes to take these words, "In the chapter of the book it is written of Me," literally, and to apply them to this or that special passage where Christ is spoken of, let him tell us on what principle he warrants his preference for one book over another. If any one supposes that we are doing something of this kind ourselves, and applying the words in question to the book of Psalms, we deny that we do so, and we would urge that in that case the words should have been, "In this book it is written of Me." But He speaks of all the books as one chapter, thus summing up in one all that is spoken of Christ for our instruction. In fact the book was seen by John, "written within and without, and sealed; and no one could open it to read it, and to loose the seals thereof, but the Lion of the tribe of Judah, the root of David, who has the key of David, he that opened and none shall shut, and that shut and none shall open." For the book here spoken of means the whole of Scripture; and it is written within (lit. in front), on account of the meaning which is obvious, and on the back, on account of its remoter and spiritual sense. Observe, in addition to this, if a proof that the sacred writings are one book, and those of an opposite character many, may not be found in the fact that there is one book of the living from which those who have proved unworthy to be in it are blotted out, as it is written: "Let them be blotted out of the book of the living," while of those who are to undergo the judgment, there are books in the plural, as Daniel says: "The judgment was set, and the books were opened." But Moses also bears witness to the unity of the sacred book, when he says: "If Thou forgive the people their sins, forgive, but if not, then wipe me out of the book which Thou hast written." The passage in Isaiah, too, I read in the same way. It is not peculiar to his prophecy that the words of the book should be sealed, and should neither be read by him who does not know letters, because he is ignorant of letters, nor by him who is learned, because the book is sealed. This is true of every writing, for every written work needs the reason (Logos) which closed it to open it. "He shall shut, and none shall open," and when He opens no one can cast doubt on the interpretation He brings. Hence it is said that He shall open and no man shall shut. I infer a similar lesson from the book spoken of in Ezekiel, in which was written lamentation, and a song, and woe. For the whole book is full of the woe of the lost, and the song of the saved, and the lamentation of those between these two. And John, too, when he speaks of his eating the one roll, in which both front and back were written on, means the whole of Scripture, one book which is, at first, most sweet when one begins, as it were, to chew it, but bitter in the revelation of himself which it makes to the conscience of each one who knows it. I will add to the proof of this an apostolic saying which has been quite misunderstood by the disciples of Marcion, who, therefore, set the Gospels at naught. The Apostle says: "According to my Gospel in Christ Jesus;" he does not speak of Gospels in the plural, and, hence, they argue that as the Apostle only speaks of one Gospel in the singular, there was only one in existence. But they fail to see that, as He is one of whom all the evangelists write, so the Gospel, though written by several hands, is, in effect, one. And, in fact, the Gospel, though written by four, is one. From these considerations, then, we learn what the one book is, and what the many books, and what I am now concerned about is, not the quantity I may write, but the effect of what I say, lest, if I fail in this point, and set forth anything against the truth itself, even in one of my writings, I should prove to have transgressed the commandment, and to be a writer of "many books." Yet I see the heterodox assailing the holy Church of God in these days, under the presence of higher wisdom, and bringing forward works in many volumes in which they offer expositions of the evangelical and apostolic writings, and I fear that if I should be silent and should not put before our members the saving and true doctrines, these teachers might get a hold of curious souls, which, in the absence of wholesome nourishment, might go after food that is forbidden, and, in fact, unclean and horrible. It appears to me, therefore, to be necessary that one who is able to represent in a genuine manner the doctrine of the Church, and to refute those dealers in knowledge, falsely so-called, should take his stand against historical fictions, and oppose to them the true and lofty evangelical message in which the agreement of the doctrines, found both in the so-called Old Testament and in the so-called New, appears so plainly and fully. You yourself felt at one time the lack of good representatives of the better cause, and were impatient of a faith which was at issue with reason and absurd, and you then, for the love you bore to the Lord, gave yourself to composition from which, however, in the exercise of the judgment with which you are endowed, you afterwards desisted. This is the defense which I think admits of being made for those who have the faculty of speaking and writing. But I am also pleading my own cause, as I now devote myself with what boldness I may to the work of exposition; for it may be that I am not endowed with that habit and disposition which he ought to have who is fitted by God to be a minister of the New Covenant, not of the letter but of the spirit.

Sixth Book.
1. The Work is taken up after a Violent Interruption, Which Has Driven the Writer from

Alexandria. He Addresses Himself to It Again, with Thanks for His Deliverance, and Prayer for Guidance.

When a house is being built which is to be made as strong as possible, the building takes place in fine weather and in calm, so that nothing may hinder the structure from acquiring the needed solidity. And thus it turns out so strong and stable that it is able to withstand the rush of the flood, and the dashing of the river, and all the agencies accompanying a storm which are apt to find out what is rotten in a building and to show what parts of it have been properly put together. And more particularly should that house which is capable of sheltering the speculations of truth, the house of reason, as it were, in promise or in letters, be built at a time when God can add His free co-operation to the projector of so noble a work, when the soul is quiet and in the enjoyment of that peace which passes all understanding, when she is turned away from all disturbance and not buffeted by any billows. This, it appears to me, was well understood by the servants of the prophetic spirit and the ministers of the Gospel message; they made themselves worthy to receive that peace which is in secret from Him who ever gives it to them that are worthy and who said, "Peace I leave with you, My peace I give unto you; not as the world giveth give I unto you." And look if some similar lesson is not taught under the surface with regard to David and Solomon in the narrative about the temple. David, who fought the wars of the Lord and stood firm against many enemies, his own and those of Israel, desired to build a temple for God. But God, through Nathan, prevents him from doing so, and Nathan says to him, "Thou shalt not build me an house, because thou art a man of blood." But Solomon, on the other hand, saw God in a dream, and in a dream received wisdom, for the reality of the vision was kept for him who said, "Behold a greater than Solomon is here." The time was one of the profoundest peace, so that it was possible for every man to rest under his own vine and his own fig-tree, and Solomon's very name was significant of the peace which was in his days, for Solomon means peaceful; and so he was at liberty to build the famous temple of God. About the time of Ezra, also, when "truth conquers wine and the hostile king and women," the temple of God is restored again. All this is said by way of apology to you, reverend Ambrosius. It is at your sacred encouragement that I have made up my mind to build up in writing the tower of the Gospel; and I have therefore sate down to count the cost, if I have sufficient to finish it, lest I should be mocked by the beholders, because I laid the foundation but was not able to finish the work. The result of my counting, it is true, has been that I do not possess what is required to finish it; yet I have put my trust in God, who enriches us with all wisdom and all knowledge. If we strive to keep His spiritual laws we believe that He does enrich us; He will supply what is necessary so that we shall get on with our building, and shall even come to the parapet of the structure. That parapet it is which keeps from falling those who go up on the house of the Word; for people only fall off those houses which have no parapet, so that the buildings themselves are to blame for their fall and for their death. We proceeded as far as the fifth volume in spite of the obstacles presented by the storm in Alexandria, and spoke what was given us to speak, for Jesus rebuked the winds and the waves of the sea. We emerged from the storm, we were brought out of Egypt, that God delivering us who led His people forth from there. Then, when the enemy assailed us with all bitterness by his new writings, so directly hostile to the Gospel, and stirred up against us all the winds of wickedness in Egypt, I felt that reason called me rather to stand fast for the conflict, and to save the higher part in me, lest evil counsels should succeed in directing the storm so as to overwhelm my soul, rather to do this than to finish my work at an unsuitable season, before my mind had recovered its calm. Indeed, the ready writers who usually attended me brought my work to a stand by failing to appear to take down my words. But now that the many fiery darts directed against me have lost their edge, for God extinguished them, and my soul has grown accustomed to the dispensation sent me for the sake of the heavenly word, and has learned from necessity to disregard the snares of my enemies, it is as if a great calm had settled on me, and I defer no longer the continuation of this work. I pray that God will be with me, and will speak as a teacher in the porch of my soul, so that the building I have begun of the exposition of the Gospel of John may arrive at completion. May God hear my prayer and grant that the body of the whole work may now be brought together, and that no interruption may intervene which might prevent me from following the sequence of Scripture. And be assured that it is with great readiness that I now make this second beginning and enter on my sixth volume, because what I wrote before at Alexandria has not, I know not by what chance, been brought with me. I feared I might neglect this work, if I were not engaged on it at once, and therefore thought it better to make use of this present time and begin without delay the part which remains. I am not certain if the part formerly written will come to light, and would be very unwilling to waste time in waiting to see if it does. Enough of preamble, let us now attend to our text.

2. How the Prophets and Holy Men of the Old Testament Knew the Things of Christ. "And this is the witness of John." This is the second recorded testimony of John the Baptist to Christ. The first begins with "This was He of whom I said, He that cometh after me," and goes down to "The only-begotten Son of God who is in the bosom of the Father, He hath declared him." Heracleon supposes the words, "No one has seen God at any time," etc., to have been spoken, not by the Baptist, but by the disciple. But in this he is not sound. He himself allows the words, "Of his fullness we all received, and grace for grace; for the law was given by Moses, but grace and truth came by Jesus Christ," to have been spoken by the Baptist. And does it not follow that the person who received of the fullness of Christ, and a second grace in addition to that he had before, and who declared the law to have been given by Moses, but grace and truth to have come through Jesus Christ, is it not clear that this is the person who understood, from what he received from the fullness of Christ, how "no one hath seen God at any time," and how "the only-begotten who is in the bosom of the Father" had delivered the declaration about God to him and to all those who had received of His fullness? He was not declaring here for the first time Him that is in the bosom of the Father, as if there had never before been any one fit to receive what he told His Apostles. Does he not teach us that he was before Abraham, and that Abraham rejoiced and was glad to see his day? The words "Of his fullness all we received," and "Grace for grace," show, as we have already made clear, that the prophets also

received their gift from the fullness of Christ and received a second grace in place of that they had before; for they also, led by the Spirit, advanced from the introduction they had in types to the vision of truth. Hence not all the prophets, but many of them, desired to see the things, which the Apostles saw. For if there was a difference among the prophets, those who were perfect and more distinguished of them did not desire to see what the Apostles saw, but actually beheld them, while those who rose less fully than these to the height of the Word were filled with longing for the things which the Apostles knew through Christ. The word "saw" we have not taken in a physical sense, and the word "heard" we have taken to refer to a spiritual communication; only he who has ears is prepared to hear the words of Jesus—a thing which does not happen too frequently. There is the further point, that the saints before the bodily advent of Jesus had an advantage over most believers in their insight into the mysteries of divinity, since the Word of God was their teacher before He became flesh, for He was always working, in imitation of His Father, of whom He says, "My father worked hitherto." On this point we may adduce the words He addresses to the Sadducees, who do not believe the doctrine of the resurrection. "Have you not read," He says, "what is said by God at the Bush, I am the God of Abraham, and the God of Isaac, and the God of Jacob; He is not the God of the dead but of the living." If, then, God is not ashamed to be called the God of these men, and if they are counted by Christ among the living, and if all believers are sons of Abraham, since all the Gentiles are blessed with faithful Abraham, who is appointed by God to be a father of the Gentiles, can we hesitate to admit that those living persons made acquaintance with the learning of living men, and were taught by Christ who was born before the daystar, before He became flesh? And for this cause they lived, because they had part in Him who said, "I am the life," and as the heirs of so great promises received the vision, not only of angels, but of God in Christ. For they saw, it may be, the image of the invisible God, since he who hath seen the Son hath seen the Father, and so they are recorded to have known God, and to have heard God's words worthily, and, therefore, to have seen God and heard Him. Now, I consider that those who are fully and really sons of Abraham are sons of his actions, spiritually understood, and of the knowledge which was made manifest to him. What he knew and what he did appears again in those who are his sons, as the Scripture teaches those who have ears to hear, "If ye were the children of Abraham, ye would do the works of Abraham." And if it is a true proverb which says, "A wise man will understand that which proceeds from his own mouth, and on his lips he will bear prudence," then we must at once repudiate some things which have been said about the prophets, as if they were not wise men, and did not understand what proceeded from their own mouths. We must believe what is good and true about the prophets, that they were sages, that they did understand what proceeded from their mouths, and that they bore prudence on their lips. It is clear indeed that Moses understood in his mind the truth (real meaning) of the law, and the higher interpretations of the stories recorded in his books. Joshua, too, understood the meaning of the allotment of the land after the destruction of the nine and twenty kings, and could see better than we can the realities of which his achievements were the shadows. It is clear, too, that

Isaiah saw the mystery of Him who sat upon the throne, and of the two seraphim, and of the veiling of their faces and their feet, and of their wings, and of the altar and of the tongs. Ezekiel, too, understood the true significance of the cherubim and of their goings, and of the firmament that was above them, and of Him that sat on the throne, than all which what could be loftier or more splendid? I need not enter into more particulars; the point I aim at establishing is clear enough already, namely, that those who were made perfect in earlier generations knew not less than the Apostles did of what Christ revealed to them, since the same teacher was with them as He who revealed to the Apostles the unspeakable mysteries of godliness. I will add but a few points, and then leave it to the reader to judge and to form what views he pleases on this subject. Paul says in his Epistle to the Romans, "Now, to him who is able to establish you according to my Gospel, according to the revelation of the mystery which hath been kept in silence through times eternal, but is now made manifest by the prophetic Scriptures and the appearance of our Lord Jesus Christ." For if the mystery concealed of old is made manifest to the Apostles through the prophetic writings, and if the prophets, being wise men, understood what proceeded from their own mouths, then the prophets knew what was made manifest to the Apostles. But to many it was not revealed, as Paul says, "In other generations it was not made known to the sons of men as it hath now been revealed unto His holy Apostles and prophets by the Spirit, that the Gentiles are fellow-heirs and members of the same body." Here an objection may be raised by those who do not share the view we have propounded; and it becomes of importance to define what is meant by the word "revealed." It is capable of two meanings: firstly, that the thing in question is understood, but secondly, if a prophecy is spoken of, that it is accomplished. Now, the fact that the Gentiles were to be fellow-heirs and members of the same body, and partakers of the promise, was known to the prophets to this extent, that they knew the Gentiles were to fellow heirs and members of the same body, and partakers of the promise in Christ. When this should be, and why, and what Gentiles were spoken of, and how, though strangers from the covenants, and aliens to the promises, they were yet to be members of one body and sharers of the blessings; all this was known to the prophets, being revealed to them. But the things prophesied belong to the future, and are not revealed to those who know them, but do not witness their fulfilment, as they are to those who have the event before their eyes. And this was the position of the Apostles. Thus, I conceive, they knew the events no more than the fathers and the prophets did; and yet it is truly said of them that "what to other generations was not revealed was now revealed to the Apostles and prophets, that the Gentiles were fellow- heirs and members of the same body, and partakers in the promise of Christ." For, in addition to knowing these mysteries, they saw the power at work in the accomplished fact. The passage, "Many prophets and righteous men desired to see the things ye see and did not see them; and to hear the things ye hear and did not hear them," may be interpreted in the same way. They also desired to see the mystery of the incarnation of the Son of God, and of His coming down to carry out the design of His suffering for the salvation of many, actually put in operation. This may be illustrated from another quarter. Suppose one of the Apostles to have understood the "unspeakable words which it is not lawful for a man to utter," but not to witness the glorious bodily appearing of Jesus to the faithful. Which is promised, although He desired to see it and suppose another had not only not marked and seen what that Apostle marked and saw, but had a much feebler grasp of the divine hope, and yet is present at the second coming of our Savior, which the Apostle, as in the parallel above, had desired, but had not seen. We shall not err from the truth if we say that both of these have seen what the Apostle, or indeed the Apostles, desired to see, and yet that they are not on that account to be deemed wiser or more blessed than the Apostles. In the same way, also, the Apostles are not to be deemed wiser than the fathers, or than Moses and the prophets, than those in fact who, for their virtue, were found worthy of epiphanies and of divine manifestations and of revelations of mysteries.

3. "Grace and Truth Came Through Jesus Christ." These Words Belong to the Baptist, Not the Evangelist. What the Baptist Testifies by Them.

We have lingered rather long over these discussions, but there is a reason for it. There are many who, under the presence of glorifying the advent of Christ, declare the Apostles to be wiser than the fathers or the prophets; and of these teachers some have invented a greater God for the later period, while some, not venturing so far, but moved, according to their own account of the matter, by the difficulty connected with doctrine, cancel the whole of the gift conferred by God on the fathers and the prophets, through Christ, through whom all things were made. If all things were made through Him, clearly so must the splendid revelations have been which were made to the fathers and prophets, and became to them the symbols of the sacred mysteries of religion. Now the true soldiers of Christ must always be prepared to do battle for the truth, and must never, so far as lies with them, allow false convictions to creep in. We must not, therefore, neglect this matter. It may be said that John's earlier testimony to Christ is to be found in the words, "He who cometh after me exists before me, for He was before me," and that the words, "For of His fullness we all received, and grace for grace," are in the mouth of John the disciple. Now, we must show this exposition to be a forced one, and one which does violence to the context; it is rather a strong proceeding to suppose the speech of the Baptist to be so suddenly and, as it were, inopportunely interrupted by that of the disciple, and it is quite apparent to anyone who can judge, in whatever small degree, of a context, that the speech goes on continuously after the words, "This is He of whom I spoke, He that cometh after me exists before me, for He was before me." The Baptist brings a proof that Jesus existed before him because He was before him, since He is the first-born of all creation; he says, "For of His fullness all we received." That is the reason why he says, "He exists before me, for He was before me." That is how I know that He is first and in higher honor with the Father, since of His fullness both I and the prophets before me received the more divine prophetic grace instead of the grace we received at His hands before in respect of our election. That is why I say, "He exists before me, for He was before me," because we know what we have received from His fullness; namely, that the law was given through Moses, not by Moses, while grace and truth not only were given but came into existence through Jesus Christ. For His God and Father both gave the law through Moses, and made grace and truth through Jesus Christ, that grace and truth which came to man. If we give a reasonable interpretation to the words, "Grace and truth came through Jesus Christ," we shall not be alarmed at the possible discrepancy with them of that other saying, "I am the way and the truth and the life." If it is Jesus who says, "I am the truth," then how does the truth come through Jesus Christ, since no one comes into existence through himself? We must recognize that this very truth, the essential truth, which is prototypal, so to speak, of that truth which exists in souls endowed with reason, that truth from which, as it were, images are impressed on those who care for truth, was not made through Jesus Christ, nor indeed through any one, but by God;—just as the Word was not made through any one which was in the beginning with the Father;—and as wisdom which God created the beginning of His ways was not made through any one, so the truth also was not made through any one. That truth, however, which is with men came through Jesus Christ, as the truth in Paul and the Apostles came through Jesus Christ. And it is no wonder, since truth is one, that many truths should flow from that one. The prophet David certainly knew many truths, as he says, "The Lord searches out truths," for the Father of truth searches out not the one truth but the many through which those are saved who possess them. And as with the one truth and many truths, so also with righteousness and righteousnesses. For the very essential righteousness is Christ, "Who was made to us of God wisdom and righteousness and sanctification and redemption." But from that righteousness is formed the righteousness which is in each individual, so that there are in the saved many righteousnesses, whence also it is written, "For the Lord is righteous, and He loved righteousnesses." This is the reading in the exact copies, and in the other versions besides the Septuagint, and in the Hebrew. Consider if the other things which Christ is said to be in a unity admit of being multiplied in the same way and spoken of in the plural. For example, Christ is our life as the Savior Himself says, "I am the way and the truth and the life." The Apostle, too, says, "When Christ our life shall appear, then shall ye also appear with Him in glory." And in the Psalms again we find, "Thy mercy is better than life;" for it is on account of Christ who is life in every one that there are many lives. This, perhaps, is also the key to the passage, "If ye seek a proof of the Christ that speaks in me." For Christ is found in every saint, and so from the one Christ there come to be many Christs, imitators of Him and formed after Him who is the image of God; whence God says through the prophet, "Touch not my Christs." Thus we have explained in passing the passage which we appeared to have omitted from our exposition, viz.: "Grace and truth came through Jesus Christ;" and we have also shown that the words belong to John the Baptist and form part of his testimony to the Son of God.

4. John Denies that He is Elijah or "The" Prophet. Yet He Was "A" Prophet.

Now let us consider John's second testimony. Jews from Jerusalem, kindred to John the Baptist, since he also belonged to a priestly race, send priests and Levites to ask John who he is. In saying, "I am not the Christ," he made a confession of the truth. The words are not, as one might suppose, a negation; for it is no negation to say, in the honor of Christ, that one is not Christ. The priests and Levites sent from Jerusalem, having there heard in the first place that he is not the expected Messiah, put a question about the second great personage whom they expected, namely, Elijah, whether John were he, and he says he is not Elijah, and by his "I am not" makes a second confession of the truth. And, as many prophets had appeared in Israel, and one in particular was looked for according to the prophecy of Moses, who said, "A prophet shall the Lord your God raise up to you of your brethren, like unto me, him shall ye hear; and it shall come to pass that every soul that shall not hear that prophet shall be destroyed from among the people," they, therefore, ask a third question, not whether he is a prophet, but whether he is the prophet. Now, they did not apply this name to the Christ, but supposed the prophet to be a second figure beside the Christ. But John, on the contrary, who knew that He whose forerunner he was was both the Christ and the prophet thus foretold, answered "No;" whereas, if they had asked if he was a prophet, he would have answered "Yes;" for he was not unconscious that he was a prophet. In all these answers John's second testimony to Christ was not yet completed; he had still to give his questioners the answer they were to take back to those who sent them, and to declare himself in the terms of the prophecy of Isaiah, which says, "The voice of one crying in the wilderness, Prepare ye the way of the Lord."

5. There Were Two Embassies to John the Baptist; The Different Characters of These.

Here the enquiry suggests itself whether the second testimony is concluded, and whether there is a third, addressed to those who were sent from the Pharisees. They wished to know why he baptized, if he was neither the Christ, nor Elijah, nor the prophet; and he said: "I baptize with water; but there stands one among you whom you know not, He that cometh after me, the latchet of whose shoe I am not worthy to unloose." Is this a third testimony, or is this which they were to report to the Pharisees a part of the second? As far as the words allow me to conjecture I should say that the word to the emissaries of the Pharisees was a third testimony. It is to be observed, however, that the first testimony asserts the divinity of the Savior, while the second disposes of the suspicion of those who were in doubt whether John could be the Christ, and the third declares one who was already present with men although they saw Him not, and whose coming was no longer in the future. Before going on to the subsequent testimonies in which he points out Christ and witnesses to Him, let us look at the second and third, word for word, and let us, in the first place, observe that there are two embassies to the Baptist, one "from Jerusalem" from the Jews, who send priests and Levites, to ask him, "Who art thou?" the second sent by the Pharisees, who were in doubt about the answer which had been made to the priests and Levites. Observe how what is said by the first envoys is in keeping with the character of priests and Levites, and shows gentleness and a willingness to learn. "Who art thou?" they say, and "What then? Art thou Elijah?" and "Art thou that prophet?" and then, "Who art thou, that we may give an answer to them that sent us? What says thou of thyself?" There is nothing harsh or arrogant in the enquiries of these men; everything agrees well with the character of true and careful servants of God; and they raise no difficulties about the replies made to them. Those, on the contrary, who are sent from the Pharisees assail the Baptist, as it were, with arrogant and unsympathetic words: "Why then baptizes thou if thou be not the Christ nor Elijah nor the prophet?" This mission is sent scarcely for the sake of information, as in the former case of the priests and Levites, but rather to debar the Baptist from baptizing, as if it were thought that no one was entitled to baptize but Christ and Elijah and the prophet. The student who desires to understand the Scripture must always proceed in this careful way; he must ask with regard to each speech, who is the speaker and on what occasion it was spoken. Thus only can we discern how speech harmonizes with the character of the speaker, as it does all through the sacred books.

6. Messianic Discussion with John the Baptist.

Then the Jews sent priests and Levites from Jerusalem to ask him, Who art thou? And he confessed and denied not; and he confessed, I am not the Christ. What legates should have been sent from the Jews to John, and where should they have been sent from? Should they not have been men held to stand by the election of God above their fellows, and should they not have come from that place which was chosen out of the whole of the earth, though it is all called good, from Jerusalem where was the temple of God? With such honor, then, do they enquire of John. In the case of Christ nothing of this sort is reported to have been done by the Jews; but what the Jews do to John, John does to Christ, sending his own disciples to ask him, "Art thou He that should come, or do we look for another?" John confesses to those sent to him, and denies not, and he afterwards declares, "I am the voice of one crying in the wilderness;" but Christ, as having a greater testimony than John the Baptist, makes His answer by words and deeds, saying, "Go and tell John those things which ye do hear and see; the blind receive their sight, and the lame walk, the lepers are cleansed and the deaf hear, and the poor have the Gospel preached to them." On this passage I shall, if God permit, enlarge in its proper place. Here, however, it might be asked reasonably enough why John gives such an answer to the question put to him. The priests and Levites do not ask him, "Art thou the Christ?" but "Who art thou?" and the Baptist's reply to this question should have been, "I am the voice of one crying in the wilderness." The proper reply to the question, "Art thou the Christ?" is, "I am not the Christ;" and to the question, "Who art thou?"—"The voice of one crying in the wilderness." To this we may say that he probably discerned in the question of the priests and Levites a cautious reverence, which led them to hint the idea in their minds that he who was baptizing might be the Christ, but withheld them from openly saying so, which might have been presumptuous. He quite naturally, therefore, proceeds in the first place to remove any false impressions they might have taken up about him, and declares publicly the true state of the matter, "I am not the Christ." Their second question, and also their third, show that they had conceived some such surmise about him. They supposed that he might be that second in honor to whom their hopes pointed, namely, Elijah, who held with them the next position after Christ; and so when John had answered, "I am not the Christ," they asked, "What then? Art thou Elijah?" And he said, "I am not." They wish to know, in the third place, if he is the prophet, and on his answer, "No," they have no longer any name to give the personage whose advent they expected, and they say, "Who art thou, then, that we may give an answer to them that sent us. What says thou of thyself?" Their meaning is: "You are not, you say, any of those personages whose advent Israel hopes and expects, and who you are, to baptize as you do, we do not know; tell us, therefore, so that we may report to those who sent us to get light upon this point." We add, as it has some bearing on the context, that the people were moved by the thought that the period of Christ's advent was near. It was in a manner imminent in the years from the birth of Jesus and a little before, down to the publication of the preaching. Hence it was, in all likelihood, that as the scribes and lawyers had deduced the time from Holy Scripture and were expecting the Coming One, the idea was taken up by Theudas, who came forward as the Messiah and brought together a considerable multitude, and after him by the famous Judas of Galilee in the days of the taxing. Thus the coming of the Messiah was more warmly expected and discussed, and it was natural enough for the Jews to send priests and Levites from Jerusalem to John, to ask him, "Who art thou?" and learn if he professed to be the Christ.

7. Of the Birth of John, and of His Alleged Identity with Elijah. Of the Doctrine of Transcorporation.

"And they asked him, What then? Art thou Elijah? And he said, I am not." No one can fail to remember in this connection what Jesus says of John, "If ye will receive it, this is Elijah which is to come." How, then, does John come to say to those who ask him, "Art thou Elijah?"—"I am not." And how can it be true at the same time that John is Elijah who is to come, according to the words of Malachi, "And behold I send unto you Elijah the Tishbite, before the great and notable day of the Lord come, who shall restore the heart of the father to the son, and the heart of a man to his neighbor, lest I come, and utterly smite the earth." The words of the angel of the Lord, too, who appeared to Zacharias, as he stood at the right hand of the altar of incense, are somewhat to the same effect as the prophecy of Malachi: "And thy wife Elisabeth shall bear thee a son, and thou shalt call his name John." And a little further on: "And he shall go before His face in the spirit and power of Elijah to turn the hearts of the fathers to the children, and the disobedient to the wisdom of the just, to make ready for the Lord a people prepared for Him." As for the first point, one might say that John did not know that he was Elijah. This will be the explanation of those who find in our passage a support for their doctrine of transcorporation, as if the soul clothed itself in a fresh body and did not quite remember its former lives. These thinkers will also point out that some of the Jews assented to this doctrine when they spoke about the Savior as if He was one of the old prophets, and had risen not from the tomb but from His birth. His mother Mary was well known, and Joseph the carpenter was supposed to be His father, and it could readily be supposed that He was one of the old prophets risen from the dead. The same person will adduce the text in Genesis, "I will destroy the whole resurrection," and will thereby reduce those who give themselves to finding in Scripture solutions of false probabilities to a great difficulty in respect of this doctrine. Another, however, a churchman, who repudiates the doctrine of transcorporation as a false one, and does not admit that the soul of John ever was Elijah, may appeal to the above quoted words of the angel, and point out that it is not the soul of Elijah that is spoken of at John's birth, but the spirit and power of Elijah. "He shall go before him," it is said, "in the spirit and power of

Elijah, to turn the hearts of the fathers to the children." Now it can be shown from thousands of texts that the spirit is a different thing from the soul, and that what is called the power is a different thing from both the soul and the spirit. On these points I cannot now enlarge; this work must not be unduly expanded. To establish the fact that power is different from spirit, it will be enough to cite the text, "The Holy Spirit shall come upon thee, and the power of the Highest shall overshadow thee." As for the spirits of the prophets, these are given to them by God, and are spoken of as being in a manner their property (slaves), as "The spirits of the prophets are subject to the prophets," and "The spirit of Elijah rested upon Elisha." Thus, it is said, there is nothing absurd in supposing that John, "in the spirit and power of Elijah," turned the hearts of the fathers to the children, and that it was on account of this spirit that he was called "Elijah who was to come." And to reinforce this view it may be argued that if the God of the universe identified Himself with His saints to such an extent as to be called the God of Abraham and the God of Isaac and the God of Jacob, much more might the Holy Spirit so identify Himself with the prophets as to be called their spirit, so that when the spirit is spoken of it might be the spirit of Elijah or the spirit of Isaiah. Our churchman, to go on with his views, may further say that those who supposed Jesus to be one of the prophets risen from the dead were probably misled, partly by the doctrine above mentioned, and partly by supposing Him to be one of the prophets, and that as for this misconception that He was one of the prophets, these persons probably fell into their error from not knowing about Jesus' supposed father and actual mother, and considering that He had risen from the tombs. As for the text in Genesis about the resurrection, the churchman will rejoin with a text to an opposite effect, "God hath raised up for me another seed in place of Abel whom Cain slew;" showing that the resurrection occurs in Genesis. As for the first difficulty which was raised, our churchman will meet the view of the believers in transcorporation by saying that John is no doubt, in a certain sense, as he has already shown, Elijah who is to come; and that the reason why he met the enquiry of the priests and Levites with "I am not," was that he divined the object they had in view in making it. For the enquiry laid before John by the priests and Levites was not intended to bring out whether the same spirit was in both, but whether John was that very Elijah who was taken up, and who now appeared according to the expectation of the Jews without being born (for the emissaries, perhaps, did not know about John's birth); and to such all enquiry he naturally answered, "I am not;" for he who was called John was not Elijah who was taken up, and had not changed his body for his present appearance. Our first scholar, whose view of transcorporation we have seen based upon our passage, may go on with a close examination of the text, and urge against his antagonist, that if John was the son of such a man as the priest Zacharias, and if he was born when his parents were both aged, contrary to all human expectation, then it is not likely that so many Jews at Jerusalem would be so ignorant about him, or that the priests and Levites whom they sent would not be acquainted with the facts of his birth. Does not Luke declare that "fear came upon all those who lived round about,"—clearly round about Zacharias and Elisabeth—and that "all these things were noised abroad throughout the whole hill country of Judæa"? And if John's birth from Zacharias was a matter of common knowledge, and the Jews of Jerusalem yet sent priests and Levites to ask, "Art thou Elijah?" then it is clear that in saying this they assumed the doctrine of transcorporation to be true, and that it was a current doctrine of their country, and not foreign to their secret teaching. John therefore says, I am not Elijah, because he does not know about his own former life. These thinkers, accordingly, entertain an opinion which is by no means to be despised. Our churchman, however, may return to the charge, and ask if it is worthy of a prophet, who is enlightened by the Holy Spirit, who is predicted by Isaiah, and whose birth was foretold before it took place by so great an angel, one who has received of the fullness of Christ, who shares in such a grace, who knows truth to have come through Jesus Christ, and has taught such deep things about God and about the only-begotten, who is in the bosom of the Father, is it worthy of such a one to lie, or even to hesitate, out of ignorance of what he was. For with respect to what was obscure, he ought to have refrained from confessing, and to have neither affirmed nor denied the proposition put before him. If the doctrine in question really was widely current, ought not John to have hesitated to pronounce upon it, lest his soul had actually been in Elijah? And here our churchman will appeal to history, and will bid his antagonists ask experts of the secret doctrines of the Hebrews, if they do really entertain such a belief. For if it should appear that they do not, then the argument based on that supposition is shown to be quite baseless. Our churchman, however, is still free to have recourse to the solution given before, and to insist that attention be paid to the meaning with which the question was put. For if, as I showed, the senders knew

John to be the child of Zacharias and Elisabeth, and if the messengers still more, being men of priestly race, could not possibly be ignorant of the remarkable manner in which their kinsman Zacharias had received his son, then what could be the meaning of their question, "Art thou Elijah?" Had they not read that Elijah had been taken up into heaven, and did they not expect him to appear? Then, as they expect Elijah to come at the consummation before Christ, and Christ to follow him, perhaps their question was meant less in a literal than in a tropical sense: Are you he who announces beforehand the word which is to come before Christ, at the consummation? To this he very properly answers, "I am not." The adversary, however, tries to show that the priests could not be ignorant that the birth of John had taken place in so remarkable a manner, because "all these things had been much spoken of in the hill country of Judæa;" and the churchman has to meet this. He does so by showing that a similar mistake was widely current about the Savior Himself; for "some said that He was John the Baptist, others Elijah, others Jeremiah or one of the prophets." So the disciples told the Lord when He was in the parts of Cæsarea Philippi, and questioned them on that subject. And Herod, too, said, "John whom I beheaded, he is risen from the dead;" so that he appears not to have known what was said about Christ, as reported in the Gospel, "Is not this the son of the carpenter, is not His mother called Mary, and His brothers James, and Joseph, and Simon, and Judas? And His sisters, are they not all with us?" Thus in the case of the Savior, while many knew of His birth from Mary, others were under a mistake about Him; and so in the case of John, there is no wonder if, while some knew of his birth from Zacharias, others were in doubt whether the expected Elijah had appeared in him or not. There was not more room for doubt about John, whether he was Elijah, than about the Savior, whether He was John. Of the two, the question of the outward form of Elijah could be disposed of from the words of Scripture, though not from actual observation, for we read, "He was a hairy man, and girt with a leather girdle about his loins." John's outward appearance, on the contrary, was well known, and was not like that of Jesus; and yet there were those who surmised that John had risen from the dead, and taken the name of Jesus. As for the change of name, a thing which reminds us of mysteries, I do not know how the Hebrews came to tell about Phinehas, son of Eleazar, who admittedly prolonged his life to the time of many of the judges, as we read in the Book of Judges, to tell about him what I now mention. They say that he was Elijah, because he had been promised immortality (in Numbers), on account of the covenant of peace granted to him because he was jealous with a divine jealousy, and in a passion of anger pierced the Midianitish woman and the Israelite, and stayed the wrath of God as it is called, as it is written, "Phinehas, the son of Eleazar, the son of Aaron, hath turned my wrath away from the children of Israel, in that he was jealous with my jealousy among them." No wonder, then, if those who conceived Phinehas and Elijah to be the same person, whether they judged soundly in this or not, for that is not now the question, considered John and Jesus also to be the same. This, then, they doubted, and desired to know if John and Elijah were the same. At another time than this, the point would certainly call for a careful enquiry, and the argument would have to be well weighed as to the essence of the soul, as to the principle of her composition, and as to her entering into this body of earth. We should also have to enquire into the distributions of the life of each soul, and as to her departure from this life, and whether it is possible for her to enter into a second life in a body or not, and whether that takes place at the same period, and after the same arrangement in each case, or not; and whether she enters the same body, or a different one, and if the same, whether the subject remains the same while the qualities are changed, or if both subject and qualities remain the same, and if the soul will always make use of the same body or will change it. Along with these questions, it would also be necessary to ask what transcorporation is, and how it differs from incorporation, and if he who holds transcorporation must necessarily hold the world to be eternal. The views of these scholars must also be taken into account, who consider that, according to the Scriptures, the soul is sown along with the body, and the consequences of such a view must also be looked at. In fact the subject of the soul is a wide one, and hard to be unraveled, and it has to be picked out of scattered expressions of Scripture. It requires, therefore, separate treatment. The brief consideration we have been led to give to the problem in connection with Elijah and John may now suffice; we go on to what follows in the Gospel.

8. John is a Prophet, But Not the Prophet.

"Art thou that prophet? And he answered No." If the law and the prophets were until John, what can we say that John was but a prophet? His father Zacharias, indeed, says, filled with the Holy Ghost and prophesying, "And thou, child, shalt be called the prophet of the Highest, for thou shalt go before the Lord to prepare His ways." (One might indeed get past this passage by laying stress on the word called: he is to be called, he is not said to be, a prophet.) And still more weighty is it that the Savior said to those who considered John to be a prophet, "But what went ye out to see? A prophet? Yea, I say unto you, and more than a prophet." The words, Yea, I say unto you, manifestly affirm that John is a prophet, and that is nowhere denied afterwards. If, then, he is said by the Savior to be not only a prophet but "more than a prophet," how is it that when the priests and Levites come and ask him, "Art thou the Prophet?" he answers No! On this we must remark that it is not the same thing to say, "Art thou the Prophet?" and "Art thou a prophet?" The distinction between the two expressions has already been observed, when we asked what was the difference between the God and God, and between the Logos and Logos. Now it is written in Deuteronomy, "A prophet shall the Lord your God raise up unto you, like me; Him shall ye hear, and it shall be that every soul that will not hear that prophet shall be cut off from among His people." There was, therefore, an expectation of one particular prophet having a resemblance to Moses in mediating between God and the people and receiving a new covenant from God to give to those who accepted his teaching; and in the case of each of the prophets, the people of Israel recognized that he was not the person of whom Moses spoke. As, then, they doubted about John, whether he were not the Christ, so they doubted whether he could not be the prophet. And there is no wonder that those who doubted about John whether he were the Christ, did not understand that the Christ and the prophet are the same person; their doubt as to John necessarily implied that they were not clear on this point. Now the difference between "the prophet" and "a prophet" has escaped the observation of most students; this is the case with Heracleon, who says, in these very words: "As, then, John confessed that he was not the Christ, and not even a prophet, nor Elijah." If he interpreted the words before us in such a way, he ought to have examined the various passages to see whether in saying that he is not a prophet nor Elijah he is or is not saying what is true. He devotes no attention, however, to these passages, and in his remaining commentaries he passes over such points without any enquiry. In the sequel, too, his remarks, of which we shall have to speak directly, are very scanty, and do not testify to careful study.

9. John I. 22.

"They said therefore unto him, Who art thou? that we may give an answer to them that sent us. What says thou of thyself?" This speech of the emissaries amounts to the following: We had a surmise what you were and came to learn if it was so, but now we know that you are not that. It remains for us, therefore, to hear your account of yourself, so that we may report your answer to those who sent us.

10. Of the Voice John the Baptist is.

"He said, I am the voice of one crying in the wilderness: Make straight the way of the Lord, as said Isaiah the prophet." As He who is peculiarly the Son of God, being no other than the Logos, yet makes use of Logos (reason)—for He was the Logos in the beginning, and was with God, the Logos of God—so John, the servant of that Logos, being, if we take the Scripture to mean what it says, no other than a voice, yet uses his voice to point to the Logos. He, then, understanding in this way the prophecy about himself spoken by Isaiah the prophet, says he is a voice, not crying in the wilderness, but "of one crying in the wilderness," of Him, namely, who stood and cried, "If any man thirst, let him come unto Me and drink." He it was, too, who said, "Prepare ye the way of the Lord, make His paths straight. Every valley shall be filled and every mountain and hill shall be brought low; and all the crooked shall be made straight." For as we read in Exodus that God said to Moses, "Behold I have given thee for a God to Pharaoh, and Aaron thy brother shall be thy prophet;" so we are to understand—the cases are at least analogous if not altogether similar—it is with the Word in the beginning, who is God, and with John. For John's voice points to that word and demonstrates it. It is therefore a very appropriate punishment that falls on Zacharias on his saying to the angel, "Whereby shall I know this? For I am an old man and my wife well stricken in years." For his want of faith with regard to the birth of the voice, he is himself deprived of his voice, as the angel Gabriel says to him, "Behold, thou shalt be silent and not able to speak until the day that these things shall come to pass, because thou hast not believed my words, which shall be fulfilled in their season." And afterwards when he had "asked for a writing tablet and written, His name is John; and they all marveled," he recovered his voice; for "his mouth was opened immediately and his tongue, and he spoke, blessing God." We discussed above how it is to be understood that the Logos is the Son of God, and went over the ideas connected with that; and a similar sequence of ideas is to be observed at this point. John came for a witness; he was a man sent from God to bear witness of the light, that all men through him might believe; he was that voice, then, we are to understand, which alone was fitted worthily to announce the Logos. We shall understand this aright if we call to mind what was adduced in our exposition of the texts: "That all might believe through Him," and "This is he of whom it is written, Behold I send My messenger before thy face, who shall prepare thy way before thee." There is fitness, too, in his being said to be the voice, not of one saying in the wilderness, but of one crying in the wilderness. He who cries, "Prepare ye the way of the Lord," also says it; but he might say it without crying it. But he cries and shouts it, that even those may hear who are at a distance from the speaker, and that even the deaf may understand the greatness of the tidings, since it is announced in a great voice; and he thus brings help, both to those who have departed from God and to those who have lost the acuteness of their hearing. This, too, was the reason why "Jesus stood and cried, saying, If any man thirst, let him come unto Me and drink." Hence, too, "John bears witness of Him, and cried, saying," "Hence also God commands Isaiah to cry, with the voice of one saying, Cry. And I said, What shall I cry?" The physical voice we use in prayer need not be great nor startling; even should we not lift up any great cry or shout, God will yet hear us. He says to Moses, "Why cries thou unto Me?" when Moses had not cried audibly at all. It is not recorded in Exodus that he did so; but Moses had cried mightily to God in prayer with that voice which is heard by God alone. Hence David also says, "With my voice I cried unto the Lord, and He heard me." And one who cries in the desert has need of a voice, that the soul which is deprived of God and deserted of truth—and what more dreadful desert is there than a soul deserted of God and of all virtue, since it still goes crookedly and needs instruction—may be exhorted to make straight the way of the Lord. And that way is made straight by the man who, far from copying the serpent's crooked journey; while he who is of the contrary disposition perverts his way. Hence the rebuke directed to a man of this kind and to all who resemble him, "Why pervert ye the right ways of the Lord?"

11. Of the Way of the Lord, How It is Narrow, and How Jesus is the Way. Now the way of the Lord is made straight in two fashions. First, in the way of contemplation, when thought is made clear in truth without any mixture of falsehood; and then in the way of conduct, after the sound contemplation of what ought to be done, when action is produced which harmonizes with sound theory of conduct. And that we may the more clearly understand the text, "Make straight the way of the Lord," it will be well to compare with it what is said in the Proverbs, "Depart not, either to the right hand or to the left." For he who deviates in either direction has given up keeping his path straight, and is no longer worthy of regard, since he has gone apart from the straightness of the journey, for "the Lord is righteous, and loves righteousness, and His face beholds straightness." Hence he who is the object of regard, and receives the benefit that comes from this oversight, says, "The light of Thy countenance was shown upon us, O Lord." Let us stand, then, as Jeremiah4876 exhorts, upon the ways, and let us see and ask after the ancient ways of the Lord, and let us see which is the good way, and walk in it. Thus did the

Apostles stand and ask for the ancient ways of the Lord; they asked the Patriarchs and the Prophets, enquiring into their writings, and when they came to understand these writings they saw the good way, namely, Jesus Christ, who said, "I am the way," and they walked in it. For it is a good way that leads the good man to the good father, the man who, from the good treasure of his heart, brings forth good things, and who is a good and faithful servant. This way is narrow, indeed, for the many cannot bear to walk in it and are lovers of their flesh; but it is also hard-pressed by those who use violence to walk in it, for it is not called afflicting, but afflicted. For that way which is a living way, and feels the qualities of those who tread it, is pressed and afflicted, when he travels on it who has not taken off his shoes from off his feet, nor truly realized that the place on which he stands. Or indeed treads, is holy ground. And it will lead to Him who is the life, and who says, "I am the life." For the Savior, in whom all virtues are combined, has many aspects. To him who, though by no means near the end, is yet advancing, He is the way; to him who has put off all that is dead He is the life. He who travels on this way is told to take nothing with him on it, since it provides bread and all that is necessary for life, enemies are powerless on it, and he needs no staff, and since it is holy, he needs no shoes.

12. Heracleon's View of the Voice, and of John the Baptist.

The words, however, "I am the voice of one crying in the wilderness," etc., may be taken as equivalent to "I am He of whom the 'voice in the wilderness' is written." Then John would be the person crying, and his voice would be that crying in the wilderness, "Make straight the way of the Lord." Heracleon, discussing John and the prophets, says, somewhat slanderously, that "the Word is the Savior; the voice, that in the wilderness which John interpreted; the sound is the whole prophetic order." To this we may reply by reminding him of the text, "If the trumpet give an uncertain sound, who shall prepare himself for the battle," and that which says that though a man have knowledge of mysteries, or have prophecy but wants love, he is a sounding or a tinkling cymbal. If the prophetic voice be nothing but sound, how does our Lord come to refer us to it as where He says, "Search the Scriptures, for in them you think you have eternal life, and these are they which bear witness," and "If ye believed Moses, ye would believe Me," and "Well did Isaiah prophesy concerning you, saying, This people honors me with their lips"? I do not know if anyone can reasonably admit that the Savior thus spoke in praise of an uncertain sound, or that there is any preparation to be had from the Scriptures to which we are referred as from the voice of a trumpet, for our war against opposing powers, should their sound give an uncertain voice. If the prophets had not love, and if that is why they were sounding brass or a tinkling cymbal, then how does the Lord send us to their sound, as these writers will have it, as if we could get help from that? He asserts, indeed, that a voice, when well fitted to speech, becomes speech, as if one should say that a woman is turned into a man; and the assertion is not supported by argument. And, as if he were in a position to put forth a dogma on the subject and to get on in this way, he declares that sound can be changed in a similar way into voice, and the voice, which is changed into speech, he says, is in the position of a disciple, while sound passing into voice is in that of a slave. If he had taken any kind of trouble to establish these points we should have had to devote some attention to refuting them; but as it is, the bare denial is sufficient refutation. There was a point some way back which we deferred taking up, that, namely, of the motive of John's speeches. We may now take it up. The Savior, according to Heracleon, calls him both a prophet and Elijah, but he himself denies that he is either of these. When the Savior, Heracleon says, calls him a prophet and Elijah, He is speaking not of John himself, but of his surroundings; but when He calls him greater than the prophets and than those who are born of women, then He is describing the character of John himself. When John, on the other hand, is asked about himself, his answers relate to himself, not to his surroundings. This we have examined as carefully as possible, comparing each of the terms in question with the statements of Heracleon, lest he should not have expressed himself quite accurately. For how it comes that the statements that he is Elijah and that he is a prophet apply to those about him, but the statement that he is the voice of one crying in the wilderness, to himself, no attempt whatever is made to show. Heracleon only gives an illustration, namely, this: His surroundings were, so to speak, his clothes, and other than himself, and when he was asked about his clothes, if he were his clothes, he could not answer "Yes." Now that his being Elijah, who was to come, was his clothes, is scarcely consistent, so far as I can see, with Heracleon's views; it might consist, perhaps, with the exposition we ourselves gave of the words, "In the spirit and power of Elijah;" it might, in a sense, be said that this spirit of Elijah is equivalent to the soul of John. He then goes on to try to determine why those who were sent by the Jews to question John were priests and Levites, and he answers by no means badly, that it was incumbent on such persons, being devoted to the service of God, to busy themselves and to make enquiries about such matters. When he goes on, however, to say that it was "because John was of the Levitical tribe," this is less well considered. We raised the question ourselves above, and saw that if the Jews who were sent knew John's birth, it was not open to them to ask if he was Elijah. Then, again, in dealing with the question, "Art thou the prophet?" Heracleon does not regard the addition of the article as having any special force, and says, "They asked him if he were a prophet, wishing to know this more general fact." Again, not Heracleon alone, but, so far as I am informed, all those who diverge from our views, as if they had not been able to deal with a trifling ambiguity and to draw the proper distinction, suppose John to be greater than Elijah and than all the prophets. The words are, "Of those born of women there is none greater than John;" but this admits of two meanings, that John is greater than they all, or again, that some of them are equal to him. For though many of the prophets were equal to him, still it might be true in respect of the grace bestowed on him, that none of them was greater than he. He regards it as confirming the view that John was greater, that "he is predicted by Isaiah;" for no other of all those who uttered prophecies was held worthy by God of this distinction. This, however, is a venturesome statement and implies some disrespect of what is called the Old Testament, and total disregard of the fact that Elijah himself was the subject of prophecy. For Elijah is prophesied by Malachi, who says, "Behold, I send unto you Elijah, the Tishbite, who shall restore the heart of the father to the son." Josiah, too, as we read in third Kings, was predicted by name by the prophet who came out of

Judah; for he said, Jeroboam also being present at the altar, "Thus says the Lord, Behold a son is born to David, his name is Josiah." There are some also who say that Samson was predicted by Jacob, when he said, "Dan shall judge his own people, he is as one tribe in Israel," for Samson who judged Israel was of the tribe of Dan. So much by way of evidence of the rashness of the statement that John alone was the subject of prophecy, made by Heracleon in his attempted explanation of the words, "I am the voice of one crying in the wilderness."

13. John I. 24, 25. Of the Baptism of John, that of Elijah, and that of Christ.

And they that were sent were of the Pharisees. And they asked him, and said unto him, "Why baptizes thou then, if thou art not the Christ, nor Elijah, nor the prophet?" Those who sent from Jerusalem the priests and Levites who asked John these questions, having learned who John was not, and who he was, preserve a decent silence, as if tacitly assenting and indicating that they accepted what was said, and saw that baptism was suited to a voice crying in the wilderness for the preparing of the way of the Lord. But the Pharisees being, as their name indicates, a divided and seditious set of people, show that they do not agree with the Jews of the metropolis and with the ministers of the service of God, the priests and Levites. They send envoys who deal in rebukes, and so far as their power extends debar him from baptizing; their envoys ask, Why baptizes thou, then, if thou art not the Christ, nor Elijah, nor the prophet? And if we were to stitch together into one statement what is written in the various Gospels, we should say that at this time they spoke as is here reported, but that at a later time, when they wished to received baptism, they heard the address of John: "Generations of vipers, who hath warned you to flee from the wrath to come? Bring forth therefore fruits worthy of repentance." This is what the Baptist says in Matthew, when he sees many of the Pharisees and Sadducees coming to his baptism, without, it is clear, having the fruits of repentance, and pharisaically boasting in themselves that they had Abraham for their father. For this they are rebuked by John, who has the zeal of Elijah according to the communication of the Holy Spirit. For that is a rebuking word, "Think not to say within yourselves, We have Abraham for our father," and that is the word of a teacher, when he speaks of those who for their stony hearts are called unbelieving stones, and says that by the power of God these stones may be changed into children of Abraham; for they were present to the eyes of the prophet and did not shrink from his divine glance. Hence his words: "I say unto you that God is able of these stones to raise up children to Abraham." And since they came to his baptism without having done fruits meet for repentance, he says to them most appropriately, "Already is the axe laid to the root of the tree; every tree that brings not forth good fruit is hewn down and cast into the fire." This is as much as to say to them: Since you have come to baptism without having done fruits meet for repentance, you are a tree that does not bring forth good fruit and which has to be cut down by the most sharp and piercing axe of the Word which is living and powerful and sharper than every two-edged sword. The estimation in which the Pharisees held themselves is also set forth by Luke in the passage: "Two men went up to the temple to pray, the one a Pharisee and the other a publican. And the Pharisee stood and prayed thus with himself: God, I thank

Thee that I am not as other men are, extortioners, unjust, adulterers, or even as this publican." The result of this speech is that the publican goes down to his house justified rather than the Pharisee, and the lesson is drawn, that everyone who exalts himself is abased. They came, then, in the character in which the Savior's reproving words described them, as hypocrites to John's baptism, nor does it escape the Baptist's observation that they have the poison of vipers under their tongue and the poison of asps, for "the poison of asps is under their tongue." The figure of serpents rightly indicates their temper, and it is plainly revealed in their better question: "Why baptizes thou then, if thou art not the Christ, nor Elijah, nor the prophet?" To these I would fain reply, if it be the case that the Christ and Elijah and the prophet baptize, but that the voice crying in the wilderness has no authority to do so, "Most harshly, my friends, do you question the messenger sent before the face of Christ to prepare His way before Him. The mysteries which belong to this point are all hidden to you; for Jesus being, whether you will or not, the Christ, did not Himself baptize but His disciples, He who was Himself the prophet. And how have you come to believe that Elijah who is to come will baptize?" He did not baptize the logs upon the altar in the times of Ahab, though they needed such a bath to be burned up, what time the Lord appeared in fire. No, he commands the priests to do this for him, and that not only once; for he says, "Do it a second time," upon which they did it a second time, and "Do it a third time," and they did it a third time. If, then, he did not at that time himself baptize but left the work to others, how was he to baptize at the time spoken of by Malachi? Christ, then, does not baptize with water, but His disciples. He reserves for Himself to baptize with the Holy Spirit and with fire. Now Heracleon accepts the speech of the Pharisees as distinctly implying that the office of baptizing belonged to the Christ and Elijah and to every prophet, for he uses these words, "Whose office alone it is to baptize." He is refuted by what we have just said, and especially by the consideration that he takes the word "prophet" in a general sense; for he cannot show that any of the prophets baptized. He adds, not incorrectly, that the Pharisees put the question from malice, and not from a desire to learn.

14. Comparison of the Statements of the Four Evangelists Respecting John the Baptist, the Prophecies Regarding Him, His Addresses to the Multitude and to the Pharisees, Etc.

We deem it necessary to compare with the expression of the passage we are considering the similar expressions found elsewhere in the Gospels. This we shall continue to do point by point to the end of this work, so that terms which appear to disagree may be shown to be in harmony, and that the peculiar meanings present in each may be explained. This we shall do in the present passage. The words, "The voice of one crying in the wilderness, Make straight the way of the Lord," are placed by John, who was a disciple, in the mouth of the Baptist. In Mark, on the other hand, the same words are recorded at the beginning of the Gospel of Jesus Christ, in accordance with the Scripture of Isaiah, as thus: "The beginning of the Gospel of Jesus Christ, as it is written in Isaiah the prophet, Behold, I send My messenger before thy face, who shall prepare thy way before thee. The voice of one crying in the wilderness, Prepare ye the way of the Lord, make His paths straight." Now the words,

"Make straight the way of the Lord," added by John, are not found in the prophet. Perhaps John was seeking to compress the "Prepare ye the way of the Lord, make straight the paths of our God," and so wrote, "Make straight the way of the Lord;" while Mark combined two prophecies spoken by two different prophets in different places, and made one prophecy out of them, "As it is written in Isaiah the prophet, Behold I send My messenger before thy face, who shall prepare thy way. The voice of one crying in the wilderness, Prepare ye the way of the Lord, make His paths straight." The words, "The voice of one crying in the wilderness," are written immediately after the narrative of Hezekiah's recovery from his sickness, while the words, "Behold I send My messenger before thy face," are written by Malachi. What John does here, abbreviating the text he quotes, we find done by Mark also at another point. For while the words of the prophet are, "Prepare ye the way of the Lord, make straight the paths of our God," Mark writes, "Prepare ye the way of the Lord, make His paths straight." And John practices a similar abbreviation in the text, "Behold I send My messenger before thy face, who shall prepare thy way before thee," when he does not add the words "before thee," as in the original. Coming now to the statement, "They were sent from the Pharisees and they asked Him," we have been led by our examination of the passage to prefix the enquiry of the Pharisees—which Matthew does not mention—to the occurrence recorded in Matthew, when John saw many of the Pharisees and Sadducees coming to his baptism, and said to them, "Ye generations of vipers," etc. For the natural sequence is that they should first enquire and then come. And we have to observe how, when Matthew reports that there went out to

John Jerusalem and all Judæa, and all the region round about Jordan, to be baptized by him in Jordan, confessing their sins, it was not these people who heard from the Baptist any word of rebuke or refutation, but only those many Pharisees and Sadducees whom he saw coming. They it was who were greeted with the address, "Ye offspring of vipers," etc. Mark, again, does not record any words of reproof as having been used by John to those who came to him, being all the country of Judæa and all of them of Jerusalem, who were baptized by him in the Jordan and confessed their sins. This is because Mark does not mention the Pharisees and Sadducees as having come to John. A further circumstance which we must mention is that both Matthew and Mark state that, in the one case, all Jerusalem and all Judæa, and the whole region round about Jordan, in the other, the whole land of Judæa and all they of Jerusalem, were baptized, confessing their sins; but when Matthew introduces the Pharisees and Sadducees as coming to the baptism, he does not say that they confessed their sins, and this might very likely and very naturally be the reason why they were addressed as "offspring of vipers." Do not suppose, reader, that there is anything improper in our adducing in our discussion of the question of those who were sent from the Pharisees and put questions to John, the parallel passages from the other Gospels too. For if we have indicated the proper connection between the enquiry of the Pharisees, recorded by the disciple John, and their baptism which is found in Matthew, we could scarcely avoid inquiring into the passages in question, nor recording the observations made on them. Luke, like Mark, remembers the passage, "The voice of one crying in the wilderness," but he for his part treats it as follows:

"The word of God came unto John, the son of Zacharias, in the wilderness. And he came into all the region round about Jordan preaching the baptism of repentance unto remission of sins; as it is written in the book of the words of Isaiah the prophet, The voice of one crying in the wilderness, Prepare ye the way of the Lord, make His paths straight." Luke, however, added the continuation of the prophecy: "Every valley shall be filled, and every mountain and hill shall be brought low, and the crooked shall become straight, and the rough ways smooth, and all flesh shall see the salvation of God." He writes, like Mark, "Make His ways straight;" curtailing, as we saw before, the text, "Make straight the ways of our God." In the phrase, "And all the crooked shall become straight," he leaves out the "all," and the word "straight" he converts from a plural into a singular. Instead of the phrase, moreover, "The rough land into a plain," he gives, "The rough ways into smooth ways," and he leaves out "And the glory of the Lord shall be revealed," and gives what follows, "And all flesh shall see the salvation of God." These observations are of use as showing how the evangelists are accustomed to abbreviate the sayings of the prophets. It has also to be observed that the speech, "Offspring of vipers," etc., is said by Matthew to have been spoken to the Pharisees and Sadducees when coming to baptism, they being a different set of people from those who confessed their sins, and to whom no words of this kind were spoken. With Luke, on the contrary, these words were addressed to the multitudes who came out to be baptized by John, and there were not two divisions of those who were baptized, as we found in Matthew. But Matthew, as the careful observer will see, does not speak of the multitudes in the way of praise, and he probably means the Baptist's address, Offspring of vipers, etc., to be understood as addressed to them also. Another point is, that to the Pharisees and Sadducees he says, "Bring forth a fruit," in the singular, "worthy of repentance," but to the multitudes he uses the plural, "Bring forth fruits worthy of repentance." Perhaps the Pharisees are required to yield the special fruit of repentance, which is no other than the Son and faith in Him, while the multitudes, who have not even a beginning of good things, are asked for all the fruits of repentance, and so the plural is used to them. Further, it is said to the Pharisees, "Think not to say within yourselves, We have Abraham for our father." For the multitudes now have a beginning, appearing as they do to be introduced into the divine Word, and to approach the truth; and thus they begin to say within themselves, "We have Abraham for our father." The Pharisees, on the contrary, are not beginning to this, but have long held it to be so. But both classes see John point to the stones aforesaid and declare that even from these children can be raised up to Abraham, rising up out of unconsciousness and deadness. And observe how it is said to the Pharisees, according to the word of the prophet, "Ye have eaten false fruit," and they have false fruit,—"Every tree which brings not forth good fruit is hewn down and cast into the fire," while to the multitudes which do not bear fruit at all, "Every tree which brings not forth fruit is hewn down." For that which has no fruit at all has not good fruit, and, therefore, it is worthy to be hewn down. But that which bears fruit has by no means good fruit, whence it also calls for the axe to lay it low. But, if we look more closely into this about the fruit, we shall find that it is impossible that that which has just begun to be cultivated, even should it not prove fruitless, should bear the first good fruits. The husbandman is content that the tree just coming into cultivation should bear him at first such fruits as it may; afterwards, when he has pruned and trained it according to his art, he will receive, not the fruits it chanced to bear at first, but good fruits. The law itself favors this interpretation, for it says that the planter is to wait for three years, having the trees pruned and not eating the fruit of them. "Three years," it says, "the fruit shall be unpurified to you, and shall not be eaten, but in the fourth year all the fruit shall be holy, for giving praise unto the Lord." This explains how the word "good" is omitted from the address to the multitudes, "Every tree, therefore, which bears not fruit is hewn down and cast into the fire." The tree which goes on bearing such fruit as it did at first, is a tree which does not bear good fruit, and is, therefore, cut down, and cast into the fire, since, when the three years have passed and the fourth comes round, it does not bear good fruit, for praise unto the Lord. In thus adducing the passages from the other Gospels I may appear to be digressing, but I cannot think it useless, or without bearing on our present subject. For the Pharisees send to John, after the priests and Levites who came from Jerusalem, men who came to ask him who he was, and enquire, Why baptizes thou then, if thou be not the Christ, nor Elijah, nor the prophet? After making this enquiry they straightway come for baptism, as Matthew records, and then they hear words suited to their quackery and hypocrisy. But the words addressed to them were very similar to those spoken to the multitudes, and hence the necessity to look carefully at both speeches, and to compare them together. It was while we were so engaged that various points arose in the sequence of the matter, which we had to consider. To what has been said we must add the following. We find mention made in John of two orders of persons sending: the one, that of the Jews from Jerusalem sending priests and Levites; the other, that of the Pharisees who want to know why he baptizes. And we found that, after the enquiry, the Pharisees present themselves for baptism. May it not be that the Jews, who had sent the earlier mission from Jerusalem, received John's words before those who sent the second mission, namely, the Pharisees, and hence arrived before them? For Jerusalem and all Judæa, and, in consequence, the whole region round about Jordan, were being baptized by him in the river Jordan, confessing their sins; or, as Mark says, "There went out to him the whole land of Judæa, and all they of Jerusalem, and were baptized of him in the river Jordan, confessing their sins." Now, neither does Matthew introduce the Pharisees and Sadducees, to whom the words, "Offspring of vipers," etc., are addressed; nor does Luke introduce the multitudes who meet with the same rebuke, as confessing their sins. And the question may be raised how, if the whole city of Jerusalem, and the whole of Judæa, and the whole region round about Jordan, were baptized of John in Jordan, the Savior could say, "John the Baptist came neither eating nor drinking, and ye say he hath a devil;" and how could He say to those who asked Him, "By what authority does thou these things? I also will ask you one word, which if ye tell me, I also will tell you by what authority I do these things. The baptism of John, whence was it? From heaven or of men? And they reason, and say, If we shall say, From heaven, He will say, Why did ye not believe him?" The solution of the difficulty is this. The Pharisees, addressed by John, as we saw before, with his "Offspring of vipers," etc., came to the baptism, without believing in him, probably because they feared the multitudes, and, with their accustomed hypocrisy towards them, deemed it right to undergo the washing, so as not to appear hostile to those who did so. Their belief was, then, that he derived his baptism from men, and not from heaven, but, on account of the multitude, lest they should be stoned, they are afraid to say what they think. Thus there is no contradiction between the Savior's speech to the Pharisees and the narratives in the Gospels about the multitudes who frequented John's baptism. It was part of the effrontery of the Pharisees that they declared John to have a devil, as, also, that they declared Jesus to have performed His wonderful works by Beelzebub, the prince of the devils.

15. How the Baptist Answers the Question of the Pharisees and Exalts the Nature of Christ. Of the Shoe-Latchet Which He is Unable to Untie.

John answered them, saying, "I baptize with water, but in the midst of you stands one whom ye know not, even He who cometh after me, the latchet of whose shoe I am not worthy to unloose." Heracleon considers that John's answers to those sent by the Pharisees refer not to what they asked, but to what he wished, not observing that he accuses the prophet of a want of manners, by making him, when asked about one thing, answer about another; for this is a fault to be guarded against in conversation. We assert, on the contrary, that the reply accurately takes up the question. It is asked, "Why baptizes thou then, if thou art not the Christ?" And what other answer could be given to this than to show that his baptism was in its nature a bodily thing? I, he says, "baptize with water;" this is his answer to, "Why baptizes thou." And to the second part of their question, "If thou art not the Christ," he answers by exalting the superior nature of Christ, that He has such virtue as to be invisible in His deity, though present to every man and extending over the whole universe. This is what is indicated in the words, "There stands one among you." The Pharisees, moreover, though expecting the advent of Christ, saw nothing in Him of such a nature as John speaks of; they believed Him to be simply a perfect and holy man. John, therefore, rebukes their ignorance of His superiority, and adds to the words, "There stands one among you," the clause, "whom ye know not." And, lest anyone should suppose the invisible One who extends to every man, or, indeed, to the whole world, to be a different person from Him who became man, and appeared upon the earth and conversed with men, he adds to the words, "There stands one among you whom you know not," the further words, "Who cometh after me," that is, He who is to be manifested after me. By whose surpassing excellence he well understood that his own nature was far surpassed, though some doubted whether he might be the Christ; and, therefore, desiring to show how far he is from attaining to the greatness of the Christ, that no one should think of him beyond what he sees or hears of him, he goes on: "The latchet of whose shoe I am not worthy to unloose." By which he conveys, as in a riddle, that he is not fit to solve and to explain the argument about Christ's assuming a human body, an argument tied up and hidden (like a shoe-tie) to those who do not understand it,—so as to say anything worthy of such an advent, compressed, as it was, into so short a space.

16. Comparison of John's Testimony to Jesus in the Different Gospels.

It may not be out of place, as we are examining the text, "I baptize with water," to compare the parallel utterances of the evangelists with this of John. Matthew reports that the Baptist, when he saw many of the Pharisees and Sadducees coming to his baptism, after the words of rebuke which we have already studied, went on: "I indeed baptize you with water unto repentance; but He that cometh after me is mightier than I, whose shoes I am not worthy to bear; He shall baptize you with the Holy Ghost, and with fire." This agrees with the words in John, in which the Baptist declares himself to those sent by the Pharisees, on the subject of his baptizing with water. Mark, again, says, "John preached, saying, There cometh after me He that is mightier than I, the latchet of whose shoes I am not worthy to stoop down and unloose. I baptized you with water, but He shall baptize you with the Holy Ghost." And Luke says that, as the people were in expectation, and all were reasoning in their hearts concerning John, whether haply he were the Christ, John answered them all, saying, "I indeed baptize you with water; but there cometh one mightier than I, whose shoe-latchet I am not worthy to unloose; He shall baptize you with the Holy Ghost, and with fire."

17. Of the Testimony of John to Jesus in Matthew's Gospel,

These, then, are the parallel passages of the four; let us try to see as clearly as we can what is the purport of each and wherein they differ from each other. And we will begin with Matthew, who is reported by tradition to have published his Gospel before the others, to the Hebrews, those, namely, of the circumcision who believed. I, he says, baptize you with water unto repentance, purifying you, as it were, and turning you away from evil courses and calling you to repentance; for I am come to make ready for the Lord a people prepared for Him, and by my baptism of repentance to prepare the ground for Him who is to come after me, and who will thus benefit you much more effectively and powerfully than my strength could. For His baptism is not that of the body only; He fills the penitent with the Holy Ghost, and His diviner fire does away with everything material and consumes everything that is earthy, not only from him who admits it to his life, but even from him who hears of it from those who have it. So much stronger than I is He who is coming after me, that I am not able to bear even the outskirts of the powers round Him which are furthest from Him (they are not open and exposed, so that anyone could see them), nor even to bear those who support them. I know not of which I should speak. Should I speak of my own great weakness, which is not able to bear even these things about Christ which in comparison with the greater things in Him are least, or should I speak of His transcendent Deity, greater than all the world? If I who have received such grace, as to be thought worthy of prophecy predicting my arrival in this human life, in the words, "The voice of one crying in the wilderness," and "Behold I send my messenger before thy face;" if I whose birth Gabriel who stands before God announced to my father so advanced in years, so much against his expectation, I at whose name Zacharias recovered his voice and was enabled to use it to prophesy, I to whom my Lord bears witness that among them that are born of women there is none greater than I, I am not able so much as to bear His shoes! And if not His shoes, what can be said about His garments? Who is so great as to be able to guard His coat? Who can suppose that He can understand the meaning contained in His tunic which is without seam from the top because it is woven throughout? It is to be observed that while the four represent John as declaring himself to have come to baptize with water, Matthew alone adds the words "to repentance," teaching that the benefit of baptism is connected with the intention of the baptized person; to him who repents it is salutary, but to him who comes to it without repentance it will turn to greater condemnation. And here we must note that as the wonderful works done by the Savior in the cures He wrought, which are symbolical of those who at any time are set free by the word of God from any sickness or disease, though they were done to the body and brought a bodily relief, yet also called those who were benefited by them to an exercise of faith, so the washing with water which is symbolic of the soul cleansing herself from every stain of wickedness, is no less in itself to him who yields himself to the divine power of the invocation of the Adorable Trinity, the beginning and source of divine gifts; for "there are diversities of gifts." This view receives confirmation from the narrative recorded in the Acts of the Apostles, which shows the Spirit to have descended so manifestly on those who receive baptism, after the water had prepared the way for him in those who properly approached the rite. Simon Magus, astonished at what he saw, desired to receive from Peter this gift, but though it was a good thing he desired, he thought to attain it by the mammon of unrighteousness. We next remark in passing that the baptism of John was inferior to the baptism of Jesus which was given through His disciples. Those persons in the Acts who were baptized to John's baptism and who had not heard if there was any Holy Ghost are baptized over again by the Apostle. Regeneration did not take place with John, but with Jesus through His disciples it does so, and what is called the laver of regeneration takes place with renewal of the Spirit; for the Spirit now comes in addition since it comes from God and is over and above the water and does not come to all after the water. So far, then, our examination of the statements in the Gospel according to Matthew.

18. Of the Testimony in Mark. What is Meant by the Savior's Shoes and by Untying His Shoe-Latchets.

Now let us consider what is stated by Mark. Mark's account of John's preaching agrees with the other. The words are, "There cometh after me He that is mightier than I," which amounts to the same thing as "He that cometh after me is mightier than I." There is a difference, however, in what follows, "The latchets of His shoes I am not worthy to stoop down and untie." For it is one thing to bear a person's shoes,—they must, it is evident, have been untied already from the feet of the wearer,—and it is another thing to stoop down and untie the latchet of his shoes. And it follows, since believers cannot think that either of the Evangelists made any mistake or misrepresentation, that the Baptist must have made these two utterances at different times and have meant them to express different things. It is not the case, as some suppose. That the reports refer to the same incident and turned out differently because of a looseness of memory as to some of the facts or words. Now it is a great thing to bear the shoes of Jesus, a great thing to stoop down to the bodily features of His mission, to that which took place in some lower region, so as to contemplate His image in the lower sphere, and to untie each difficulty connected with the mystery of His incarnation, such being as it were His shoe-latchets. For the fetter of obscurity is one as the key of knowledge also is one; not even He who is greatest among those born of women is sufficient of Himself to loose such things or to open them, for He who tied and locked at first, He also grants to whom He will to loose His shoe-latchet and to unlock what He has shut. If the passage about the shoes has a mystic meaning we ought not to scorn to consider it. Now I consider that the inhumanisation when the Son of God assumes flesh and bones is one of His shoes, and that the other is the descent to Hades, whatever that Hades be, and the journey with the Spirit to the prison. As to the descent into Hades, we read in the sixteenth Psalm, "Thou wilt not leave my soul in Hades," and as for the journey in prison with the Spirit we read in Peter in his Catholic Epistle, "Put to death," he says, "in the flesh, but quickened in the Spirit; in which also He went and preached unto the spirits in prison, which at one time were disobedient, when the long-suffering of God once waited in the days of Noah while the ark was a preparing." He, then, who is able worthily to set forth the meaning of these two journeys is able to untie the latchet of the shoes of Jesus; he, bending down in his mind and going with Jesus as He goes down into Hades, and descending from heaven and the mysteries of Christ's deity to the advent He of necessity made with us when He took on man (as His shoes). Now He who put on man also put on the dead, for "for this end Jesus both died and revived, that He might be Lord both of dead and living." This is why He put on both living and dead, that is, the inhabitants of the earth and those of Hades, that He might be the Lord of both dead and living. Who, then, is able to stoop down and untie the latchet of such shoes, and having untied them not to let them drop, but by the second faculty he has received to take them up and bear them, by bearing the meaning of them in his memory?

19. Luke and John Suggest that One May Loose the Shoe-Latchets of the Logos Without Stooping Down.

We must not, however, omit to ask how it comes that Luke and John give the speech without the phrase "to stoop down." He, perhaps, who stoops down may be held to unloose in the sense which we have stated. On the other hand, it may be that one who fixes his eyes on the height of the exaltation of the Logos, may find the loosing of those shoes which when one is seeking them seem to be bound, so that He also looses those shoes which are separable from the Logos, and beholds the Logos divested of inferior things, as He is, the Son of God.

20. The Difference between Not Being "Sufficient" And Not Being "Worthy."

John records that the Baptist said he was not worthy, Mark that he was not sufficient, and these two are not the same. One who was not worthy might yet be sufficient, and one who was worthy might not be sufficient. For even if it be the case that gifts are bestowed to profit withal and not merely according to the proportion of faith, yet it would seem to be the part of a God who loves men and who sees before what harm must come from the rise of self-opinion or conceit, not to bestow sufficiency even on the worthy. But it belongs to the goodness of God by conferring bounties to conquer the object of His bounty, taking in advance him who is destined to be worthy, and adorning him even before he becomes worthy with sufficiency, so that after his sufficiency he may come to be worthy; he is not first to be worthy and then to anticipate the giver and take His gifts before the time and so arrive at being sufficient. Now with the three the Baptist says he is not sufficient, while in John he says he is not worthy. But it may be that he who formerly declared that he was not sufficient became sufficient afterwards, even though perhaps he was not worthy, or again that while he was saying he was not worthy, and was in fact not worthy, he arrived at being worthy, unless one should say that human nature can never come to perform worthily this loosing or this bearing, and that John, therefore, says truly that he never became sufficient to loose the latchets of the Savior's shoes, nor worthy of it either. However much we take into our minds there are still left things not yet understood; for, as we read in the wisdom of Jesus, son of Sirach, "When a man hath done, then he begins, and when he leaves off, then he shall be doubtful."

21. The Fourth Gospel Speaks of Only One Shoe, the Others of Both. The Significance of This.

As to the shoes, too, which are spoken of in the three Gospels, we have a question to consider; we must compare them with the single shoe named by the disciple John. "I am not worthy," we read there, "to untie the latchet of His shoe." Perhaps he was conquered by the grace of God, and received the gift of doing that which of himself he would not have been worthy to do, of untying, namely, the latchet of one of the shoes, namely, after he had seen the Savior's sojourn among men, of which he bears witness. But he did not know the things which were to follow, namely, whether Jesus was to come to that place also, to which he was to go after being beheaded in prison, or whether he was to look for another; and hence he alludes enigmatically to that doubt which was afterwards cleared up to us, and says, "I am not worthy to untie His shoe-latchet." If any one considers this to be a superfluous speculation, he can combine in one the speech about the shoes and that about the shoe, as if John said, I am by no means worthy to loose His shoestring, not even at the beginning, the string of one of His shoes. Or the following may be a way to combine what is said in the Four. If John understands about Jesus' sojourn here, but is in doubt about the future, then he says with perfect truth that he is not worthy to loose the latchet of His shoes; for though he loosed that of one shoe, he did not loose both. And on the other hand, what he says about the latchet of the shoe is quite true also; since as we saw he is still in doubt whether Jesus is He that was to come, or whether another is to be looked for, in that other region.

22. How the Word Stands in the Midst of Men Without Being Known of Them.

As for the saying, "There stands one among you whom you know not," we are led by it to consider the Son of God, the Word, by whom all things were made, since He exists in substance throughout the underlying nature of things, being the same as wisdom. For He permeated, from the beginning, all creation, so that what is made at any time should be made through Him, and that it might be always true of anything so ever, that "All things were made by Him, and without Him was not anything made that was made;" and this saying also, "By wisdom didst thou make them all." Now, if He permeates all creation, then He is also in those questioners who ask, "Why baptizes thou, if thou art not the Christ, nor Elijah, nor the prophet?" In the midst of them stands the Word, who is the same and steadfast, being everywhere established by the Father. Or the words, "There stands among you," may be understood to say, In the midst of you men, because you are reasonable beings, stands He who is proved by Scripture to be the sovereign principle in the midst of everybody, and so to be present in your heart. Those, therefore, who have the Word in the midst of them, but who do not consider His nature, nor from what spring and principle He came, nor how He gave them the nature they have, these, while having Him in the midst of them, know Him not. But John knew Him: for the words, "Whom you know not," used in reproach to the Pharisees, show that he well knew the Word whom they did not know. And the Baptist, therefore, knowing Him, saw Him coming after himself, who was now in the midst of them, that is to say, dwelling after him and the teaching he gave in his baptism, in those who, according to reason (or the Word), submitted to that purifying rite. The word "after," however, has not the same meaning here as it has when Jesus commands us to come "after" Him; for in this case we are bidden to go after Him, so that, treading in His steps, we may come to the Father; but in the other case, the meaning is that after the teachings of John (since "He came in order that all men through Him might believe"), the Word dwells with those who have prepared themselves, purified as they are by the lesser words for the perfect Word. Firstly, then, stands the Father, being without any turning or change; and then stands also His Word, always carrying on His work of salvation, and even when He is in the midst of men, not comprehended, and not even seen. He stands, also, teaching, and inviting all to drink from His abundant spring, for "Jesus stood and cried, saying, if any man thirst, let him come unto Me and drink."

23. Heracleon's View of This Utterance of John the Baptist, and Interpretation of the Shoe of Jesus.

But Heracleon declares the words, "There stands one among you," to be equivalent to "He is already here, and He is in the world and in men, and He is already manifest to you all." By this He does away with the meaning which is also present in the words, that the Word had permeated the whole world. For we must say to him, When is He not present, and when is He not in the world? Does not this Gospel say, "He was in the world, and the world was made by Him, and the world knew Him not." And this is why those to whom the Logos is He "whom you know not," do not know Him: they have never gone out of the world, but the world does not know Him. But at what time did He cease to be among men? Was He not in Isaiah, when He said, "The Spirit of the Lord is upon me, because He hath anointed me," and "I became manifest to those who sought me not." Let them say, too, if He was not in David when he said, not from himself, "But I was established by Him a king in Zion His holy hill," and the other words spoken in the Psalms in the person of Christ. And why should I go over the details of this proof, truly they are hard to be numbered, when I can show quite clearly that He was always in men? And that is enough to show Heracleon's interpretation of "There stands in the midst of you," to be unsound, when he says it is equivalent to "He is already here, and He is in the world and in men." We are disposed to agree with him when he says that the words, "Who cometh after me," show John to be the forerunner of Christ, for he is in fact a kind of servant running before his master. The words, however, "Whose shoe-latchet I am not worthy to unloose," receive much too simple an interpretation when it is said that "in these words the Baptist confesses that he is not worthy even of the least honorable ministration to Christ." After this interpretation he adds, not without sense, "I am not worthy that for my sake He should come down from His greatness and should take flesh as His footgear, concerning which I am not able to give any explanation or description, nor to unloose the arrangement of it." In understanding the world by his shoe, Heracleon shows some largeness of mind, but immediately after he verges on impiety in declaring that all this is to be understood of that person whom John here has in his mind. For he considers that it is the demiurge of the world who confesses by these words that he is a lesser person than the Christ; and this is the height of impiety. For the Father who sent Him, He who is the God of the living as Jesus Himself testifies, of Abraham and of Isaac and of Jacob, and He who is greater than heaven and earth for the reason that He is the Maker of them, He also alone is good and is greater than He who was was the shoe of Jesus, yet I think we ought not to agree with him. For how can it be harmonized with such a view, that "Heaven is My throne and the earth My footstool," a testimony which Jesus accepts as said of the Father? "Swear not by heaven," He says, "for it is God's throne, nor by the earth, for it is the footstool of His feet." How, if he takes the whole world to be the shoe of Jesus, can he also accept the text, "Do not I fill heaven and earth?" says the Lord. It is also worthwhile to enquire, whether as the Word and wisdom permeated the whole world, and as the Father was in the Son, the words are to be understood as above or in this way, that He who first of all was girded about with the whole creation, in addition to the Son's being in Him, granted to the Savior, as being second after Him and being God the Word, to pervade the whole creation. To those who have it in them to take note of the uninterrupted movement of the great heaven, how it carries with it from East to West so great a multitude of stars, to them most of all it will seem needful to enquire what that force is, how great and of what nature, which is present in the whole world. For to pronounce that force to be other than the Father and the Son, that perhaps might be inconsistent with piety.

24. The Name of the Place Where John Baptized is Not Bethany, as in Most Copies, But Bethabara. Proof of This. Similarly "Gergesa" Should Be Read for "Gerasa," In the Story of the Swine. Attention is to Be Paid to the Proper Names in Scripture, Which are Often Written Inaccurately, and are of Importance for Interpretation.

"These things were done in Bethabara, beyond Jordan, where John was baptizing." We are aware of the reading which is found in almost all the copies, "These things were done in Bethany." This appears, moreover, to have been the reading at an earlier time; and in Heracleon we read "Bethany." We are convinced, however, that we should not read "Bethany," but "Bethabara." We have visited the places to enquire as to the footsteps of Jesus and His disciples, and of the prophets. Now, Bethany, as the same evangelist tells us, was the town of Lazarus, and of Martha and Mary; it is fifteen stadia from Jerusalem, and the river Jordan is about a hundred and eighty stadia distant from it. Nor is there any other place of the same name in the neighborhood of the Jordan, but they say that Bethabara is pointed out on the banks of the Jordan, and that John is said to have baptized there. The etymology of the name, too, corresponds with the baptism of him who made ready for the Lord a people prepared for Him; for it yields the meaning "House of preparation," while Bethany means "House of obedience." Where else was it fitting that he should baptize, who was sent as a messenger before the face of the Christ, to prepare His way before Him, but at the House of preparation? And what more fitting home for Mary, who chose the good part, which was not taken away from her, and for Martha, who was cumbered for the reception of Jesus, and for their brother, who is called the friend of the Savior, than Bethany, the House of obedience? Thus we see that he who aims at a complete understanding of the Holy Scriptures must not neglect the careful examination of the proper names in it. In the matter of proper names the Greek copies are often incorrect, and in the Gospels one might be misled by their authority. The transaction about the swine, which were driven down a steep place by the demons and drowned in the sea, is said to have taken place in the country of the Gerasenes. Now, Gerasa is a town of Arabia, and has near it neither sea nor lake. And the Evangelists would not have made a statement so obviously and demonstrably false; for they were men who informed themselves carefully of all matters connected with Judæa. But in a few copies we have found, "into the country of the Gadarenes;" and, on this reading, it is to be stated that Gadara is a town of Judæa, in the neighborhood of which are the well-known hot springs, and that there is no lake there with overhanging banks, nor any sea. But Gergesa, from which the name Gergesenes is taken, is an old town in the neighborhood of the lake now called Tiberias, and on the edge of it there is a steep place abutting on the lake, from which it is pointed out that the swine were cast down by the demons. Now, the meaning of Gergesa is "dwelling of the casters-out," and it contains a prophetic reference to the conduct towards the Savior of the citizens of those places, who "besought Him to depart out of their coasts." The same inaccuracy with regard to proper names is also to be observed in many passages of the law and the prophets, as we have been at pains to learn from the Hebrews, comparing our own copies with theirs which have the confirmation of the versions, never subjected to corruption, of Aquila and Theodotion and Symmachus. We add a few instances to encourage students to pay more attention to such points. One of the sons of Levi, the first, is called Geson in most copies, instead of Gerson. His name is the same as that of the first-born of Moses; it was given appropriately in each case, both children being born, because of the sojourn in Egypt, in a strange land. The second son of Juda, again, has with us the name Annan, but with the Hebrews Onan, "their labor." Once more, in the departures of the children of Israel in Numbers, we find, "They departed from Sochoth and pitched in Buthan;" but the Hebrew, instead of Buthan, reads Aiman. And why should I add more points like these, when anyone who desires it can examine into the proper names and find out for himself how they stand? The place names of Scripture are specially to be suspected where many of them occur in a catalogue, as in the account of the partition of the country in Joshua, and in the first Book of Chronicles from the beginning down to, say, the passage about Dan, and similarly in Ezra. Names are not to be neglected, since indications may be gathered from them which help in the interpretation of the passages where they occur. We cannot, however, leave our proper subject to examine in this place into the philosophy of names.

25. Jordan Means "Their Going Down." Spiritual Meanings and Application of This.

Let us look at the words of the Gospel now before us. "Jordan" means "their going down." The name "Jared" is etymologically akin to it, if I may say so; it also yields the meaning "going down;" for Jared was born to Maleleel, as it is written in the Book of Enoch—if anyone cares to accept that book as sacred—in the days when the sons of God came down to the daughters of men. Under this descent some have supposed that there is an enigmatical reference to the descent of souls into bodies, taking the phrase "daughters of men" as a tropical expression for this earthly tabernacle. Should this be so, what river will "their going down" be, to which one must come to be purified, a river going down, not with its own descent, but "theirs," that, namely, of men, what but our Savior who separates those who received their lots from Moses from those who obtained their own portions through Jesus (Joshua)? His current, flowing in the descending stream, makes glad, as we find in the Psalms, the city of God, not the visible Jerusalem—for it has no river beside it—but the blameless Church of God, built on the foundation of the Apostles and Prophets, Christ Jesus our Lord being the chief corner-stone. Under the Jordan, accordingly, we have to understand the Word of God who became flesh and tabernacled among us, Jesus who gives us as our inheritance the humanity which He assumed, for that is the head cornerstone, which being taken up into the deity of the Son of God, is washed by being so assumed, and then receives into itself the pure and guileless dove of the Spirit, bound to it and no longer able to fly away from it. For "Upon whomsoever," we read, "thou shalt see the Spirit descending and abiding upon Him, the same is He that baptizes with the Holy Spirit." Hence, he who receives the Spirit abiding on Jesus Himself is able to baptize those who come to him in that abiding Spirit. But John baptizes beyond Jordan, in the regions verging on the outside of Judæa, in Bethabara, being the forerunner of Him who came to call not the righteous but sinners, and who taught that the whole have no need of a physician, but they that are sick. For it is for forgiveness of sins that this washing is given.

26. The Story of Israel Crossing Jordan under Joshua is Typical of Christian Things, and is written for Our Instruction.

Now, it may very well be that someone not versed in the various aspects of the Savior may stumble at the interpretation given above of the Jordan; because John says, "I baptize with water, but He that cometh after me is stronger than I; He shall baptize you with the Holy Spirit." To this we reply that, as the Word of God in His character as something to be drunk is to one set of men water, and to another wine, making glad the heart of man, and to others blood, since it is said, "Except ye drink My blood, ye have no life in you," and as in His character as food He is variously conceived as living bread or as flesh, so also He, the same person, is baptism of water, and baptism of Holy Spirit and of fire, and to some, also, of blood. It is of His last baptism, as some hold, that He speaks in the words, "I have a baptism to be baptized with, and how am I straitened till it be accomplished?" And it agrees with this that the disciple John speaks in his Epistle of the Spirit, and the water, and the blood, as being one. And again He declares Himself to be the way and the door, but clearly He is not the door to those to whom He is the way, and He is no longer the way to those to whom He is the door. All those, then, who are being initiated in the beginning of the oracles of God, and come to the voice of him who cries in the wilderness, "Make straight the way of the Lord," the voice which sounds beyond Jordan at the house of preparation, let them prepare themselves so that they may be in a state to receive the spiritual word, brought home to them by the enlightenment of the Spirit. As we are now, as our subject requires, bringing together all that relates to the Jordan, let us look at the "river." God, by Moses, carried the people through the Red Sea, making the water a wall for them on the right hand and on the left, and by Joshua He carried them through Jordan. Now, Paul deals with this Scripture, and his warfare is not according to the flesh of it, for he knew that the law is spiritual in a spiritual sense. And he shows us that he understood what is said about the passage of the Red Sea; for he says in his first Epistle to the Corinthians, "I would not, brethren, have you ignorant, how that our fathers were all under the cloud, and all passed through the sea, and were all baptized into Moses in the cloud and in the sea, and did all eat the same spiritual meat, and drink the same spiritual drink; for they drank of the spiritual rock which followed them, and the rock was Christ." In the spirit of this passage let us also pray that we may receive from God to understand the spiritual meaning of Joshua's passage through Jordan. Of it, also, Paul would have said, "I would not, brethren, have you ignorant, that all our fathers went through Jordan, and were all baptized into Jesus in the spirit and in the river." And Joshua, who succeeded Moses, was a type of Jesus Christ, who succeeds the dispensation through the law, and replaces it by the preaching of the Gospel. And even if those Paul speaks of were baptized in the cloud and in the sea, there is something harsh and salt in their baptism. They are still in fear of their enemies, and crying to the Lord and to Moses, saying, "Because there were no graves in Egypt, hast thou brought us forth to slay us in the wilderness? Why hast thou dealt thus with us, to bring us forth out of Egypt?" But the baptism to Joshua, which takes place in quite sweet and drinkable water, is in many ways superior to that earlier one, religion having by this time grown clearer and assuming a becoming order. For the ark of the covenant of the Lord our God is carried in procession by the priests and Levites, the people following the ministers of God, it, also, accepting the law of holiness. For Joshua says to the people, "Sanctify yourselves against tomorrow; the Lord will do wonders among you." And he commands the priests to go before the people with the ark of the covenant, wherein is plainly showed forth the mystery of the Father's economy about the Son, which is highly exalted by Him who gave the Son this office; "That at the name of Jesus every knee should bow, of things in heaven and things on earth and things under the earth, and that every tongue should confess that Jesus Christ is Lord, to the glory of God the Father." This is pointed out by what we find in the book called Joshua, "In that day I will begin to exalt thee before the children of Israel." And we hear our Lord Jesus saying to the children of Israel, "Come hither and hear the words of the Lord your God. Hereby ye shall know that the living God is in (among) you;" for when we are baptized to Jesus, we know that the living God is in us. And, in the former case, they kept the Passover in Egypt, and then began their journey, but with Joshua, after crossing Jordan on the tenth day of the first month they pitched their camp in Galgala; for a sheep had to be procured before invitations could be issued to the banquet after Joshua's baptism. Then the children of Israel, since the children of those who came out of Egypt had not received circumcision, were circumcised by Joshua with a very sharp stone; the Lord declares that He takes away the reproach of Egypt on the day of Joshua's baptism, when Joshua purified the children of Israel. For it is written: "And the Lord said to Joshua, the son of Nun, This day have I taken away the reproach of Egypt from off you." Then the children of Israel kept the Passover on the fourteenth day of the month, with much greater gladness than in Egypt, for they ate unleavened bread of the corn of the holy land, and fresh food better than manna. For when they received the land of promise God did not entertain them with scantier food, nor when such a one as Joshua was their leader do they get inferior bread. This will be plain to him who thinks of the true holy land and of the Jerusalem above. Hence it is written in this same Gospel: Your fathers did eat bread in the wilderness, and are dead; he that eats of this bread shall live forever. For the manna, though it was given by God, yet was bread of travel, bread supplied to those still under discipline, well fitted for those who were under tutors and governors. And the new bread Joshua managed to get from corn they cut in the country, in the land of promise, others having labored and his disciples reaping,—that was bread more full of life, distributed as it was to those who, for their perfection, were able to receive the inheritance of their fathers. Hence, he who is still under discipline to that bread may receive death as far as it is concerned, but he who has attained to the bread that follows that, eating it, shall live forever. All this has been added, not, I conceive, without appropriateness, to our study of the baptism at the Jordan, administered by John at Bethabara.

27. Of Elijah and Elisha Crossing the Jordan.

Another point which we must not fail to notice is that when Elijah was about to be taken up in a whirlwind, as if to heaven,4942 he took his mantle and wrapped it together and smote the water, which was divided hither and thither, and they went over both of them, that is, he and Elisha. His baptism in the Jordan made him fitter to be taken up, for, as we showed before, Paul gives the name of baptism to such a remarkable passage through the water. And through this same Jordan Elisha receives, through Elijah, the gift he desired, saying, "Let a double portion of thy spirit be upon me." What enabled him to receive this gift of the spirit of Elijah was, perhaps, that he had passed through Jordan twice, once with Elijah, and the second time, when, after receiving the mantle of Elijah, he smote the water and said, "Where is the God of Elijah, even He? And he smote the waters, and they were divided hither and thither."

28. Naaman the Syrian and the Jordan. No Other Stream Has the Same Healing Power.

Should anyone object to the expression "He smote the water," on account of the conclusion we arrived at above with respect to the Jordan, that it is a type of the Word who descended for us our descending, we rejoin that with the Apostle the rock is plainly said to be Christ, and that it is smitten twice with the rod, so that the people may drink of the spiritual rock which follows them. The "smiting" in this new difficulty is that of those who are fond of suggesting something that contradicts the conclusion even before they have learned what the question is which is in hand. From such God sets us free, since, on the one hand, He gives us to drink when we are thirsty, and on the other He prepares for us, in the immense and trackless deep, a road to pass over, namely, by the dividing of His Word, since it is by the reason which distinguishes (divides) that most things are made plain to us. But that we may receive the right interpretation about this Jordan, so good to drink, so full of grace, it may be of use to compare the cleansing of Naaman the Syrian from his leprosy, and what is said of the rivers of religion of the enemies of Israel. It is recorded of Naaman that he came with horse and chariot, and stood at the door of the house of Elisha. And Elisha sent a messenger to him, saying, "Go, wash seven times in the Jordan, and thy flesh shall come again unto thee, and thou shalt be cleansed." Then Naaman is angry; he does not see that our Jordan is the cleanser of those who are impure from leprosy, from that impurity, and their restorer to health; it is the Jordan that does this, and not the prophet; the office of the prophet is to direct to the healing agency. Naaman then says, not understanding the great mystery of the Jordan, "Behold, I said that he will certainly come out to me, and will call upon the name of the Lord his God, and lay his hand upon the place, and restore the leper." For to put his hand on the leprosy and cleanse it is a work belonging to our Lord Jesus only; for when the leper appealed to Him with faith, saying, "If Thou wilt Thou canst make me clean," He not only said, "I will, be thou clean," but in addition to the word He touched him, and he was cleansed from his leprosy. Naaman, then, is still in error, and does not see how far inferior other rivers are to the Jordan for the cure of the suffering; he extols the rivers of Damascus, Arbana, and Pharpha, saying, "Are not Arbana and Pharpha, rivers of Damascus, better than all the waters of Israel? Shall I not wash in them and be clean?" For as none is good but one, God the Father, so among rivers none is good but the Jordan, nor able to cleanse from his leprosy him who with faith washes his soul in Jesus. And this, I suppose, is the reason why the Israelites are recorded to have wept when they sat by the rivers of Babylon and remembered Zion; those who are carried captive, on account of their wickedness, when they taste other waters after sacred Jordan, are led to remember with longing their own river of salvation. Therefore it is said of the rivers of Babylon, "There we sat down," clearly because they were unable to stand, "and wept." And Jeremiah rebukes those who wish to drink the waters of Egypt, and desert the water which comes down from heaven, and is named from its so coming down—namely, the Jordan. He says, "What hast thou to do with the way of Egypt, to drink the water of Geon, and to drink the water of the river," or, as it is in the Hebrew, "to drink the water of Sion." Of which water we have now to speak.

29. The River of Egypt and Its Dragon, Contrasted with the Jordan.

But that the Spirit in the inspired Scriptures is not speaking mainly of rivers to be seen with the eyes, may be gathered from Ezekiel's prophecies against Pharaoh, king of Egypt: "Behold I am against thee, Pharaoh, king of Egypt, the great dragon, seated in the midst of rivers, who says, Mine are the rivers, and I made them. And I will put traps in thy jaws, and I will make the fishes of the river to stick to thy fins, and I will bring thee up from the midst of thy river, and all the fish of the river, and I will cast thee down quickly and all the fish of the river; thou shalt fall upon the face of thy land, and thou shalt not be gathered together, and thou shalt not be adorned." For what real bodily dragon has ever been reported as having been seen in the material river of Egypt? But consider if the river of Egypt be not the dwelling of the dragon who is our enemy, who was not even able to kill the child Moses. But as the dragon is in the river of Egypt, so is God in the river which makes glad the city of God; for the Father is in the Son. Hence those who come to wash themselves in Him put away the reproach of Egypt, and become more fit to be restored. They are cleansed from that foulest leprosy, receive a double portion of spiritual gifts, and are made ready to receive the Holy Spirit, since the spiritual dove does not light on any other stream. Thus we have considered in a way more worthy of the sacred subject the Jordan and the purification that is in it, and Jesus being washed in it, and the house of preparation. Let us, then, draw from the river as much help as we require.

30. Of What John Learned from Jesus When Mary Visited Elisabeth in the Hill Country.

"The next day John sees Jesus coming unto him."4948 The mother of Jesus had formerly, as soon as she conceived, stayed with the mother of John, also at that time with child, and the Former then communicated to the Formed with some exactness His own image, and caused him to be conformed to His glory. And from this outward similarity it came that with those who did not distinguish between the image itself and that which was according to the image, John was thought to be Christ4949 and Jesus was supposed4950 to be John risen from the dead. So now Jesus, after the testimonies of John to Him which we have examined, is Himself seen by the Baptist coming to him. It is to be noticed that on the former occasion, when the voice of Mary's salutation came to the ears of Elisabeth, the babe John leaped in the womb of his mother, who then received the Holy Spirit, as it were, from the ground. For it came to pass, we read,4951 "when Elisabeth heard the salutation of Mary, the babe leaped in her womb; and Elisabeth was filled with the Holy Spirit, and she lifted up her voice with a loud cry and said," etc. On this occasion, similarly, John sees Jesus coming to him and says, "Behold the Lamb of God which taketh away the sin of the world." For with regard to matters of great moment one is first instructed by hearing and afterwards one sees them with one's own eyes. That John was helped to the shape he was to wear by the Lord who, still in the process of formation and in His mother's womb, approached Elisabeth, will be clear to anyone who has grasped our proof that John is a voice but that Jesus is the Word, for when Elisabeth was filled with the Holy Spirit at the salutation of Mary there was a great voice in her, as the words themselves bear; for they say, "And she spoke out with a loud voice." Elisabeth, it is plain, did this, "and she spoke." For the voice of Mary's salutation coming to the ears of Elisabeth filled John with itself; hence John leaps, and his mother becomes, as it were, the mouth of her son and a prophetess, crying out with a loud voice and saying, "Blessed art thou among women, and blessed is the fruit of thy womb." Now we see clearly how it was with Mary's hasty journey to the hill country, and her entrance into the house of Zacharias, and the greeting with which she salutes Elisabeth; it was that she might communicate some of the power she derived from Him she had conceived, to John, yet in his mother's womb, and that John too might communicate to his mother some of the prophetic grace which had come to him, that all these things were done. And most rightly was it in the hill country that these transactions took place, since no great thing can be entertained by those who are low and may be thence called valleys. Here, then, after the testimonies of John,—the first, when he cried and spoke about His deity; the second, addressed to the priests and Levites who were sent by the Jews from Jerusalem; and the third, in answer to the sharper questions of those from the Pharisees,—Jesus is seen by the witness bearer coming to him while he is still advancing and growing better. This advance and improvement is symbolically indicated in the phrase, "On the morrow." For Jesus came in the consequent illumination, as it were, and on the day after what had preceded, not only known as standing in the midst even of those who knew Him not, but now plainly seen advancing to him who had formerly made such declarations about Him. On the first day the testimonies take place, and on the second Jesus comes to John. On the third John, standing with two of his disciples and looking upon Jesus as He walked, said, "Behold the

Lamb of God," thus urging those who were there to follow the Son of God. On the fourth day, too, He was minded to go forth into Galilee, and He who came forth to seek that which was lost finds Philip and says to him, "Follow Me." And on that day, after the fourth, which is the sixth from the beginning of those we have enumerated, the marriage takes place in Cana of Galilee, which we shall have to consider when we get to the passage. Note this, too, that Mary being the greater comes to Elisabeth, who is the less, and the Son of God comes to the Baptist; which should encourage us to render help without delay to those who are in a lower position, and to cultivate for ourselves a moderate station.

31. Of the Conversation between John and Jesus at the Baptism, Recorded by Matthew Only.

John the disciple does not tell us where the Savior comes from to John the Baptist, but we learn this from Matthew, who writes: "Then cometh Jesus from Galilee to Jordan to John, to be baptized of him." And Mark adds the place in Galilee; he says, "And it came to pass in those days, that Jesus came from Nazareth in Galilee and was baptized by John in Jordan." Luke does not mention the place Jesus came from, but on the other hand he tells us what we do not learn from the others, that immediately after the baptism, as He was coming up, heaven was opened to Him, and the Holy Spirit descended on Him in bodily form like a dove. Again, it is Matthew alone who tells us of John's preventing the Lord, saying to the Savior, "I have need to be baptized of Thee, and comes Thou to me?" None of the others added this after Matthew, so that they might not be saying just the same as he. And what the Lord rejoined, "Suffer it now, for thus it becomes us to fulfil all righteousness," this also Matthew alone recorded.

32. John Calls Jesus a "Lamb." Why Does He Name This Animal Specially? Of the Typology of the Sacrifices, Generally.

"And he sayeth, Behold the Lamb of God, which taketh away the sin of the world." There were five animals which were brought to the altar, three that walk and two that fly; and it seems to be worth asking why John calls the Savior a lamb and not any of these other creatures, and why, when each of the animals that walk is offered of three kinds he used for the sheep-kind the term "lamb." The five animals are as follows: the bullock, the sheep, the goat, the turtle-dove, the pigeon. And of the walking animals these are the three kinds—bullock, ox, calf; ram, sheep, lamb; he-goat, goat, kid. Of the flying animals, of pigeons we only hear of two young ones; of turtle doves only of a pair. He, then, who would accurately understand the spiritual rationale of the sacrifices must enquire of what heavenly things these were the pattern and the shadow, and also for what end the sacrifice of each victim is prescribed, and he must specially collect the points connected with the lamb. Now that the principle of the sacrifice must be apprehended with reference to certain heavenly mysteries, appears from the words of the Apostle, who somewhere says, "Who serve a pattern and shadow of heavenly things," and again, "It was necessary that the patterns of the things in the heavens should be purified with these, but the heavenly things themselves with better sacrifices than these." Now to find out all the particulars of these and to state in its relation to them that sacrifice of the spiritual law which took place in Jesus Christ (a truth greater than human nature can comprehend)—to do this belongs to no other than the perfect man, who, by reason of use, has his senses exercised to discern good and evil, and who is able to say, from a truth-loving disposition, "We speak wisdom among them that are perfect." Of these things truly and things like these, we can say, "Which none of the rulers of this world knew."

33. A Lamb Was Offered at the Morning and Evening Sacrifice. Significance of This.

Now we find the lamb offered in the continual (daily) sacrifice. Thus it is written, "This is that which thou shalt offer upon the altar; two lambs of the first year day by day continually, for a continual sacrifice. The one lamb thou shalt offer in the morning, and the other lamb thou shalt offer at even, and a tenth part of fine flour mingled with beaten oil, the fourth part of a hin; and for a drink-offering the fourth part of a bin of wine to the first lamb. And the other lamb thou shalt offer in the evening, according to the first sacrifice and according to its drink-offering. Thou shalt offer a sweet savor, an offering to the Lord, a continual burnt offering throughout your generations at the door of tent of witness before the Lord, where I will make myself known to thee, to speak unto thee. And I will appoint thee for the children of Israel, and I will be sanctified in my glory, and with sanctification I will sanctify the tent of witness." But what other continual sacrifice can there be to the man of reason in the world of mind, but the Word growing to maturity, the Word who is symbolically called a lamb and who is offered as soon as the soul receives illumination. This would be the continual sacrifice of the morning, and it is offered again when the sojourn of the mind with divine things comes to an end. For it cannot maintain forever its intercourse with higher things, seeing that the soul is appointed to be yoked together with the body which is of earth and heavy.

34. The Morning and Evening Sacrifices of the Saint in His Life of Thought.
But if anyone asks what the saint is to do in the time between morning and evening, let him follow what takes place in the cultus and infer from it the principle he asks for. In that case the priests begin their offerings with the continual sacrifice, and before they come to the continuous one of the evening they offer the other sacrifices which the law prescribes, as, for example, that for transgression, or that for involuntary offences, or that connected with a prayer for salvation, or that of jealousy, or that of the Sabbath, or of the new moon, and so on, which it would take too long to mention. So we, beginning our oblation with the discourse of that type which is Christ, can go on to discourse about many other most useful things. And drawing to a close still in the things of Christ, we come, as it were, to evening and night, when we arrive at the bodily features of His manifestation.

35. Jesus is a Lamb in Respect of His Human Nature.
If we enquire further into the significance of Jesus being pointed out by John, when he says, "This is the Lamb of God which taketh away the sin of the world," we may take our stand at the dispensation of the bodily advent of the Son of God in human life, and in that case we shall conceive the lamb to be no other than the man.

For the man "was led like a sheep to the slaughter, and as a lamb, dumb before his shearers," saying, "I was as like a gentle lamb led to the slaughter." Hence, too, in the Apocalypse a lamb is seen, standing as if slain. This slain lamb has been made, according to certain hidden reasons, a purification of the whole world, for which, according to the Father's love to man, He submitted to death, purchasing us back by His own blood from him who had got us into his power, sold under sin. And He who led this lamb to the slaughter was God in man, the great High-Priest, as he shows by the words: "No one taketh My life away from Me, but I lay it down of Myself. I have power to lay it down, and I have power to take it again."

36. Of the Death of the Martyrs Considered as a Sacrifice, and in What Way It Operates to the Benefit of Others.

Akin to this sacrifice are the others of which the sacrifices of the law are symbols, and another kind of sacrifice also appears to me to be of the same nature; namely, the shedding of the blood of the noble martyrs, whom the disciple John saw, for this is not without significance, standing beside the heavenly altar. "Who is wise, and he shall understand these things, prudent, and he shall know them?" It is a matter of higher speculation to consider even slightly the rationale of those sacrifices which cleanse those for whom they are offered. Jephthah's sacrifice of his daughter should receive attention; it was by vowing it that he conquered the children of Ammon, and the victim approved his vow, for when her father said, "I have opened my mouth unto the Lord against thee," she answered, "If thou hast opened thy mouth unto the Lord against me, do that which thou hast vowed." The story suggests that the being must be a very cruel one to whom such sacrifices are offered for the salvation of men; and we require some breadth of mind and some ability to solve the difficulties raised against Providence, to be able to account for such things and to see that they are mysteries and exceed our human nature. Then we shall say, "Great are the judgments of God, and hard to be described; for this cause untutored souls have gone astray." Among the Gentiles, too, it is recorded that many a one, when pestilential disease broke out in his country, offered himself a victim for the public good. That this was the case the faithful Clement assumes, on the faith of the narratives, to whom Paul bears witness when he says, "With Clement also, and the others, my fellow-laborers, whose names are in the book of life." If there is anything in these narratives that appears incongruous to one who is minded to carp at mysteries revealed to few, the same difficulty attaches to the office that was laid on the martyrs, for it was God's will that we should rather endure all the dreadful reproaches connected with confessing Him as God, than escape for a short time from such sufferings (which men count evil) by allowing ourselves by our words to conform to the will of the enemies of the truth. We are, therefore, led to believe that the powers of evil do suffer defeat by the death of the holy martyrs; as if their patience, their confession, even unto death, and their zeal for piety blunted the edge of the onset of evil powers against the sufferer, and their might being thus dulled and exhausted, many others of those whom they had conquered raised their heads and were set free from the weight with which the evil powers formerly oppressed and injured them. And even the martyrs themselves are no longer involved in suffering, even though those agents which formerly wrought ill to others are not exhausted; for he who has offered such a sacrifice overcomes the power which opposed him, as I may show by an illustration which is suited to this subject. He who destroys a poisonous animal, or lulls it to sleep with charms, or by any means deprives it of its venom, he does good to many who would otherwise have suffered from that animal had it not been destroyed, or charmed, or emptied of its venom. Moreover, if one of those who were formerly bitten should come to know of this, and should be cured of his malady and look upon the death of that which injured him, or tread on it, or touch it when dead, or taste a part of it, then he, who was formerly a sufferer, would owe cure and benefit to the destroyer of the poisonous animal. In some such way must we suppose the death of the most holy martyrs to operate, many receiving benefit from it by an influence we cannot describe.

37. Of the Effects of the Death of Christ, of His Triumph after It, and of the Removal by His Death of the Sins of Men.

We have lingered over this subject of the martyrs and over the record of those who died on account of pestilence, because this lets us see the excellence of Him who was led as a sheep to the slaughter and was dumb as a lamb before the shearer. For if there is any point in these stories of the Greeks, and if what we have said of the martyrs is well founded,—the Apostles, too, were for the same reason the filth of the world and the off scouring of all things,—what and how great things must be said of the Lamb of God, who was sacrificed for this very reason, that He might take away the sin not of a few but of the whole world, for the sake of which also He suffered? If anyone sin, we read, "We have an advocate with the Father, Jesus Christ the righteous; and He is the propitiation for our sins, and not for ours only, but for those of the whole world," since He is the Savior of all men, especially of them that believe, who blotted out the written bond that was against us by His own blood, and took it out of the way, so that not even a trace, not even of our blotted-out sins, might still be found, and nailed it to His cross; who having put off from Himself the principalities and powers, made a show of them openly, triumphing over them by His cross. And we are taught to rejoice when we suffer afflictions in the world, knowing the ground of our rejoicing to be this, that the world has been conquered and has manifestly been subjected to its conqueror. Hence all the nations, released from their former rulers, serve Him, because He saved the poor from his tyrant by His own passion, and the needy who had no helper. This Savior, then, having humbled the calumniator by humbling Himself, abides with the visible sun before His illustrious church, tropically called the moon, from generation to generation. And having by His passion destroyed His enemies, He who is strong in battle and a mighty Lord required after His mighty deeds a purification which could only be given Him by His Father alone; and this is why He forbids Mary to touch Him, saying, "Touch Me not, for I am not yet ascended to My Father; but go and tell My disciples, I go to My Father and your Father, to My God and your God." And when He comes, loaded with victory and with trophies, with His body which has risen from the dead,—for what other meaning can we see in the words, "I am not yet ascended to My Father," and "I go unto My Father,"—then there are certain powers which say, Who is this that cometh from Edom, red garments from Bosor; this that is beautiful? Then those who escort Him say to those that are upon the heavenly gates, "Lift up your gates, ye rulers, and be ye lifted up, ye everlasting doors, and the king of glory shall come in." But they ask again, seeing as it were His right hand red with blood and His whole person covered with the marks of His valor, "Why are Thy garments red, and Thy clothes like the treading of the full wine fat when it is trodden?" And to this He answers, "I have crushed them." For this cause He had need to wash "His robe in wine, and His garment in the blood of the grape." For when He had taken up our infirmities and carried our diseases, and had borne the sin of the whole world, and had conferred blessings on so many, then, perhaps, He received that baptism which is greater than any that could ever be conceived among men, and of which I think He speaks when He says, "I have a baptism to be baptized with, and how am I straitened till it be accomplished?" I enquire here with boldness and I challenge the ideas put forward by most writers. They say that the greatest baptism, beyond which no greater can be conceived, is His passion. But if this be so, why should He say to Mary after it, "Touch Me not"? He should rather have offered Himself to her touch, when by His passion He had received His perfect baptism. But if it was the case, as we said before, that after all His deeds of valor done against His enemies, He had need to wash "His robe in wine, His garment in the blood of the grape," then He was on His way up to the husbandman of the true vine, the Father, so that having washed there and after having gone up on high, He might lead captivity captive and come down bearing manifold gifts—the tongues, as of fire, which were divided to the Apostles, and the holy angels which are to be present with them in each action and to deliver them. For before these economies they were not yet cleansed and angels could not dwell with them, for they too perhaps do not desire to be with those who have not prepared themselves nor been cleansed by Jesus. For it was of Jesus' benignity alone that He ate and drank with publicans and sinners, and suffered the penitent woman who was a sinner to wash His feet with her tears, and went down even to death for the ungodly, counting it not robbery to be equal with God, and emptied Himself, assuming the form of a servant. And in accomplishing all this He fulfils rather the will of the Father who gave Him up for sinners than His own. For the Father is good, but the Savior is the image of His goodness; and doing good to the world in all things, since God was in Christ reconciling the world to Himself, which formerly for its wickedness was all enemy to Him, He accomplishes His good deeds in order and succession, and does not all at once take all His enemies for His footstool. For the Father says to Him, to the Lord of us all, "Sit Thou on My right hand, until I make Thy enemies the footstool of Thy feet." And this goes on till the last enemy, Death, is overcome by Him. And if we consider what is meant by this subjection to Christ and find an explanation of this mainly from the saying, "When all things shall have been put under Him, then shall the Son Himself be subjected to Him who put all things under Him," then we shall see how the conception agrees with the goodness of the God of all, since it is that of the Lamb of God, taking away the sin of the world. Not all men's sin, however, is taken away by the Lamb of God, not the sin of those who do not grieve and suffer affliction till it be taken away. For thorns are not only fixed but deeply rooted in the hand of everyone who is intoxicated by wickedness and has parted with sobriety, as it is said in the Proverbs, "Thorns grow in the hand of the drunkard," and what pain they must cause him who has admitted such growth in the substance of his soul, it is hard even to tell. Who has allowed wickedness to establish itself so deeply in his soul as to be a ground full of thorns, he must be cut down by the quick and powerful word of God, which is sharper than a two-edged sword, and which is more caustic than any fire. To such a soul that fire must be sent which finds out thorns, and by its divine virtue stands where they are and does not also burn up the threshing-floors or standing corn. But of the Lamb which takes away the sin of the world and begins to do so by His own death there are several ways, some of which are capable of being clearly understood by most, but others are concealed from most, and are known to those only who are worthy of divine wisdom. Why should we count up all the ways by which we come to believe among men? That is a thing which everyone living in the body is able to see for himself. And in the ways in which we believe in these also, sin is taken away; by afflictions and evil spirits and dangerous diseases and grievous sicknesses. And who knows what follows after this? So much as we have said was not unnecessary—we could not neglect the thought which is so clearly connected with that of the words, "Behold the Lamb of God that taketh away the sin of the world," and had therefore to attend somewhat closely to this part of our subject. This has brought us to see that God convicts some by His wrath and chastens them by His anger, since His love to men is so great that He will not leave any without conviction and chastening; so that we should do what in us lies to be spared such conviction and such chastening by the sorest trials.

38. The World, of which the Sin is Taken Away, is said to be the Church. Reasons for Not Agreeing with This Opinion.

The reader will do well to consider what was said above and illustrated from various quarters on the question what is meant in Scripture by the word "world"; and I think it proper to repeat this. I am aware that a certain scholar understands by the world the Church alone, since the Church is the adornment of the world, and is said to be the light of the world. "You," he says, "are the light of the world." Now, the adornment of the world is the Church, Christ being her adornment, who is the first light of the world. We must consider if Christ is said to be the light of the same world as His disciples. When Christ is the light of the world, perhaps it is meant that He is the light of the Church, but when His disciples are the light of the world, perhaps they are the light of others who call on the Lord, others in addition to the Church, as Paul says on this point in the beginning of his first Epistle to the Corinthians, where he writes, "To the Church of God, with all who call on the name of the Lord Jesus Christ." Should anyone consider that the Church is called the light of the world, meaning thereby of the rest of the race of men, including unbelievers, this may be true if the assertion is taken prophetically and theologically; but if it is to be taken of the present, we remind him that the light of a thing illuminates that thing, and would ask him to show how the remainder of the race is illuminated by the Church's presence in the world. If those who hold the view in question cannot show this, then let them consider if our interpretation is not a sound one, that the light is the Church, and the world those others who call on the Name. The words which follow the above in Matthew will point out to the careful enquirer the proper interpretation. "You," it is said, "are the salt of the earth," the rest of mankind being conceived as the earth, and believers are their salt; it is because they believe that the earth is preserved. For the end will come if the salt loses its savor, and ceases to salt and preserve the earth, since it is clear that if iniquity is multiplied and love waxes cold upon the earth, as the Savior Himself uttered an expression of doubt as to those who would witness His coming, saying, "When the Son of man cometh, shall He find faith upon the earth?" then the end of the age will come. Supposing, then, the Church to be called the world, since the Savior's light shines on it—we have to ask in connection with the text, "Behold the Lamb of God, which taketh away the sin of the world," whether the world here is to be taken intellectually of the Church, and the taking away of sin is limited to the Church. In that case what are we to make of the saying of the same disciple with regard to the Savior, as the propitiation for sin? "If any man sin," we read, "we have an advocate with the Father, Jesus Christ the righteous; and He is the propitiation for our sins, and not for our sins only, but for the sins of the whole world?" Paul's dictum appears to me to be to the same effect, when he says, "Who is the Savior of all men, especially of the faithful." Again, Heracleon, dealing with our passage, declares, without any proof or any citation of witnesses to that effect, that the words, "Lamb of God," are spoken by John as a prophet, but the words, "who taketh away the sin of the world," by John as more than a prophet. The former expression he considers to be used of His body, but the latter of Him who was in that body, because the lamb is an imperfect member of the genus sheep; the same being true of the body as compared with the dweller in it. Had he meant to attribute perfection to the body he would have spoken of a ram as about to be sacrificed. After the careful discussions given above, I do not think it necessary to enter into repetitions on this passage, or to controvert Heracleon's careless utterances. One point only may be noted, that as the world was scarcely able to contain Him who had emptied Himself, it required a lamb and not a ram, that its sin might be taken away.

Tenth Book.
1. Jesus Comes to Capernaum. Statements of the Four Evangelists Regarding This.
"After this He went down to Capernaum, He and His mother and His brothers and His disciples; and there they abode not many days. And the Passover of the Jews was at hand, and Jesus went up to Jerusalem, and He found in the temple those that sold oxen and sheep and doves, and the changers of money sitting, and He made a sort of scourge of cords, and cast them all out of the temple, and the sheep and the oxen, and He poured out the small money of the changers and overthrew their tables, and to those that sold the doves He said, Take these things hence; make not My Father's house a house of merchandize. Then His disciples remembered that it was written, that the zeal of thy house shall eat me up. The Jews therefore answered and said unto Him, What sign shows Thou unto us, that Thou does such things? Jesus answered and said unto them, Destroy this temple, and in three days I will raise it up. The Jews therefore answered, Forty-six years was this temple in building, and

wilt thou raise it up in three days? But He spoke of the temple of His body. When therefore He rose from the dead, His disciples remembered that He said this, and they believed the Scripture and the word which Jesus said. Now when He was at Jerusalem at the Passover at the feast, many believed in His name, beholding His signs which He did. But Jesus Himself did not trust Himself to them, for that He knew all men, and because He had no need that any should bear witness concerning man. For He Himself knew what was in man."

The numbers which are recorded in the book of that name obtained a place in Scripture in accordance with some principle which determines their proportion to each thing. We ought therefore to enquire whether the book of Moses which is called Numbers teaches us, should we be able to trace it out, in some special way, the principle with regard to this matter. This remark I make to you at the outset of my tenth book, for in many passages of Scripture I have observed the number ten to have a peculiar privilege, and you may consider carefully whether the hope is justified that this volume will bring you from God some special benefit. That this may prove to be the case, we will seek to yield ourselves as fully as we can to God, who loves to bestow His choicest gifts. The book begins at the words: "After this He went down to Capernaum, He and His mother and His brothers and His disciples, and there they abode not many days." The other three Evangelists say that the Lord, after His conflict with the devil, departed into Galilee. Matthew and Luke represent that he was first at Nazara, and then left them and came and dwelt in Capernaum. Matthew and Mark also state a certain reason why He departed thither, namely, that He had heard that John was cast into prison. The words are as follows: Matthew says, "Then the devil leaves Him, and behold, angels came and ministered unto Him. But when He heard that John was delivered up, He departed into Galilee, and leaving Nazareth He came and dwelt at Capernaum on the seashore in the borders of Zebulun and Naphtali, that it might be fulfilled which was spoken by Isaiah the prophet, saying, The land of Zebulun and the land of Naphtali;" and after the quotation from Isaiah: "From that time Jesus began to preach and to say, Repent ye; for the kingdom of heaven is at hand." Mark has the following: "And He was in the desert forty days and forty nights tempted by Satan, and He was with the wild beasts; and the angels ministered unto Him. But after John was delivered up Jesus came into Galilee, preaching the Gospel of God, that the time is fulfilled and the kingdom of God is at hand; repent ye, and believe in the Gospel." Then after the narrative about Andrew and Peter and James and John, Mark writes: "And He entered into Capernaum, and straightway on the Sabbath He was teaching in the synagogue." Luke has, "And having finished the temptation the devil departed from Him for a season. And Jesus returned in the power of the Spirit into Galilee, and a fame went out concerning Him into all the region round about, and He taught in their synagogues being glorified of all. And He came to Nazara, where He had been brought up, and He entered as His custom was into the synagogue on the Sabbath day." Then Luke gives what He said at Nazara, and how those in the synagogue were enraged at Him and cast Him out of the city and brought Him to the brow of the hill on which their cities were built, to cast Him down headlong, and how going through the midst of them the Lord went His way; and with this he connects the statement, "And He came down to Capernaum, a city of Galilee, and He was teaching them on the Sabbath day."

2. The Discrepancy between John and the First Three Gospels at This Part of the Narrative, Literally Read, the Narratives Cannot Be Harmonized: They Must Be Interpreted Spiritually.

The truth of these matters must lie in that which is seen by the mind. If the discrepancy between the Gospels is not solved, we must give up our trust in the Gospels, as being true and written by a divine spirit, or as records worthy of credence, for both these characters are held to belong to these works. Those who accept the four Gospels, and who do not consider that their apparent discrepancy is to be solved anagogically (by mystical interpretation), will have to clear up the difficulty, raised above, about the forty days of the temptation, a period for which no room can be found in any way in John's narrative; and they will also have to tell us when it was that the Lord came to Capernaum. If it was after the six days of the period of His baptism, the sixth being that of the marriage at Cana of Galilee, then it is clear that the temptation never took place, and that He never was at Nazara, and that John was not yet delivered up. Now, after Capernaum, where He abode not many days, the Passover of the Jews was at hand, and He went up to Jerusalem, where He cast the sheep and oxen out of the temple, and poured out the small change of the bankers. In Jerusalem, too, it appears that Nicodemus, the ruler and Pharisee, first came to Him by night, and heard what we may read in the Gospel. "After these things, Jesus came, and His disciples, into the land of Judæa, and there He tarried with them and baptized, at the same time at which John also was baptizing in Ænon near Salim, because there were many waters there, and they came and were baptized; for John was not yet cast into prison." On this occasion, too, there was a questioning on the part of John's disciples with the Jews about purification, and they came to John, saying of the Savior, "Behold, He baptizes, and all come to Him." They had heard words from the Baptist, the exact tenor of which it is better to take from Scripture itself. Now, if we ask when Christ was first in Capernaum, our respondents, if they follow the words of Matthew, and of the other two, will say, After the temptation, when, "leaving Nazareth, He came and dwelt in Capernaum by the sea." But how can they show both the statements to be true, that of Matthew and Mark, that it was because He heard that John was delivered up that He departed into Galilee, and that of John, found there, after a number of other transactions, subsequent to His stay at Capernaum, after His going to Jerusalem, and His journey from there to Judæa, that John was not yet cast into prison, but was baptizing in Ænon near Salim? There are many other points on which the careful student of the Gospels will find that their narratives do not agree; and these we shall place before the reader, according to our power, as they occur. The student, staggered at the consideration of these things, will either renounce the attempt to find all the Gospels true, and not venturing to conclude that all our information about our Lord is untrustworthy, will choose at random one of them to be his guide; or he will accept the four, and will consider that their truth is not to be sought for in the outward and material letter.

## 3. What We are to Think of the Discrepancies Between the Different Gospels.

We must, however, try to obtain some notion of the intention of the Evangelists in such matters, and we direct ourselves to this. Suppose there are several men who, by the spirit, see God, and know His words addressed to His saints, and His presence which He vouchsafes to them, appearing to them at chosen times for their advancement. There are several such men, and they are in different places, and the benefits they receive from above vary in shape and character. And let these men report, each of them separately, what he sees in spirit about God and His words, and His appearances to His saints, so that one of them speaks of God's appearances and words and acts to one righteous man in such a place, and another about other oracles and great works of the Lord, and a third of something else than what the former two have dealt with. And let there be a fourth, doing with regard to some particular matter something of the same kind as these three. And let the four agree with each other about something the Spirit has suggested to them all, and let them also make brief reports of other matters besides that one; then their narratives will fall out something on this wise: God appeared to such a one at such a time and in such a place, and did to him thus and thus; as if He had appeared to him in such a form, and had led him by the hand to such a place, and then done to him thus and thus. The second will report that God appeared at the very time of the foresaid occurrences, in a certain town, to a person who is named, a second person, and in a place far removed from that of the former account, and he will report a different set of words spoken at the same time to this second person. And let the same be supposed to be the case with the third and with the fourth. And let them, as we said, agree, these witnesses who report true things about God, and about His benefits conferred on certain men, let them agree with each other in some of the narratives they report. He, then, who takes the writings of these men for history, or for a representation of real things by a historical image, and who supposes God to be within certain limits in space, and to be unable to present to several persons in different places several visions of Himself at the same time, or to be making several speeches at the same moment, he will deem it impossible that our four writers are all speaking truth. To him it is impossible that God, who is in certain limits in space, could at the same set time be saying one thing to one man and another to another, and that He should be doing a thing and the opposite thing as well, and, to put it bluntly, that He should be both sitting and standing, should one of the writers represent Him as standing at the time, and making a certain speech in such a place to such a man, while a second writer speaks of Him as sitting.

4. Scripture Contains Many Contradictions, and Many Statements Which are Not Literally True, But Must Be Read Spiritually and Mystically.

In the case I have supposed where the historians desire to teach us by an image what they have seen in their mind, their meaning would be found, if the four were wise, to exhibit no disagreement; and we must understand that with the four Evangelists it is not otherwise. They made full use for their purpose of things done by Jesus in the exercise of His wonderful and extraordinary power; they use in the same way His sayings, and in some places they tack on to their writing, with language apparently implying things of sense, things made manifest to them in a purely intellectual way. I do not condemn them if they even sometimes dealt freely with things which to the eye of history happened differently, and changed them so as to subserve the mystical aims they had in view; so as to speak of a thing which happened in a certain place, as if it had happened in another, or of what took place at a certain time, as if it had taken place at another time, and to introduce into what was spoken in a certain way some changes of their own. They proposed to speak the truth where it was possible both materially and spiritually, and where this was not possible it was their intention to prefer the spiritual to the material. The spiritual truth was often preserved, as one might say, in the material falsehood. As, for example, we might judge of the story of Jacob and Esau. Jacob says to Isaac, "I am Esau thy firstborn son," and spiritually he spoke the truth, for he already partook of the rights of the first-born, which were perishing in his brother, and clothing himself with the goatskins he assumed the outward semblance of Esau, and was Esau all but the voice praising God, so that Esau might afterward find a place to receive a blessing. For if Jacob had not been blessed as Esau, neither would Esau perhaps have been able to receive a blessing of his own. And Jesus too is many things, according to the conceptions of Him, of which it is quite likely that the Evangelists took up different notions; while yet they were in agreement with each other in the different things they wrote. Statements which are verbally contrary to each other, are made about our Lord, namely, that He was descended from David and that He was not descended from David. The statement is true, "He was descended from David," as the Apostle says, "born of the seed of David according to the flesh," if we apply this to the bodily part of Him; but the self-same statement is untrue if we understand His being born of the seed of David of His diviner power; for He was declared to be the Son of God with power. And for this reason too, perhaps, the sacred prophecies speak of Him now as a servant, and now as a Son. They call Him a servant on account of the form of a servant which he wore, and because He was of the seed of David, but they call Him the Son of God according to His character as first-born. Thus it is true to call Him man and to call Him not man; man, because He was capable of death; not man, on account of His being diviner than man. Marcion, I suppose, took sound words in a wrong sense, when he rejected His birth from Mary, and declared that as to His divine nature He was not born of Mary, and hence made bold to delete from the Gospel the passages which have this effect. And a like fate seems to have overtaken those who make away with His humanity and receive His deity alone; and also those opposites of these who cancel His deity and confess Him as a man to be a holy man, and the most righteous of all men. And those who hold the doctrine of Dokesis, not remembering that He humbled Himself even unto death and became obedient even to the cross, but only imagining in Him the absence of suffering, the superiority to all such accidents, they do what they can to deprive us of the man who is more just than all men, and are left with a figure which cannot save them, for as by one man came death, so also by one man is the justification of life. We could not have received such benefit as we have from the Logos had He not assumed the man, had He remained such as He was from the beginning with God the Father, and had He not taken up man, the first man of all, the man more precious than all others, purer than all others and capable of receiving Him. But after that man we also shall be able to receive Him, to receive Him so great and of such nature as He was, if we prepare a place in proportion to Him in our soul. So much I have said of the apparent discrepancies in the Gospels, and of my desire to have them treated in the way of spiritual interpretation.

5. Paul Also Makes Contradictory Statements About Himself, and Acts in Opposite Ways at Different Times.

On the same passage one may also make use of such an example as that of Paul, who at one place says that he is carnal, sold under sin, and thus was not able to judge anything, while in another place he is the spiritual man who is able to judge all things and himself to be judged by no man. Of the carnal one are the words, "Not what I would that do I practice, but what I hate that do I." And he too who was caught up to the third heaven and heard unspeakable words is a different Paul from him who says, Of such an one I will glory, but of myself I will not glory. If he becomes to the Jews as a Jew that he may gain the Jews, and to those under the law as under the law that he may gain those under the law, and to them that are without law as without law, not being without law to God, but under law to Christ, that he may gain those without law, and if to the weak he becomes weak that he may gain the weak, it is clear that these statements must be examined each by itself, that he becomes a Jew, and that sometimes he is under the law and at another time without law, and that sometimes he is weak. Where, for example, he says something by way of permission and not by commandment, there we may recognize that he is weak;

for who, he says, is weak, and I am not weak? When he shaves his head and makes an offering, or when he circumcises Timothy, he is a Jew; but when he says to the Athenians, "I found an altar with the inscription, To the unknown God. That, then, which ye worship not knowing it, that declare I unto you," and, "As also some of your own poets have said, For we also are His offspring," then he becomes to those without the law as without the law, adjuring the least religious of men to espouse religion, and turning to his own purpose the saying of the poet, "From Love do we begin; his race are we." And instances might perhaps be found where, to men not Jews and yet under the law, he is under the law.

6. Different Accounts of the Call of Peter, and of the Imprisonment of the Baptist. The Meaning of "Capernaum."

These examples may be serviceable to illustrate statements not only about the Savior, but about the disciples too, for here also there is some discrepancy of statement. For there is a difference in thought perhaps between Simon who is found by his own brother Andrew, and who is addressed "Thou shalt be called Cephas," and him who is seen by Jesus when walking by the sea of Galilee, along with his brother, and addressed conjointly with that brother, "Come after Me, and I will make you fishers of men." There was some fitness in the fact that the writer who goes more to the root of the matter and tells of the Word becoming flesh, and hence does not record the human generation of the Word who was in the beginning with God, should not tell us of Simon's being found at the seashore and called away from there, but of his being found by his brother who had been staying with

Jesus at the tenth hour, and of his receiving the name Cephas in connection with his being thus found out. If he was seen by Jesus when walking by the sea of Galilee, it would scarcely be on a later occasion that he was addressed, "Thou art Peter and upon this rock I will build My church." With John again the Pharisees know Jesus to be baptizing with His disciples, adding this to His other great activities; but the Jesus of the three does not baptize at all. John the Baptist, too, with the Evangelist of the same name, goes on a long time without being cast into prison. With Matthew, on the contrary, he is put in prison almost at the time of the temptation of Jesus, and this is the occasion of Jesus retiring to Galilee, to avoid being put in prison. But in John there is nothing at all about John's being put in prison. Who is so wise and so able as to learn all the things that are recorded about Jesus in the four Evangelists, and both to understand each incident by itself, and have a connected view of all His sojourning and words and acts at each place? As for the passage presently before us, it gives in the order of events that on the sixth day the Savior, after the business of the marriage at Cana of Galilee, went down with His mother and His brothers and His disciples to Capernaum, which means "field of consolation." For after the feasting and the wine it was fitting that the Savior should come to the field of consolation with His mother and His disciples, to console those whom He was training for disciples and the soul which had conceived Him by the Holy Ghost, with the fruits which were to stand in that full field.

7. Why His Brothers are Not Called to the Wedding; and Why He Abides at Capernaum Not Many Days.

But we must ask why His brothers are not called to the wedding: they were not there, for it is not said they were; but they go down to Capernaum with Him and His mother and His disciples. We must also examine why on this occasion they do not "*go in to*" Capernaum, nor "*go up to*," but "go down to" it. Consider if we must not understand by His brothers here the powers which went down along with Him, not called to the wedding according to the explanations given above, since it is in lower and humbler places than those who are called disciples of Christ, and in another way, that these brothers receive assistance. For if His mother is called, then there are some bearing fruit, and even to these the Lord goes down with the servants and disciples of the Word, to help such persons, His mother also being with Him. Those indeed who are called Capernaum appear not to be able to allow Jesus and those who went down with Him to make a longer stay with them: hence they remain with them not many days. For the lower field of consolation does not admit the illumination of many doctrines, but is only capable of a few. To get a clear view of the difference between those who receive Jesus for longer and for shorter time, we may compare with this, "They abode there not many days," the words recorded in Matthew as spoken by Christ when risen from the dead to His disciples who were being sent out to teach all nations, "Behold, I am with you always, even to the end of the world." To those who are to know all that human nature can know while it still is here, is said with emphasis, "I am with you;" and as the rise of each new day upon the field of contemplation brings more days before the eyes of the blessed, therefore He says, "All the days till the end of the world." As for those in Capernaum, on the contrary, to whom they go down as to the more needy, not only Jesus, but also His mother and His brothers and His disciples "abode there not many days."

8. How Christ Abides with Believers to the End of the Age, and Whether He Abides with Them After that Consummation.

Some may very likely and not unreasonably ask, whether, when all the days of this age are over, there will no longer be any one to say, "Lo, I am with you," with those, namely, who received Him till the fulfilment of the age, for the "until" seems to indicate a certain limit of time. To this we must say that the phrase, "I am with you," is not the same as "I am in you." We might say more properly that the Savior was not in His disciples but with them, so long as they had not arrived in their minds at the consummation of the age. But when they see to be at hand, as far as their effort is concerned, the consummation of the world which is crucified to them, then Jesus will be no longer with them, but in them, and they will say, "It is no longer I that live but Christ that lives in me," and "If ye seek a proof of Christ that speaks in me." In saying this we are keeping for our part also to the ordinary interpretation which makes the "always" the time down to the consummation of the age, and are not asking more than is attainable to human nature as it is here. That interpretation may be adhered to and justice yet be done to the "I." He who is with His disciples who are sent out to teach all the nations, until the consummation, maybe He who emptied Himself and took the form of a servant, and yet afterwards may be another in point of state; afterwards He may be such as He was before He emptied Himself, until all His enemies are made by His

Father the footstool of His feet; and after this, when the Son has delivered up the kingdom to God and the Father, it may be the Father who says to them, "Behold, I am with you." But whether it is "all the days" up to that time, or simply "all the days," or not "all days" but "every day," anyone may consider that likes. Our plan does not allow us at present to digress so far.

9. Heracleon Says that Jesus is Not Stated to Have Done Anything at Capernaum. But in the Other Gospels He Does Many Things There.

But Heracleon, dealing with the words, "After this He went down to Capernaum," declares that they indicate the introduction of another transaction, and that the word "went down" is not without significance. "Capernaum," he says, "means these farthest-out parts of the world, these districts of matter, into which He descended, and because the place was not suitable, he says, He is not reported either to have done anything or said anything in it." Now if the Lord had not been reported in the other Gospels either as having done or said anything at Capernaum, we might perhaps have hesitated whether this view ought or ought not to be received. But that is far from being the case. Matthew says our Lord left Nazareth and came and dwelt at Capernaum on the seaside, and that from that time He began to preach, saying, "Repent ye, for the kingdom of heaven is at hand." And Mark, starting in his narrative from the temptation by the devil, relates that after John was cast into prison, Jesus came into Galilee, proclaiming the Gospel of God, and after the call of the four fishermen to the Apostleship, "they enter into Capernaum; and straightway on the Sabbath day He taught in the synagogue, and they were astonished at His doctrine." And Mark records an action of Jesus also which took place at Capernaum, for he goes on to say, "In their synagogue there was a man with an unclean spirit, and he cried out, saying, Ah! What have we to do with Thee, Thou Jesus of Nazareth? Art Thou come to destroy us? We know Thee who Thou art, the Son of God. And Jesus rebuked him, saying, Hold thy peace and come out of him; and the unclean spirit, tearing him and crying with a loud voice, came out of him. And they were all amazed." And at Capernaum Simon's mother-in-law is cured of her fever. And Mark adds that when evening was come all those were cured who were sick and who were possessed with demons. Luke's report is very like Mark's about Capernaum. He says, "And He came to Capernaum, a city of Galilee, and He was teaching them on the Sabbath day, and they were astonished at His teachings, for His word was with power. And in the synagogue there was a man having a spirit of an unclean demon, and he cried out with a loud voice, Ah! What have we to do with Thee, Thou Jesus of Nazareth? Hast Thou come to destroy us? I know Thee who Thou art, the holy one of God. And Jesus rebuked him, saying, Hold thy peace and come out of him. Then the demon having thrown him down in the midst, went out of him, doing him no harm." And then Luke reports how the Lord rose up from the synagogue and went into the house of Simon, and rebuked the fever in his mother-in-law, and cured her of her disease; and after this cure, "when the sun was setting," he says, "all, as many as had persons sick with divers diseases, brought them to Him, and He laid his hands on each one of them and cured them. And demons also went out from many, crying and saying, Thou art the Son of God, and He rebuked them and suffered them not to speak because they knew that He was the Christ." We have presented all these statements as to the Savior's sayings and doings at Capernaum in order to refute Heracleon's interpretation of our passage, "Hence He is not said to have done or to have spoken anything there." He must either give two meanings to Capernaum, and show us his reasons for them, or if he cannot do this he must give up saying that the Savior visited any place to no purpose. We, for our part, should we come to passages where even a comparison of the other Gospels fails to show that Jesus' visit to this place or that was not accompanied by any results, will seek with the divine assistance to make it clear that His coming was not in vain.

10. Significance of Capernaum.

Matthew for his part adds, that when the Lord had entered into Capernaum the centurion came to him, saying, "My boy is lying in my house sick of the palsy, grievously tormented," and after telling the Lord some more about him, received the reply, "Go, and as thou hast believed, so be it unto thee." And Matthew then gives us the story of Peter's mother-in-law, in close agreement with the other two. I conceive it to be a creditable piece of work and becoming to one who is anxious to hear about Christ, to collect from the four Gospels all that is related about Capernaum, and the discourses spoken, and the works done there, and how many visits the Lord paid to the place, and how, at one time, He is said to have gone down to it, and at another to have entered into it, and where He came from when He did so. If we compare all these points together, we shall not go astray in the meaning we ascribe to Capernaum. On the one hand, the sick are healed, and other works of power are done there, and on the other, the preaching, Repent ye, for the kingdom of heaven is at hand, begins there, and this appears to be a sign, as we showed when entering on this subject, of some more needy place of consolation, made so perhaps by Jesus, who comforted men by what He taught and by what He did there, in that place of consolation. For we know that the names of places agree in their meaning with the things connected with Jesus; as Gergesa, where the citizens of these parts besought Him to depart out of their coasts, means, "The dwelling of the casters-out." And this, also, we have noticed about Capernaum, that not only did the preaching, "Repent ye, for the kingdom of heaven is at hand," begin there, but that according to the three Evangelists Jesus performed there His first miracles. None of the three, however, added to the first wonders which he records as done in Capernaum, that note attached by John the disciple to the first work of Jesus, "This beginning of His signs did Jesus in Cana of Galilee." For that which was done in Capernaum was not the beginning of the signs, since the leading sign of the Son of God was good cheer, and in the light of human experience it is also the most representative of Him. For the Word of God does not show forth His own beauty so much in healing the sick, as in His tendering the temperate draught to make glad those who are in good health and are able to join in the banquet.

11. Why the Passover is Said to Be that of the "Jews." Its Institution: and the Distinction Between "Feasts of the Lord" And Feasts Not So Spoken of.

"And the Passover of the Jews was at hand." Inquiring into the accuracy of the most wise John (on this passage), I put myself the question, What is indicated by the addition "of the Jews"? Of what other nation was the Passover a festival? Would it not have been enough to say, "And the Passover was at hand"? It may, however, be the case that the human Passover is one thing when kept by men not as Scripture intended, and that the divine Passover is another thing, the true Passover, observed in spirit and truth by those who worship God in spirit and in truth; and then the distinction indicated in the text may be that between the divine Passover and that said to be of the Jews. We should attend to the Passover law and observe what the Lord says of it when it is first mentioned in Scripture. "And the Lord spoke unto Moses and Aaron in the land of Egypt, saying, This month is to you the beginning of months, it is the first for you among the months of the year. Speak thou to all the congregation of the children of Israel, saying, On the tenth of this month shall every man take a sheep, according to the houses of your families;" then after some directions in which the word Passover does not occur again, he adds, "Thus shall ye eat it, your loins girt and your shoes on your feet, and your staves in your hands, and ye shall eat it with haste. It is the Passover of the Lord." He does not say, "It is your Passover." And a little further on He names the festival again in the same way, "And it shall come to pass, when your sons say to you, What is this service? And ye shall say to them, It is the sacrifice, the Passover of the Lord, how He guarded the houses of the children of Israel." And again, a little further on, "And the Lord spoke to Moses and Aaron, saying, This is the law of the Passover. No alien shall eat of it." And again in a little, "But if a proselyte come to you, and keep the Passover of the Lord, every male of him shall be circumcised." Observe that in the law we never find it said, "Your Passover;" but in all the passages quoted the phrase occurs once without any adjunct, while we have three times "The Passover of the Lord." To make sure that there is such a distinction between the Passover of the Lord and the Passover of the Jews, we may consider the way in which Isaiah speaks of the matter: "Your new moons and your Sabbaths and your great day I cannot bear; your fast and your holiday and your new moons and your feasts my soul hates." The Lord does not call them His own, these observances of sinners (they are hated of His soul, if such there be); neither the new moons, nor the Sabbaths, nor the great day, nor the fast, nor the festivals. And in the legislation about the Sabbath in Exodus, we read, "And Moses said unto them, This is the word which the Lord spoke, The Sabbath is a holy rest unto the Lord." And a little further on, "And Moses said, Eat ye; for to-day is a Sabbath unto the Lord." And in Numbers, before the sacrifices which are offered at each festival, as if all the festivals came under the law of the continuous and daily sacrifice, we find it written, "And the Lord spoke unto Moses, Announce to the children of Israel, and thus shalt thou say unto them, My gifts, My offerings, My fruits for a smell of sweet savor, ye shall observe to offer unto Me at My festivals. And thou shalt say unto them, These are the offerings which ye shall offer unto the Lord." The festival set forth in Scripture He calls His own, not those of the people receiving the law, He speaks of *His* gifts, *His* offerings. A similar way of speaking is that in Exodus with regard to the people; it is said by God to be His own people, when it does not sin; but in the section about the calf He abjures it and calls it the people of Moses. On the one hand, "Thou shalt say to Pharaoh, Thus says the Lord, Let My people go, that they may serve Me in the wilderness. But if thou wilt not let My people go, behold, I will send against thee and against thy servants, and against thy people and against thy houses, the dog-fly; and the houses of the Egyptians shall be full of the dog-fly, and on the land on which they are, against it will I send them. And I will glorify on that day the land of Gesem, on which My people are; on it there shall be no dog-fly, that thou may know that I am the Lord, the Lord of all the earth. And I will make a distinction between My people and thy people." To Moses, on the other hand, He says, "Go, descend quickly, for thy people hath transgressed, which thou leads out of the land of Egypt." As, then, the people when it does not sin is the people of God, but when it sins is no longer spoken of as His, thus, also, the feasts when they are hated by the Lord's soul are said to be feasts of sinners, but when the law is given regarding them, they are called feasts of the Lord. Now of these feasts Passover is one, which in the passage before us is said to be that not of the Lord, but of the Jews. In another passage, too, we find it said, "These are the feasts of the Lord, which ye shall call chosen, holy." From the mouth of the Lord Himself, then, we see that there is no gainsaying our statement on this point. Someone, no doubt, will ask about the words of the Apostle, where he writes to the Corinthians: "For our Passover also was sacrificed for us, namely, Christ;" he does not say, "The Passover of the Lord was sacrificed, even Christ." To this we must say, either that the Apostle simply calls the Passover our Passover because it was sacrificed for us, or that every sacrifice which is really the Lord's, and the Passover is one of these, awaits its consummation not in this age nor upon earth, but in the coming age and in heaven when the kingdom of heaven appears. As for those feasts, one of the twelve prophets says, "What will ye do in the days of assembly, and in the days of the feast of the Lord?" But Paul says in the Epistle to the Hebrews: "But ye are come unto Mount Zion, and to the city of the living God, the heavenly Jerusalem, and to ten thousands of angels, the assembly and church of the firstborn, who are written in heaven." And in the Epistle to the Colossians: "Let no one judge you in meat and in drink, or in respect of a feast-day or a new moon, or a Sabbath day; which are a shadow of the things to come."

12. Of the Heavenly Festivals, of which those on Earth are Typical.

Now in what manner, in those heavenly things of which the shadow was present to the Jews on earth, those will celebrate festivals who have first been trained by tutors and governors under the true law, until the fullness of the time should come, namely, above, when we shall be able to receive into ourselves the perfect measure of the Son of God, this it is the work of that wisdom to make plain which has been hidden in a mystery; and it also may show to our thought how the laws about meats are symbols of those things which will there nourish and strengthen our soul. But it is vain to think that one desiring to work out in his fancy the great sea of such ideas, even if he wished to show how local worship is still a pattern and shadow of heavenly things, and that the sacrifices and the sheep are full of meaning, that he should advance further than the Apostle, who seeks indeed to lift our minds above earthly views of the law, but who does not show us to any extent how these things are to be. Even if we look at the festivals, of which Passover is one, from the point of view of the age to come, we have still to ask how it is that our Passover is now sacrificed, namely, Christ, and not only so, but is to be sacrificed hereafter.

### 13. Spiritual Meaning of the Passover.

A few points may be added in connection with the doctrines now under consideration, though it would require a special discussion in many volumes to treat of all the mystical statements about the law, and especially of those connected with the festivals, and more particularly still with the Passover. The Passover of the Jews consists of a sheep which is sacrificed, each taking a sheep according to his father's house; and the Passover is accompanied by the slaughter of thousands of rams and goats, in proportion to the number of the houses of the people. But our Passover is sacrificed for us, namely, Christ. Another feature of the Jewish festival is unleavened bread; all leaven is made to disappear out of their houses; but "we keep the feast not with the old leaven, nor with the leaven of malice and wickedness, but with the unleavened bread of sincerity and truth." Whether there be any Passover and any feast of leaven beyond the two we have mentioned, is a point we must examine more carefully, since these serve for a pattern and a shadow of the heavenly ones we spoke of, and not only such things as food and drink and new moons and Sabbaths, but the festivals also, are a shadow of the things to come. In the first place, when the Apostle says, "Our Passover is sacrificed, Christ," one may feel with regard to this such doubts as these. If the sheep with the Jews is a type of the sacrifice of Christ, then one should have been offered and not a multitude, as Christ is one; or if many sheep were offered it is to follow out the type, as if many

Christs were sacrificed. But not to dwell on this, we may ask how the sheep, which was the victim, contains an image of Christ, when the sheep was sacrificed by men who were observing the law, but Christ was put to death by transgressors of the law, and what application can be found in Christ of the direction, "They shall eat the flesh this night, roast with fire, and unleavened bread on bitter herbs shall they eat," and "Eat not of it raw, nor sodden with water, but roast with fire; the head with the feet and the entrails; ye shall not set any of it apart till the morning, and a bone thereof ye shall not break. But that which is left thereof till the morning ye shall burn." The sentence, "A bone of it ye shall not break," John appears to have made use of in his Gospel, as applying to the transactions connected with Christ, and connecting with them the occasion spoken of in the law when those eating the sheep are bidden not to break a bone of it. He writes as follows: "The soldiers therefore came and brake the legs of the first, and of the other who was crucified with him; but when they came to Jesus and saw that He was already dead, they brake not His legs, but one of the soldiers with a spear pierced His side, and straightway there came out blood and water. And he that hath seen hath borne witness and his witness is true, and he knows that he sayeth truth that ye also may believe. And these things took place that the Scripture might be fulfilled, "A bone of Him ye shall not break." There are a myriad other points besides this in the Apostle's language which would call for inquiry, both about the Passover and the unleavened bread, but they would have to be dealt with, as we said above, in a special work of great length. At present we can only give an epitome of them as they bear on the text presently before us, and aim at a short solution of the principal problem. We call to mind the words, "This is the Lamb of God that taketh away the sin of the world," for it is said of the Passover, "Ye shall take it of the lambs or of the goats." The Evangelist here agrees with Paul, and both are involved in the difficulties we spoke of above. But on the other hand we have to say that if the Word became flesh, and the Lord says, "Unless ye eat the flesh of the Son of Man, and drink His blood, ye have no life in you. He that eats My flesh and drinks My blood, hath eternal life, and I will raise him up at the last day. For My flesh is meat indeed and My blood is drink indeed. He that eats My flesh and drinks My blood abides in Me, and I in him,"—then the flesh thus spoken of is that of the Lamb that takes away the sin of the world; and this is the blood, some of which was to be put on the two side posts of the door, and on the lintels in the houses, in which we eat the Passover. Of the flesh of this Lamb it is necessary that we should eat in the time of the world, which is night, and the flesh is to be roast with fire, and eaten with unleavened bread; for the Word of God is not flesh and flesh only. He says, in fact, Himself, "I am the bread of life," and "This is the bread of life which came down from heaven, that a man should eat of it, and not die. I am the bread of life that came down from heaven; if a man eat of this bread, he shall live forever." We must not overlook, however, that by a loose use of words, any food is called bread, as we read in Moses in Deuteronomy, "Forty days He ate no bread and drank no water," instead of, He took no food, either wet or dry. I am led to this observation by John's saying, "And the bread which I will give is My flesh, for the life of the world." Again, we eat the flesh of the Lamb, with bitter herbs, and unleavened bread, when we repent of our sins and grieve with the sorrow which is according to God, a repentance which operates for our salvation, and is not to be repented of; or when, on account of our trials, we turn to the speculations which are found to be those of truth, and are nourished by them. We are not, however, to eat the flesh of the Lamb raw, as those do who are slaves of the letter, like irrational animals, and those who are enraged at men truly reasonable, because they desire to understand spiritual things; truly, they share the nature of savage beasts. But we must strive to convert the rawness of Scripture into well-cooked food, not letting what is written grow flabby and wet and thin, as those do who have itching ears, and turn away their ears from the truth; their methods tend to a loose and flabby conduct of life. But let us be of a fervent spirit and keep hold of the fiery words given to us of God, such as Jeremiah received from Him who spoke to him, "Behold, I have made My words in thy mouth like fire," and let us see that the flesh of the Lamb be well cooked, so that those who partake of it may say, as Christ speaks in us, "Our heart burned by the way, as He opened to us the Scriptures." Further, if it is our duty to enquire into such a point as the roasting of the flesh of the Lamb with fire, we must not forget the parallel of what Jeremiah suffered on account of the words of God, as he says: "And it was as a glowing fire, burning in my bones, and I am without any strength, and I cannot bear it." But, in this eating, we must begin at the head, that is to say, at the principal and the most essential doctrines about heavenly things, and we must end at the feet, the last branches of learning which enquire as to the final nature in things, or about more material things, or about things under the earth, or about wicked spirits and unclean demons. For it may be that the account of these things is not obvious, like themselves, but is laid away among the mysteries of Scripture, so that it may be called, tropically, the feet of the Lamb. Nor must we fail to deal with the entrails, which are within and hidden from us; we must approach the whole of Scripture as one body, we must not lacerate nor break through the strong and well-knit connections which exist in the harmony of its whole composition, as those do who lacerate, so far as they can, the unity of the Spirit that is in all the Scriptures. But this aforesaid prophecy of the Lamb is to be our nourishment only during the night of this dark life of ours; what comes after this life is, as it were, the dawn of day, and why should we leave over till then the food which can only be useful to us now? But when the night is passed, and the day which succeeds it is at hand, then we shall have bread to eat which has nothing to do with the leavened bread of the older and lower state of things, but is unleavened, and that will serve our turn until that which comes after the unleavened bread is given us, the manna, which is food for angels rather than men. Every one of us, then, may sacrifice his lamb in every house of our fathers; and while one breaks the law, not sacrificing the lamb at all, another may keep the commandment entirely, offering his sacrifice, and cooking it aright, and not breaking a bone of it. This, then, in brief, is the interpretation of the Passover sacrificed for us, which is Christ, in accordance with the view taken of it by the Apostles, and with the Lamb in the Gospel. For we ought not to suppose that historical things are types of historical things, and material things of material, but that material things are typical of spiritual things, and historical things of intellectual. It is not necessary that our discourse should now ascend to that third Passover which is to be celebrated with myriads of

Origen of Alexandra

angels in the most perfect and most blessed exodus; we have already spoken of these things to a greater extent than the passage demands.

14. In the First Three Gospels the Passover is Spoken of Only at the Close of the Ministry; In John at the Beginning. Remarks on This. Heracleon on the Passover.

We must not, however, fail to enquire into the statement that the Passover of the Jews was at hand, when the Lord was at Capernaum with His mother and His brothers and His disciples. In the Gospel according to Matthew, after being left by the devil, and after the angels came and ministered to Him, when He heard that John was delivered up He withdrew into Galilee, and leaving Nazara He came and dwelt in Capernaum. Then He began to preach, and chose the four fishermen for His Apostles, and taught in the synagogues of the whole of Galilee and healed those who were brought to Him. Then He goes up into the mountain and speaks the beatitudes and what follows them; and after finishing that instruction He comes down from the mountain and enters Capernaum a second time. Then He embarked in a ship and crossed over to the other side to the country of the Gergesenes. On their beseeching Him to depart out of their coasts He embarked in a ship and crossed over and came to His own city. Then He wrought certain cures and went about all the cities and the villages, teaching in their synagogues; after this most of the events of the Gospels take place, before Matthew indicates the approach of the time of Passover. With the other Evangelists also, after the stay at Capernaum it is long till we come to any mention of the Passover; which may confirm in their opinion those who take the view about Capernaum which was set forth above. That stay, in the neighborhood of the Passover of the Jews, is set in a brighter light by that nearness, both because it was better in itself, and still more because at the Passover of the Jews there are found in the temple those who sell oxen and sheep and doves. This adds emphasis to the statement that the Passover was not that of the Lord but that of the Jews; the Father's house was made, in the eyes of those who did not hallow it, a house of merchandise, and the Passover of the Lord became for those who took a low and material view of it a Jewish Passover. A fitter occasion than the present will occur for enquiring as to the time of the Passover, which took place about the spring equinox, and for any other enquiry which may arise in connection with it. As for Heracleon, he says, "This is the great festival; for it was a type of the passion of the Savior; not only was the lamb put to death, the eating of it afforded relaxation, the killing it pointed to what of the passion of the Savior was in this world, and the eating it to the rest at the marriage." We have given his words, that it may be seen with what a want of caution and how loosely he proceeds, and with what an absence of constructive skill even on such a theme as this; and how little regard in consequence is to be paid to him.

15. Discrepancy of the Gospel Narratives Connected with the Cleansing of the Temple.

"And Jesus went up to Jerusalem. And He found in the temple those that sold oxen and sheep and doves and the changers of money sitting; and He made a scourge of cords, and cast out of the temple the sheep and the oxen, and poured out the small coin of the changers, and overturned their tables, and to those who sold the doves

He said, Take these things hence; make not My Father's house a house of merchandise. Then His disciples remembered that it was written, the zeal of thy house shall eat me up." It is to be noted that John makes this transaction of Jesus with those He found selling oxen and sheep and doves in the temple His second work; while the other Evangelists narrate a similar incident almost at the end and in connection with the story of the passion. Matthew has it thus: "At Jesus' entry into Jerusalem the whole city was stirred, saying, Who is this? And the multitudes said, This is Jesus the prophet, from Nazareth of Galilee. And Jesus went into the temple and cast out all them that sold and bought in the temple, and He overturned the tables of the money-changers and the seats of them that sold doves. And He says to them, It is written, My house shall be called a house of prayer, but you make it a den of robbers." Mark has the following: "And they came to Jerusalem. And having entered into the temple He began to cast out those that sold and bought in the temple, and the tables of the money-changers He overthrew and the seats of them that sold doves. And He suffered not that any should carry a vessel through the temple; and He taught and said unto them, Is it not written that My house shall be called a house of prayer for all the nations? But you have made it a den of robbers." And Luke: "And when he came near, He beheld the city and wept over it, saying that, if thou had known in this day, even thou, the things that belong to peace; but now they are hid from thine eyes. For the days shall come upon thee, when they shall surround thee and shut thee in on every side, and shall dash thee to the ground and thy children, and they shall not leave in thee one stone upon another, because thou knew not the time of thy visitation.

And He entered into the temple and began to cast out those that sold, saying to them, It is written, My house shall be a house of prayer, but ye have made it a den of robbers." It is further to be observed that what is recorded by the three as having taken place in connection with the Lord's going up to Jerusalem, when He did these things in the temple, is narrated in a very similar manner by John as taking place long after this, after another visit to Jerusalem different from this one. We must consider the statements, and in the first place that of Matthew, where we read: "When He drew nigh to Jerusalem and came to Bethphage over against the Mount of Olives, then Jesus sent two disciples, saying unto them, Go ye into the village over against you, and straightway ye shall find an ass tied and a colt with her; loose them and bring them to Me. And if any man say unto you, What are you doing? You shall say, The Lord hath need of them, and straightway he will send them. But this was done that it might be fulfilled which was spoken by the prophet, saying, Say you to the daughter of Zion, Behold, thy king cometh, meek and seated upon an ass and upon the colt of an ass. And the disciples went and did as Jesus commanded them; they brought the ass and the foal, and they placed on them their garments, and He sat thereon. And the most part of the multitude spread their garments on the road, but the multitudes that went before Him, and they that followed, cried, Hosanna to the Son of David, blessed is He that cometh in the name of the Lord. Hosanna in the highest." After this comes, "And when He had entered into Jerusalem the whole city was stirred," which we cited above. Then we have Mark's account: "And when they drew nigh unto Jerusalem, to Bethphage and Bethany, to the Mount of Olives, He sends two of His disciples and says to them, Go ye into the village over against you. And straightway as ye enter into it ye shall find a colt tied, on which no man hath ever sat, loose it and bring it. And if anyone say to you, Why do ye this? say, Because the Lord hath need of him, and straightway he will send him back hither. And they went and found the colt tied at the door outside on the road, and they loose him. And some of them that stood there said to them, What do ye, loosing the colt? And they said to them as Jesus told them, and they let them go. And they brought the colt to Jesus, and cast on it their garments. But others cut down branches from the field and spread them in the way. And they that went before and they that followed cried, Hosanna, blessed is He that cometh in the name of the Lord; blessed be the kingdom that cometh, of our father David! Hosanna in the highest! And He went into Jerusalem to the temple, and looked round about on all things, and as it was already evening, He went out to Bethany with the twelve. And on the morrow when they were come forth from Bethany He was hungry." Then, after the affair of the withered fig tree, "They came to Jerusalem. And He went into the temple and began to cast out them that sold." Luke narrates as follows: "And it came to pass, when He drew near to Bethphage and Bethany at the mount that is called the Mount of Olives, He sent two of his disciples, saying, Go ye into the village over against you, in which when ye enter, ye shall find a colt tied, on which no man ever hath sate; loose him and bring him. And if any man asks you, Why do ye loose him? Ye shall say thus, The Lord hath need of him. And the disciples went and found as He said to them. And when they were loosing the colt its owners said to them, Why loose ye the colt? And they said, Because the Lord hath need of him. And they brought him to Jesus, and they threw their garments on the colt, and set Jesus thereon. And as He went, they strewed their garments in the way. And when He was drawing near, being now at the descent of the Mount of Olives, the whole multitude of the disciples began to rejoice and praise God with a loud voice for all the mighty works which they had seen, saying, Blessed is the King in the name of the Lord; peace in heaven and glory in the highest. And some of the Pharisees from the multitude said unto Him, Master, rebuke Thy disciples. And He answered and said, I say unto you, If these shall hold their peace, the stones will cry out. And when He drew near He beheld the city and wept over it," and so on, as we cited above. John, on the contrary, after giving an account nearly identical with this, as far as, "And Jesus went up to Jerusalem, and He found in the temple those who were selling oxen and sheep," gives a second account of an ascent of the Lord to Jerusalem, and then goes on to tell of the supper in Bethany six days before the Passover, at which Martha served and Lazarus was at table. "On the morrow, a great multitude that had come to the feast, having heard that Jesus was coming to Jerusalem, took branches of palm trees and went forth to meet Him; and they cried, Hosanna, blessed be the King of Israel in the name of the Lord. And Jesus, having found a young ass, sat thereon, as it is written, Fear not, daughter of Zion; behold thy King cometh, sitting on the foal of an ass." I have written out long sections from the Gospels, but I have thought it necessary to do so, in order to exhibit the discrepancy at this part of our Gospel. Three of the Gospels place these incidents, which we supposed to be the same as those narrated by John, in connection with one visit of the Lord to Jerusalem. While John, on the other hand, places them in connection with two visits which are widely separated from each other and between which were various journeys of the Lord to other places. I conceive it to be impossible for those who admit nothing more than the history in their interpretation to show that these discrepant statements are in harmony with each other. If any one considers that we have not given a sound exposition, let him write a reasoned rejoinder to this declaration of ours.

16. The Story of the Purging of the Temple Spiritualized. Taken Literally, It Presents Some Very Difficult and Unlikely Features.

We shall, however, expound according to the strength that is given to us the reasons which move us to recognize here a harmony; and in doing so we entreat Him who gives to everyone that asks and strives acutely to enquire, and we knock that by the keys of higher knowledge the hidden things of Scripture may be opened to us. And first, let us fix our attention on the words of John, beginning, "And Jesus went up to Jerusalem." Now Jerusalem, as the Lord Himself teaches in the Gospel according to Matthew, "is the city of the great King." It does not lie in a depression, or in a low situation, but is built on a high mountain, and there are mountains round about it, and the participation of it is to the same place, and thither the tribes of the Lord went up, a testimony for Israel. But that city also is called Jerusalem, to which none of those upon the earth ascends, nor goes in; but every soul that possesses by nature some elevation and some acuteness to perceive the things of the mind is a citizen of that city. And it is possible even for a dweller in Jerusalem to be in sin (for it is possible for even the acutest minds to sin), should they not turn round quickly after their sin, when they have lost their power of mind and are on the point not only of dwelling in one of those strange cities of Judæa, but even of being inscribed as its citizens. Jesus goes up to Jerusalem, after bringing help to those in Cana of Galilee, and then going down to Capernaum, that He may do in Jerusalem the things which are written. He found in the temple, certainly, which is said to be the house of the Father of the Savior, that is, in the church or in the preaching of the ecclesiastical and sound word, some who were making His Father's house a house of merchandise. And at all times Jesus finds some of this sort in the temple. For in that which is called the church, which is the house of the living God, the pillar and ground of the truth, when are there not some money-changers sitting who need the strokes of the scourge Jesus made of small cords, and dealers in small coin who require to have their money poured out and their tables overturned? When are there not those who are inclined to merchandise, but need to be held to the plough and the oxen, that having put their hand to it and not turning round to the things behind them, they may be fit for the kingdom of God? When are there not those who prefer the mammon of unrighteousness to the sheep which give them the material for their true adornment? And there are always many who look down on what is sincere and pure and unmixed with any bitterness or gall, and who, for the sake of miserable gain, betray the care of those tropically called doves. When, therefore, the Savior finds in the temple, the house of His Father, those who are selling oxen and sheep and doves, and the changers of money sitting, He drives them out, using the scourge of small cords which He has made, along with the sheep and oxen of their trade, and pours out their stock of coin, as not deserving to be kept together, so little is it worth. He also overturns the tables in the souls of such as love money, saying even to those who sell doves, "Take these things hence," that they may no longer traffic in the house of God. But I believe that in these words He indicated also a deeper truth, and that we may regard these occurrences as a symbol of the fact that the service of that temple was not any longer to be carried on by the priests in the way of material sacrifices, and that the time was coming when the law could no longer be observed, however much the Jews according to the flesh desired it. For when Jesus casts out the oxen and sheep, and orders the doves to be taken away, it was because oxen and sheep and doves were not much longer to be sacrificed there in accordance with Jewish practices. And possibly the coins which bore the stamp of material things and not of God were poured out by way of type; because the law which appears so venerable, with its letter that kills, was, now that Jesus had come and had used His scourge to the people, to be dissolved and poured out, the sacred office (episcopate) being transferred to those from the Gentiles who believed, and the kingdom of God being taken away from the Jews and given to a nation bringing forth the fruits of it. But it may also be the case that the natural temple is the soul skilled in reason, which, because of its inborn reason, is higher than the body; to which Jesus ascends from Capernaum, the lower-lying place of less dignity, and in which, before Jesus' discipline is applied to it, are found tendencies which are earthly and senseless and dangerous, and things which have the name but not the reality of beauty, and which are driven away by Jesus with His word plaited out of doctrines of demonstration and of rebuke, to the end that His Father's house may no longer be a house of merchandize but may receive, for its own salvation and that of others, that service of God which is performed in accordance with heavenly and spiritual laws. The ox is symbolic of earthly things, for he is a husbandman. The sheep, of senseless and brutal things, because it is more servile than most of the creatures without reason. Of empty and unstable thoughts, the dove. Of things that are thought good but are not, the small change. If anyone objects to this interpretation of the passage and says that it is only pure animals that are mentioned in it, we must say that the passage would otherwise have an unlikely air. The occurrence is necessarily related according to the possibilities of the story. It could not have been narrated that a herd of any other animals than pure ones had found access to the temple, nor could any have been sold there but those used for sacrifice. The Evangelist makes use of the known practice of the merchants at the times of the Jewish feasts; they did bring in such animals to the outer court; this practice, with a real occurrence He knew of, were His materials. Anyone, however, who cares to do so may enquire whether it is in agreement with the position held by Jesus in this world, since He was reputed to be the Son of a carpenter, to venture upon such an act as to drive out a crowd of merchants from the temple? They had come up to the feast to sell to a great number of the people, the sheep, several myriads in number, which they were to sacrifice according to their fathers' houses. To the richer Jews they had oxen to sell, and there were doves for those who had vowed such animals, and many no doubt bought these with a view to their good cheer at the festival. And did not Jesus do an unwarrantable thing when He poured out the money of the money-changers, which was their own, and overthrew their tables? And who that received a blow from the scourge of small cords at the hands of One held in but slight esteem, was driven out of the temple, would not have attacked Him and raised a cry and avenged himself with his own hand, especially when there was such a multitude present who might all feel themselves insulted by Jesus in the same way? To think, moreover, of the Son of God taking the small cords in His hands and plaiting a scourge out of them for this driving out from the temple, does it not bespeak audacity and temerity and even some measure of lawlessness? One refuge remains for the writer who wishes to defend these things and is minded to treat the occurrence as real history, namely, to appeal to the divine nature of Jesus, who was able to quench, when He desired to do so, the rising anger of His foes, by divine grace to get the better of myriads, and to scatter the devices of tumultuous men; for "the Lord scatters the counsels of the nations and brings to naught devices of the peoples, but the counsel of the Lord abides forever." Thus the occurrence in our passage, if it really took place, was not second in point of the power it exhibits to any even of the most marvelous works Christ wrought, and claimed no less by its divine character the faith of the beholders. One may show it to be a greater work than that done at Cana of Galilee in the turning of water into wine; for in that case it was only soulless matter that was changed, but here it was the soul and will of thousands of men. It is, however, to be observed that at the marriage the mother of Jesus is said to be there, and Jesus to have been invited and His disciples, but that no one but Jesus is said to have descended to Capernaum. His disciples, however, appear afterwards as present with Him; they remembered that "the zeal of thine house shall devour me." And perhaps Jesus was in each of the disciples as He ascended to Jerusalem, whence it is not said, Jesus went up to "Jerusalem and His disciples," but He went down to Capernaum, "He and His mother and His brothers and His disciples."

17. Matthew's Story of the Entry into Jerusalem. Difficulties Involved in It for Those Who Take It Literally.

We have now to take into consideration the statements of the other Gospels on the expulsion from the temple of those who made it a house of merchandise. Take in the first place what we find in Matthew. On the Lord's entering Jerusalem, he says, "All the city was stirred, saying, Who is this?" But before this he has the story of the ass and the foal which were taken by command of the Lord and found by the two disciples whom he sent from Bethphage into the village over against them. These two disciples loose the ass which was tied, and they have orders, if any one says anything to them, to answer that "the Lord has need of them; and immediately he will send them." By these incidents Matthew declares that the prophecy was fulfilled which says, "Behold, the King cometh, meek and sitting on an ass and a colt the foal of an ass," which we find in Zechariah. When, then, the disciples went and did as Jesus commanded them, they brought the ass and the colt, and placed on them, he says, their own garments, and the Lord sat upon them, clearly on the ass and the colt. Then "the most part of the multitude spread their garments in the way, and others cut down branches from the trees and strewed them in the way, and the multitudes that went before and that followed cried, Hosanna to the Son of David, blessed is He that cometh in the name of the Lord. Hosanna in the highest." Hence it was that when He entered Jerusalem, the whole city was moved, saying, Who is this? "And the multitudes said," those obviously who went before Him and who followed Him, to those who were asking who He was, "This is the prophet Jesus of Nazareth of Galilee. And Jesus entered into the temple and cast out all those that sold and bought in the temple, and overthrew the tables of the moneychangers and the seats of them that sold doves: and He says unto them, It is written, My house shall be called a house of prayer; but ye make it a den of robbers." Let us ask those who consider that Matthew had nothing but the history in his mind when he wrote his Gospel, what necessity there was for two of the disciples to be sent to the village over against Bethphage, to find an ass tied and its colt with it and to loose them and bring them? And how did it deserve to be recorded that He sat upon the ass and the foal and entered into the city? And how does Zechariah prophesy about Christ when he says, "Rejoice greatly, thou daughter of Zion, proclaim it, thou daughter of Jerusalem. Behold thy king cometh unto thee, just is He and bringing salvation, meek and sitting on an ass and a young foal"? If it be the case that this prophecy predicts simply the material incident described by the Evangelists, how can those who stand on the letter maintain that this is so with regard to the following part also of the prophecy, which runs: "And He shall destroy chariots from Ephraim and horse from Jerusalem, and the bow of the warrior shall be destroyed, and a multitude and peace from the Gentiles, and He shall rule over the waters as far as the sea, and the rivers to the ends of the earth," etc. It is to be noted, too, that Matthew does not give the words as they are found in the prophet, for instead of "Rejoice greatly, thou daughter of Zion, proclaim it, thou daughter of Jerusalem," he makes it, "Tell ye the daughter of Zion." He curtails the prophetic utterance by omitting the words, "Just is He and bringing salvation," then he gives, "meek and sitting," as in the original, but instead of "on an ass and a young colt," he gives, "on an ass and a colt the foal of an ass." The Jews, examining into the application of the prophecy to what is recorded about Jesus, press us in a way we cannot overlook with the enquiry how Jesus destroyed chariots out of Ephraim and horse from Jerusalem, and how He destroyed the bow of the enemy and did the other deeds mentioned in the passage. So much with regard to the prophecy. Our literal interpreters, however, if there is nothing worthy of the appearance of the Son of God in the ass and the foal, may perhaps point to the length of the road for an explanation. But, in the first place, fifteen stades are not a great distance and afford no reasonable explanation of the matter, and, in the second place, they would have to tell us how two beasts of burden were needed for so short a journey; "He sat," it is said, "on them." And then the words: "If any man say aught unto you, say ye that the Lord hath need of them, and straightway he will send them." It does not appear to me to be worthy of the greatness of the Son's divinity to say that such a nature as His confessed that it had need of an ass to be loosed from its bonds and of a foal to come with it; for everything the Son of God has need of should be great and worthy of His goodness. And then the very great multitude strewing their garments in the way, while Jesus allows them to do so and does not rebuke them, as is clear from the words used in another passage, "If these should hold their peace, the stones will cry out." I do not know if it does not indicate a certain degree of stupidity on the part of the writer to take delight in such things, if nothing more is meant by them than what lies on the surface. And the branches being cut down from the trees and strewn on the road where the asses go by, surely they are rather a hindrance to Him who is the center of the throng than a well-devised reception of Him. The difficulties which met us on the part of those who were cast out of the temple by Jesus meet us here in a still greater degree. In the Gospel of John He casts out those who bought, but Matthew says that He cast out those who sold and those who bought in the temple. And the buyers would naturally be more numerous than the sellers. We have to consider if the casting out of buyers and sellers in the temple was not out of keeping with the reputation of one who was thought to be the Son of a carpenter, unless, as we said before, it was by a divine power that He subjected them. The words addressed to them, too, are harsher in the other Evangelists than in John. For John says that Jesus said to them, "Make not My Father's house a house of merchandise," while in the others they are rebuked for making the house of prayer a den of robbers. Now the house of His Father did not admit of being turned into a den of robbers, though by the acts of sinful men it was brought to be a house of merchandise. It was not only the house of prayer, but in fact the house of God, and by force of human neglect it harbored robbers, and was turned not only into their house but their den—a thing which no skill, either of architecture or of reason, could make it.

18. The Ass and the Colt are the Old and the New Testament. Spiritual Meaning of the Various Features of the Story. Differences between John's Narrative and that of the Other Evangelists.

Now to see into the real truth of these matters is the part of that true intelligence which is given to those who can say, "But we have the mind of Christ that we may see those things which are freely given to us of God;" and doubtless it is beyond our powers. For neither is the ruling principle in our soul free from agitation, nor are our eyes such as those of the fair bride of Christ should be, of which the bridegroom says, "Thy eyes are doves," signifying, perhaps, in a riddle, the observant power which dwells in the spiritual, because the Holy Spirit came like a dove to our Lord and to the lord in every one. Such as we are, however, we will not delay, but will feel about the words of life which have been spoken to us and strive to lay hold of that power in them which flows to him who touches them in faith. Now Jesus is the word of God which goes into the soul that is called Jerusalem, riding on the ass freed by the disciples from its bonds. That is to say, on the simple language of the Old Testament, interpreted by the two disciples who loose it: in the first place him who applies what is written to the service of the soul and shows the allegorical sense of it with reference to her, and in the second place him who brings to light by the things which lie in shadow the good and true things of the future. But He also rides on the young colt, the New Testament; for in both alike we find the word of truth which purifies us and drives away all those thoughts in us which incline to selling and buying. But He does not come alone to Jerusalem, the soul, nor only with a few companions; for many things have to enter into us before the word of God which makes us perfect, and as many things have to come after Him, all, however, hymning and glorifying Him and placing under Him their ornaments and vestures, so that the beasts He rides on may not touch the ground, when He who descended out of heaven is seated on them. But that His bearers, the old and the new words of Scripture, may be raised yet higher above the ground, branches have to be cut down from the trees that they may tread on reasonable expositions. But the multitudes which go before and follow Him may also signify the angelic ministrations, some of which prepare the way for Him in our souls, and help in their adorning, while some come after His presence in us, of which we have often spoken, so that we need not now adduce testimonies about it. And perhaps it is not without reason that I have likened to an ass the surrounding voices which conduct the Word Himself to the soul; for it is a beast of burden, and many are the burdens, heavy the loads, which are brought into view from the text, especially of the Old Testament, as he can clearly see who observes what is done in this connection on the part of the Jews. But the foal is not a beast of burden in the same way as the ass. For though every lead of the latter be heavy to those who have not in themselves the up bearing and most lightening power of the Spirit, yet the new word is less heavy than the old. I know some who interpret the tied-up ass as being believers from the circumcision, who are freed from many bonds by those who are truly and spiritually instructed in the word; and the foal they take to be those from the Gentiles, who before they receive the word of Jesus are free from any control and subject to no yoke in their unbridled and pleasure-loving existence. The writers I am speaking of do not say who those are that go before and who those follow after; but there would be no absurdity in saying that those who went before were like Moses and the prophets, and those who followed after the holy Apostles. To what Jerusalem all these go in it is now our business to enquire, and what is the house which has many sellers and buyers to be driven out by the Son of God. And perhaps the Jerusalem above to which the Lord is to ascend driving like a charioteer those of the circumcision and the believers of the Gentiles, while prophets and Apostles go before Him and follow after Him (or is it the angels who minister to Him, for they too may be meant by those who go before and those who follow), perhaps it is that city which before He ascended to it contained the so-called "spiritual hosts of wickedness in heavenly places," or the Canaanites and Hittites and Amorites and the other enemies of the people of God, and in a word, the foreigners. For in that region, too, it was possible for the prophecy to be fulfilled which says, "Your country is desolate, your cities are burned with fire, your land, strangers devour it in your presence." For these are they who defile and turn into a den of robbers, that is, of themselves the heavenly house of the Father, the holy Jerusalem, the house of prayer; having spurious money, and giving pence and small change, cheap worthless coinage, to all who come to them. These are they who, contending with the souls, take from them what is most precious, robbing them of their better part to return to them what is worth nothing. But the disciples go and find the ass tied and loose it, for it cannot have Jesus on account of the covering that is laid upon it by the law. And the colt is found with it, both having been lost till Jesus came; I mean, namely, those of the circumcision and those of the Gentiles who afterwards believed. But how these are sent back again after Jesus has ascended to Jerusalem seated upon them, it is somewhat dangerous to say; for there is something mystical about it, in connection with the change of saints into angels. After that change they will be sent back, in the age succeeding this one, like the ministering spirits, who are sent to do service for the sake of them who will thereby inherit salvation. But if the ass and the foal are the old and the new Scriptures, on which the Word of God rides, it is easy to see how, after the Word has appeared in them, they are sent back and do not wait after the Word has entered Jerusalem among those who have cast out all the thoughts of selling and buying. I consider, too, that it is not without significance that the place where the ass was found tied, and the foal, was a village, and a village without a name. For in comparison with the great world in heaven, the whole earth is a village where the ass is found tied and the colt, and it is simply called "the village" without any other designation being added to it. From Bethphage Matthew says the disciples are sent out who are to fetch the ass and the colt; and Bethphage is a priestly place, the name of which means "House of Jawbones." So much we have said, as our power allowed, on the text of Matthew, reserving for a further opportunity, when we may be permitted to take up the Gospel of Matthew by itself, a more complete and accurate discussion of his statements. Mark and Luke say that the two disciples, acting on their Master's instructions, found a foal tied, on which no one had ever sat, and that they loosed it and brought it to the Lord. Mark adds that they found the foal tied at the door, outside on the road. But who is outside? Those of the Gentiles who were strangers from the covenants, and aliens to the promise of God; they are on the road, not resting under a roof or a house, bound by their own sins, and to be loosed by the twofold knowledge spoken of above, of the friends of Jesus. And the bonds with which the foal was tied, and the sins committed against the wholesome law and reproved by it,—for it is the gate of life,—in respect of it, I say, they were not inside but outside the door, for perhaps inside the door there cannot be any such bond of wickedness. But there were some persons standing beside the tied-up foal, as Mark says; those, I suppose, who had tied it; as Luke records, it was the masters of the foal who said to the disciples, Why loose ye the foal? For those lords who subjected and bound the sinner are illegal masters and cannot look the true master in the face when he frees the foal from its bonds. Thus when the disciples say, "The Lord hath need of him," these wicked masters have nothing to say in reply. The disciples then bring the foal to Jesus naked, and put their own dress on it, so that the Lord may sit on the disciples' garments which are on it, at His ease. What is said further will not, in the light of Matthew's statements, present any difficulty; how "They come to Jerusalem, and entering into the temple He began to cast out them that sold and bought in the temple," or how "When He drew nigh and beheld the city He wept over it; and entering into the temple He began to cast out them that sold." For in some of those who have the temple in themselves He casts out all that sell and buy in the temple; but in others who do not quite obey the word of God, He only makes a beginning of casting out the sellers and buyers. There is a third class also besides these, in which He began to cast out the sellers only, and not also the buyers. With John, on the contrary, they are all cast out by the scourge woven of small cords, along with the sheep and the oxen. It should be carefully considered whether it is possible that the changes of the things described and the discrepancies found in them can be satisfactorily solved by the anagogic method. Each of the Evangelists ascribes to the Word different modes of action, which produce in souls of different tempers not the same effects but yet similar ones. The discrepancy we noticed in respect of Jesus' journeys to Jerusalem, which the Gospel now in hand reports quite differently from the other three, as we have expounded their words, cannot be made good in any other way. John gives statements which are similar to those of the other three but not the same; instead of branches cut from the trees or stubble brought from the fields and strewed on the road he says they took branches of palm trees. He says that much people had come to the feast, and that these went out to meet Him, crying, "Blessed is He that cometh in the name of the Lord," and "Blessed is the King of Israel." He also says that it was Jesus Himself who found the young ass on which Christ sat, and the phrase, young ass, doubtless conveys some additional meaning, as the small animal afforded a benefit not of men, nor through men, but through Jesus Christ. John moreover does not, any more than the others, reproduce the prophetic words exactly; instead of them he gives us "Fear not, O daughter of Zion; behold thy King cometh sitting" (instead of "mounted") "on the foal of an ass" (for "on an ass and a young foal"). The words "Fear not, daughter of Zion," are not in the prophet at all. But as the prophetic utterance has been applied by all in this way, let us see if there was not a necessity that the daughter of Zion should rejoice greatly and that the greater than she, the daughter of Jerusalem, should not only rejoice greatly but should also proclaim it when her king was coming to her, just and bringing salvation, and meek, having mounted an ass and a young colt. Whoever, then, receives Him will no longer be afraid of those who are armed with the specious discourses of the heterodox, those chariots of Ephraim said to be destroyed by the Lord, nor the horse, the vain thing for safety, that is the mad desire which has accustomed itself to the things of sense and which is injurious to many of those who desire to dwell in Jerusalem and to attend to the sound word. It is also fitting to rejoice at the destruction by Him who rides on the ass and the young foal of every hostile dart, since the fiery darts of the enemy are no longer to prevail over him who has received Jesus to his own temple. And there will also be a multitude from the Gentiles with peace at the Savior's coming to Jerusalem, when He rules over the waters that He may bruise the head of the dragon on the water, and we shall tread upon the waves of the sea and to the mouths of all the rivers on the earth. Mark, however, writing about the foal, reports the Lord to have said, "On which never man sat;" and he seems to me to hint at the circumstance that those who afterwards believed had never submitted to the Word before Jesus' coming to them. For of men, perhaps, no one had ever sate on the foal, but of hearts or of powers alien to the Word some had sate on it, since in the prophet Isaiah the wealth of opposing powers is said to be borne on asses and camels. "In the distress and the affliction," he writes, "the lion and the lion's whelp, whence also the offspring of flying asps, who carried their riches on asses and camels." The question occurs again, for those who have no mind but for the bare words, if according to their view the words, "on which never man sat," are not quite meaningless. For who but a man ever sits on a foal? So much of our views.

19. Various Views of Heracleon on Purging of the Temple.

Let us see what Heracleon makes of this. He says that the ascent to Jerusalem signifies the Lord's going up from material things to the spiritual place, which is a likeness of Jerusalem. And he considers that the words are, "He found in the temple," and not "in the sanctuary," because the Lord is not to be understood as instrumental in that call only, which takes place where the spirit is not. He considers the temple to be the Holy of Holies, into which none but the High-Priest enters, and there I believe he says that the spiritual go; while the court of the temple, where the Levites also enter, is a symbol of these psychical ones who are saved, but outside the Pleroma. Then those who are found in the temple selling oxen and sheep and doves, and the money-changers sitting, he took to represent those who attribute nothing to grace, but regard the entrance of strangers to the temple as a matter of merchandise and gain, and who minister the sacrifices for the worship of God, with a view to their own gain and love of money. And the scourge which Jesus made of small cords and did not receive from another, he expounds in a way of his own, saying that the scourge is an image of the power and energy of the Holy Spirit, driving out by His breath those who are bad. And he declares that the scourge and the linen and the napkin and other things of such a kind are symbolic of the power and energy of the Holy Spirit. Then he assumes what is not written, as that the scourge was tied to a piece of wood, and this wood he takes to be a type of the cross; on this wood the gamblers, merchants, and all evil was nailed up and done away. In searching into the act of Jesus, and discussing the composition of the scourge out of two substances, he romances in an extraordinary way; He did not make it, he says, of dead leather. He wished to make the Church no longer a den of robbers, but the house of His Father. We must here say what is most necessary on the divinity, as referred to in Heracleon's text. If Jesus calls the temple at Jerusalem the house of His Father, and that temple was made in honor of Him who made heaven and earth, why are we not at once told that He is the Son of no one else than the Maker of heaven and earth, that He is the Son of God? To this house of the Father of Jesus, as being the house of prayer, the Apostles of Christ also, as we find in their "Acts," are told by the angel to go and to stand there and preach all the words of this life. But they came to the house of prayer, through the Beautiful Gate, to pray there, a thing they would not have done had they not known Him to be the same with the God worshipped by those who had dedicated that temple. Hence, too, they say, those who obeyed God rather than men, Peter and the Apostles, "The God of our Fathers raised up Jesus, whom ye slew, hanging Him on a tree;" for they know that by no other God was Jesus raised from the dead but the God of the fathers, whom Jesus also extols as the God of Abraham and Isaac and Jacob, who are not dead but living. How, too, could the disciples, if the house was not that of the same God with the God of Christ, have remembered the saying in the sixty-ninth Psalm, "The zeal of thy house shall devour Me;" for thus it is found in the prophet, and not "hath devoured Me." Now Christ is zealous principally for that house of God which is in each of us; He does not wish that it should be a house of merchandise, nor that the house of prayer should be a den of robbers; for He is the Son of a jealous God. We ought to give a liberal interpretation to such utterances of Scripture; they speak of human things, but in the way of metaphor, to show that God desires that nothing foreign should be mixed up with His will in the soul of all men, indeed, but principally of those who are minded to accept the message of our most divine faith. But we must remember that the sixty-ninth Psalm, which contains the words, "The zeal of thy house shall devour me," and a little further on, "They gave Me gall for My drink and for My thirst they gave Me vinegar," both texts being recorded in the Gospels, that that Psalm is spoken in the person of the Christ, and nowhere shows any change of person. It shows a great want of observation on Heracleon's part that he considers the words, "The zeal of thy house shall devour Me," to be spoken in the person of those powers which were cast out and destroyed by the Savior; he fails to see the connection of the prophecy in the Psalm. For if these words are understood as spoken by the expelled and destroyed powers, it follows that he must take the words, "They gave Me vinegar to drink," which are a part of the same psalm, to be also spoken by those powers. What misled him was probably that he could not understand how the "shall devour Me" could be spoken by Christ, since He did not appreciate the way in which anthropopathic statements are applied to God and to Christ.

20. The Temple Which Christ Says He Will Raise Up is the Church. How the Dry Bones Will Be Made to Live Again.

"The Jews then answered and said unto Him, What sign shows Thou unto us, seeing that Thou does these things? Jesus answered and said unto them, destroy this temple, and in three days I will raise it up." Those of the body, and those who incline to material things, seem to me to be meant by the Jews, who, after Jesus has driven out those who make God's house a house of merchandise, are angry at Him for treating these matters in such a way, and demand a sign, a sign which will show that the Word, whom they do not receive, has a right to do such things. The Savior joins on to His statement about the temple a statement which is really one with the former, about His own body, and to the question, What sign does Thou, seeing that Thou does such things? Answers, "Destroy this temple, and in three days I will raise it up." He could have exhibited a thousand other signs, but to the question, "Seeing that Thou does such things," He could not answer anything else; He fittingly gave the answer about the sign connected with the temple, and not about signs unconnected with the temple. Now, both of these two things, the temple and the body of Jesus, appear to me, in one interpretation at least, to be types of the Church, and to signify that it is built of living stones, a spiritual house for a holy priesthood, built on the foundation of the Apostles and prophets, Christ Jesus being the head corner-stone; and it is, therefore, called a temple. Now, from the text, "Ye are the body of Christ, and members each in his part," we see that even though the harmonious fitting of the stones of the temple appear to be dissolved and scattered, as it is written in the twenty-second Psalm that all the bones of Christ are, by the plots made against it in persecutions and afflictions, on the part of those who war against the unity of the temple in persecutions, yet the temple will be raised again, and the body will rise again on the third day after the day of evil which threatens it, and the day of consummation which follows. For the third day will rise on the new heaven and the new earth, when these bones, the whole house of Israel, will rise in the great Lord's day, death having been overcome. And thus the resurrection of the Savior from the passion of the cross contains the mystery of the resurrection of the whole body of Christ. But as that material body of Jesus was sacrificed for Christ, and was buried, and was afterwards raised, so the whole body of Christ's saints is crucified along with Him, and now lives no longer; for each of them, like Paul, glories in nothing but the cross of our Lord Jesus Christ, through which He is crucified to the world, and the world to Him. Not only, therefore, is it crucified with Christ, and crucified to the world; it is also buried with Christ, for we were buried with Christ, Paul says. And then he says, as if enjoying some earnest of the resurrection, "We rose with Him," because He walks in a certain newness of life, though not yet risen in that blessed and perfect resurrection which is hoped for. Either, then, he is now crucified, and afterwards is buried, or he is now buried and taken down from the cross, and, being now buried, is to rise at some future time. But to most of us the mystery of the resurrection is a great one, and difficult of contemplation; it is spoken of in many other passages of Scripture, and is specially announced in the following passage of Ezekiel: "And the hand of the Lord was upon me, and He led me out in the Spirit of the Lord, and set me in the midst of the plain, and it was full of human bones. And He led me round about them in a circle, and behold there were very many on the face of the plain, and behold they were very dry. And He said to me,

Son of man, shall these bones live? And I said, Lord, Lord, Thou knows. And He said to me, Prophesy to these bones, and thou shalt say to them, Hear the word of the Lord, ye dry bones;" and a little further on, "And the Lord spoke to me, saying, Son of man, these bones are the house of Israel. And they say, Our bones are become dry, our hope is lost, we have breathed our last." For what bones are these which are addressed, "Hear ye the word of the Lord," as if they heard the word of the Lord? They belong to the house of Israel, or to the body of Christ, of which the Lord says, "All My bones are scattered," although the bones of His body were not scattered, and not even one of them was broken. But when the resurrection itself takes place of the true and more perfect body of Christ, then those who are now the members of Christ, for they will then be dry bones, will be brought together, bone to bone, and fitting to fitting (for none of those who are destitute of fitting (ἁρμονία) will come to the perfect man), to the measure of the stature of the fullness of the body of Christ. And then the many members will be the one body, all of them, though many, becoming members of one body. But it belongs to God alone to make the distinction of foot and hand and eye and hearing and smelling, which in one sense fill up the head, but in another the feet and the rest of the members, and the weaker and humbler ones, the more and the less honorable. God will temper the body together, and then, rather than now, He will give to that which lacks the more abundant honor, that there may be, by no means, any schism in the body, but that the members may have the same care for one another, and, if any member be well off, all the members may share in its good things, or if any member be glorified, all the members may rejoice with it.

21. That the Son Was Raised Up by the Father. The Charge Brought Against Jesus at His Trial Was Based on the Incident Now Before Us.

What I have said is not alien to the passage now engaging us, dealing as it does with the temple and those cast out from it, of which the Savior says, "The zeal of thy house shall devour Me;" and with the Jews who asked that a sign should be showed them, and the Savior's answer to them, in which He combines the discourse on the temple with that on His own body, and says, "Destroy this temple and in three days I will raise it up." For from this temple, which is the body of Christ, everything that is irrational and savors of merchandise must be driven away, that it may no longer be a house of merchandise. And this temple must be destroyed by those who plot against the Word of God, and after its destruction be raised again on that third day which we discussed above; when the disciples also will remember what He, the Word, said before the temple of God was destroyed, and will believe, not only their knowledge but their faith also being then made perfect, and that by the word which Jesus spoke. And everyone who is of this nature, Jesus purifying him, puts away things that are irrational and things that savor of selling, to be destroyed on account of the zeal of the Logos that is in Him. But they are destroyed to be raised again by Jesus, not on the third day, if we attend to the exact words before us, but "in three days." For the rising again of the temple takes place on the first day after it has been destroyed and on the second day, and its resurrection is accomplished in all the three days. Hence a resurrection both has been and is to be, if indeed we were buried with Christ, and rose with Him. And since the word, "We rose with Him," does not cover the whole of the resurrection, "in Christ shall all be made alive, but everyone in his own order, Christ the first fruits, then they that are Christ's at His coming, and then the end." It belongs to the resurrection that one should be on the first day in the paradise of God, and it belongs to the resurrection when Jesus appears and says, "Touch Me not; for I am not yet ascended to My Father," but the perfection of the resurrection was when He came to the Father. Now there are some who fall into confusion on this head of the Father and the Son, and we must devote a few words to them. They quote the text, "Yea, and we are found false witnesses for God, because we testified against God that He raised up Christ, whom He raised not up," and other similar texts which show the raiser-up to be another person than He who was raised up; and the text, "Destroy this temple and in three days I will raise it up," as if it resulted from these that the Son did not differ in number from the Father, but that both were one, not only in point of substance but in point of subject, and that the Father and the Son were said to be different in some of their aspects but not in their hypostases. Against such views we must in the first place adduce the leading texts which prove the Son to be another than the Father, and that the Son must of necessity be the son of a Father, and the Father, the father of a Son. Then we may very properly refer to Christ's declaration that He cannot do anything but what He sees the Father doing and saying, because whatever the Father does that the Son also does in like manner, and that He had raised the dead, i.e., the body, the Father granting Him this, who must be said to have been the principal agent in raising up Christ from the dead. But Heracleon says, "In three days," instead of "On the third day," not having examined the point (and yet having noted the words "in three"), that the resurrection is brought about in three days. But he also calls the third the spiritual day, in which they consider the resurrection of the Church to be indicated. It follows from this that the first day is to be called the "earthly" day, and the second the psychical, the resurrection of the Church not having taken place on them. Now the statements of the false witnesses, recorded in the Gospel according to Matthew and Mark towards the end of the Gospel, and the accusation they brought against our Lord Jesus Christ, appear to have reference to this utterance of His, "Destroy this temple, and I will build it up in three days." For He was speaking of the temple of His body, but they supposed His words to refer to the temple of stone, and so they said when accusing Him, "This man said, I am able to destroy the temple of God and to build it up in three days," or, as Mark has it, "We heard Him say, that I will destroy this temple made with hands, and in three days I will build up another temple not made with hands." Here the high-priest stood up and said to Him, "Answers Thou nothing? What do these witness against Thee? But Jesus held His peace." Or, as Mark says, "And the high-priest stood up in the midst, and asked Jesus saying, Answers Thou nothing? What do these witness against Thee? But He held His peace and answered nothing." These words must, I think, necessarily have reference to the text now before us.

22. The Temple of Solomon Did Not Take Forty-Six Years to Build. With Regard to that of Ezra We

Cannot Tell How Long It Took. Significance of the Number Forty-Six.

The Jews therefore said, "Forty and six years was this temple in building, and wilt thou raise it up in three days?" How the Jews said that the temple had been forty-six years building, we cannot tell, if we adhere to the history. For it is written in the third Book of Kings, that they prepared the stones and the wood three years, and in the fourth year, in the second month, when Solomon was king over Israel, the king commanded, and they brought great precious stones for the foundation of the house, and unhewn stones. And the sons of Solomon and the sons of Hiram hewed the stones and laid them in the fourth year, and they founded the house of the Lord in the month Nisan and the second month: in the tenth year in the month Baal, which was the eighth month, the house was finished according to the whole count and the whole plan of it. Thus comparing the time of its completion with the period of building, the building of it occupies less than eleven years. How, then, do the Jews come to say that the temple was forty-six years in building? One might, indeed, do violence to the words and make out the period of forty-six years at all costs, by counting from the time when David, after planning about the building of the temple, said to Nathan the prophet, "Behold I dwell in a house of cedar, and the ark of God dwells in the midst of the tent," for though it is true that he was prevented, as being a man of blood, from carrying out the building, he seems to have busied himself in collecting materials for it. In the first Book of Chronicles, certainly, David the king says to all the congregation, "Solomon my son, whom the Lord hath chosen, is young and tender, and the work is great, because he is not to build for man but for the Lord

God. According to my whole power I have prepared for the house of my God, gold, silver, brass, and iron, wood, stones of Soom, and stones for filling up, and precious stones of many kinds, and all sorts of precious wood, and a large quantity of Parian marble. And besides this, for the pleasure I have taken in the house of my God, the gold and the silver I possess, lo, I have given it for the house of my Lord, to the full; from such supplies I prepared for the house of the saints, three thousand talents of gold from Suphir, and seven thousand talents of stamped silver. That the houses of God may be overlaid with them by the hands of artificers." For David reigned seven years in Hebron and thirty-three years in Jerusalem; so that if it could be shown that the beginning of the preparations for the temple and of David's collecting the necessary material, was in the fifth year of his reign, then, with some forcing, the statement about forty-six years might stand. But someone else will say that the temple spoken of was not that built by Solomon, for that it was destroyed at the period of the captivity, but the temple built at the time of Ezra, with regard to which the forty-six years can be shown to be quite accurate. But in this Maccabean period things were very unsettled with regard to the people and the temple, and I do not know if the temple was really built in that number of years. Heracleon pays no attention to the history, but says that in that he was forty-six years preparing the temple, Solomon was an image of the Savior. The number six he connects with matter, that is, the image, and the number forty, which he says is the tetrad, not admitting of combination, he connects with the inspiration and the seed in the inspiration. Consider if the forty cannot be taken as due to the four elements of the world arranged in the building of the temple at the points at issue, and the six to the fact that man was created on the sixth day.

23. The Temple Spoken of by Christ is the Church. Application to the Church of the Statements Regarding the Building of Solomon's Temple, and the Numbers Stated in that Narrative.

"But He spoke of the temple of His body. When, therefore, He was raised from the dead, His disciples remembered that He said this, and they believed the Scripture and the word which Jesus had said." This refers to the statement that the body of the Son is His temple. It may be asked whether this is to be taken in its plain sense, or whether we should try to connect each statement that is recorded about the temple, with the view we take about the body of Jesus, whether the body which He received from the Virgin, or that body of Christ which the Church is said to be, as we are said by the Apostle to be all members of His body. One may, on the one hand, suppose it to be hopeless to get everything that is said about the temple properly connected with the body, in whatever sense the body be taken, and one may have recourse to a simpler explanation, and say that the body (in either of these senses) is called the temple, because as the temple had the glory of God dwelling in it, so He who was the image and glory of God, the first-born of every creature, could rightly be called, in respect of His body or the Church, the temple containing the image. We, for our part, see it to be a hard task to expound every particular of what is said about the temple in the third Book of Kings, and far beyond our powers of language, and we defer it in the meantime, as a thing beyond the scale of the present work. We also have a strong conviction that in such matters, which transcend human nature, it must be the work of divine wisdom to make plain the meaning of inspired Scripture, of that wisdom which is hidden in a mystery, which none of the rulers of this world knew. We are well aware, too, that we need the assistance of that excellent Spirit of wisdom, in order to understand such matters, as they should be understood by ministers of sacred things; and in this connection we will attempt to describe, as shortly as we may, our view of what belongs to this subject. The body is the Church, and we learn from Peter that it is a house of God, built of living stones, a spiritual house for a holy priesthood. Thus the son of David, who builds this house, is a type of Christ. He builds it when his wars are at an end, and a period of profound peace has arrived; he builds the temple for the glory of God in the Jerusalem on earth, so that worship may no longer be celebrated in a moveable erection like the tabernacle. Let us seek to find in the Church the truth of each statement made about the temple. If all Christ's enemies are made the footstool of His feet, and Death, the last enemy, is destroyed, then there will be the most perfect peace. Christ will be Solomon, which means "Peaceful," and the prophecy will find its fulfilment in Him, which says, "With those who hated peace I was peaceful." And then each of the living stones will be, according to the work of his life here, a stone of that temple, one, at the foundation, an apostle or a prophet, bearing those placed upon him, and another, after those in the foundation, and supported by the Apostles, will himself, with the Apostles, help to bear those in more need. One will be a stone of the inmost parts, where the ark is, and the cherubim, and the mercy-seat; another will be on the outer wall, and another even outside the outer wall of the Levites and priests, a stone of the altar of whole burnt offerings. And the management and service of these things will be entrusted to holy powers, angels of God, being, respectively, lordships, thrones, dominions, or powers; and there will be others subject to these, typified by three thousand six hundred chief officers, who were appointed over the works of Solomon, and the seventy thousand of those who bore burdens, and the eighty thousand stone-cutters in the mountain, who wrought in the work, and prepared the stones and the wood. It is to be remarked that those reported as bearing burdens are related to the Hebdomad. The quarrymen and stone-cutters, who make the stones fitted for the temple, have some kinship to the ogdoad. And the officers, who are six hundred in number, are connected with the perfect number six multiplied into itself. The preparation of the stones, as they are taken out and fitted for the building, extends over three years; this appears to me to point solely to the time of the eternal interval which is akin to the triad. This will come to pass when peace is consummated after the number of years of the transaction of the matters connected with the exodus from Egypt, namely, three hundred and forty, and of what took place in Egypt four hundred and thirty years after the covenant made by God with Abraham. Thus, from Abraham to the beginning of the building of the temple, there are two sabbatic numbers, the 700 and the 70; and at that time, too, our King Christ will command the seventy thousand burden-bearers not to take any chance stones for the foundation of the temple, but great stones, precious, unhewn, that they may be hewn, not by any chance workmen, but by the sons of Solomon; for so we find it written in the third Book of Kings. Then, too, on account of the profound peace, Hiram, king of Tyre, cooperates in the building of the temple, and gives his own sons to the sons of Solomon, to hew, in company with them, the great and precious stones for the holy place, which, in the fourth year, are placed in the foundation of the house of the Lord. But in an ogdoad of years the house is finished in the eighth month of the eighth year after its foundation.

24. The Account of the Building of Solomon's Temple Contains Serious Difficulties and is to Be Interpreted Spiritually.

For the sake of those, however, who consider that nothing further than the narrative itself is meant to be indicated in these words, it may not be unfitting to introduce at this point some considerations which they can scarcely withstand, to show that the words ought to be regarded as those of the Spirit, and that the mind of the Spirit should be sought for in them. Did the sons of the kings really spend their time in hewing the great and precious stones, and practice a craft so little in keeping with royal birth? And the number of the burden-bearers and of the stone-cutters and of the officers, the duration, too, of the period of preparing the stones and marking them, is all this recorded as it really was? The holy house, too, was got ready in peace and was to be built for God without hammer or axe or any iron tool, that there might be no disturbance in the house of God. And again I would ask those who are in bondage to the letter how it is possible that there should be eighty thousand stone-cutters and that the house of God should be built out of hard white stones without the noise of hammer or axe or any iron tool being heard in His house while the building was going on? Is it not living stones that are hewn without any noise or tumult somewhere outside the temple, so that they are brought ready prepared to the place which awaits them in the building? And there is some sort of an ascent about the temple of God, not with angles, but with bends of straight lines. For it is written, "And there was a winding staircase to the middle, and from the middle to the third floor;" for the staircase in the house of God had to be spiral, thus imitating in its ascent the circle, which is the most perfect figure. But that this house might be secure five ties are built in it, as fair as possible, a cubit high, that on looking up one might see it to be suggested how we rise from sensible things to the so-called divine perceptions, and so be brought to perceive those things which are seen only by the mind. But the place of the happier stones appears to be that called Dabir, where the ark of the covenant of the Lord was, and, as I may say, the handwriting of God, the tables written with His own finger. And the whole house is overlaid with gold; "the whole house," we read, "he overlaid with gold until all the house was finished." But there were two cherubim in Dabir, a word which the translators of the Hebrew Bible into Greek failed to render satisfactorily. Some, failing to do justice to the language, render it the temple; but it is more sacred than the temple. Now everything about the house was made golden, for a sign that the mind which is quite made perfect estimates accurately the things perceived by the intellect. But it is not given to all to approach and know them; and hence the veil of the court is erected, since to most of the priests and Levites the things in the inmost part of the temple are not revealed.

25. Further Spiritualizing of Solomon's Temple-Building.

It is worthwhile to enquire how, on the one hand, Solomon the king is said to have built the temple, and on the other the master-builder whom Solomon sent and fetched, "Hiram of Tyre, the son of a woman who was a widow; and he was of the tribe of Naphtali, and his father was a man of Tyre, a worker in brass, and filled with wisdom and understanding, to work all works in brass; and he was brought in to King Solomon and wrought all his works." Here I ask whether Solomon can be taken for the first-born of all creation, and Hiram for the man whom he assumed, from the constraint of men—for the word Tyrians means "constrainers"—the man who derived his birth from nature, and being filled with all manner of art and wisdom and understanding, was brought in to cooperate with the first-born of all creation, and to build the temple. In this temple there are also windows, placed obliquely and out of sight, so that the illumination of the divine light may enter for salvation, and—why should I go into particulars?—that the body of Christ, the Church, may be found having the plan of the spiritual house and temple of God. As I said before, we require that wisdom which is hidden in a mystery, and which he alone can apprehend who is able to say, "But we have the mind of Christ,"—we require that wisdom to interpret spiritually each detail of what is said in accordance with the will of Him who caused it to be written. To enter into these details is not in accordance with our present subject. What has been said may suffice to let us understand how "He spoke about the temple of His body."

26. The Promises Addressed to Jerusalem in the Prophets Refer to the Church, and are Still to Be Fulfilled.

After all this it is proper to ask whether what is narrated as having taken place about the temple has ever taken place or ever will take place about the spiritual house. The argument may seem to pinch in whichever way we take it. If we say that it is possible that something like what is told about the temple may take place with regard to the spiritual house, or has already taken place in it, then those who hear us will, with difficulty, be brought to admit that a change can take place in such good things as these, firstly, because they do not wish it, and secondly, because of the incongruity of thinking that such things admit of change. If, on the other hand, We seek to maintain the unchangeableness of the good things once given to the saints, then we cannot apply to them what we find in the history, and we shall seem to be doing what those of the heresies do, who fail to maintain the unity of the narrative of Scripture from beginning to end. If we are not to take the view proper to old wives or Jews, of the promises recorded in the prophets, and especially in Isaiah, if, that is to say, we are to look for their fulfilment in connection with the Jerusalem on earth, then, as certain remarkable things connected with the building of the temple and the restoration of the people from the captivity are spoken of as happening after the captivity and the destruction of the temple, we must say that we are now the temple and the people which was carried captive, but is to come up again to Judæa and Jerusalem, and to be built with the precious stones of Jerusalem. But I cannot tell if it be possible that, at the revolution of long periods of time, things of the same nature should take place again, but in a worse way. The prophecies of Isaiah which we mentioned are the following: "Behold I prepare for thy stone carbuncle and for thy foundation sapphire; and I will make thy battlements jasper, and thy gates stones of crystal, and thy outer wall choice stones; and all thy sons shall be taught of the Lord, and in great peace shall thy children be, and in righteousness shalt thou be built." And a little further on, to the same Jerusalem: "And the glory of Lebanon shall come to thee with cypress, and pine, and cedar, along with those who will glorify My holy place. And the sons of them that humbled thee and insulted thee shall come to thee in fear; and thou shalt be called the city of the Lord, Sion of holy Israel, because thou wert desolate and hated, and there was none to help thee. And I will make thee an eternal delight, a joy of generations of generations. And thou shalt suck the milk of the Gentiles and shall eat the riches of kings, and thou shalt know that I am the Lord that saves thee and the God of Israel that chooses thee. And instead of brass I will bring thee gold, and instead of iron I will bring thee silver, and for wood I will bring thee brass, and for stones iron. And I will establish thy rulers in peace and thy overseers in righteousness. And wickedness shall no more be heard in thy land, nor affliction and distress in thy borders, but thy walls shall be called salvation and thy gates sculpture. And the sun shall no longer be to thee for light by day, nor shall the rising of the moon give light to thee by night, but Christ shall be to thee an everlasting light and thy God thy glory. For thy sun shall no more go down, and thy moon shall not fail, for thy Lord shall be to thee an everlasting light, and the days of thy mourning shall be fulfilled." These prophecies clearly refer to the age still to come, and they are addressed to the children of Israel in their captivity, to whom He was sent and came, who said, "I am not sent but to the lost sheep of the house of Israel." Such things, though they are captives, they are to receive in their own land; and proselytes also are to come to them at that time through Christ, and are to fly to them, according to the saying, "Behold, proselytes shall come to thee through Me, and shall flee to thee for refuge." And if all this is to take place with the captives, then it is plain that they must be about their temple, and that they must go up there again to be built up, having become the most precious of stones. For we find with John in his Apocalyse, the promise made to him that overcomes, that he will be a pillar in the temple of God, and will go no more out. All this I have said with a view to our obtaining a cursory view at least of the matters pertaining to the temple, and the house of God, and the Church and Jerusalem, which we cannot now take up systematically. Those, however, who, in their reading of the prophets, do not shrink from the labor of seeking after their spiritual meaning, must enquire into these matters with the greatest particularity, and must take account of every possibility. So far of "the temple of His body."

27. Of the Belief the Disciples Afterwards Attained in the Words of Jesus.

"When He was raised from the dead, His disciples remembered that He spoke this, and they believed the Scripture and the word which Jesus had said." This tells us that after Jesus' resurrection from the dead His disciples saw that what He had said about the temple had a higher application to His passion and His resurrection; they remembered that the words, "In three days I will raise it up," pointed to the resurrection; "And they believed the Scripture and the word which Jesus had said." We are not told that they believed the Scripture or the word which Jesus said, before. For faith in its full sense is the act of him who accepts with his whole soul what is professed at baptism. As for the higher sense, as we have already spoken of the resurrection from the dead of the whole body of the Lord, we have now to note that the disciples were put in mind by the fulfilment of the Scripture which when they were in life they had not fully understood; its meaning was now brought under their eyes and made quite clear to them, and they knew of what heavenly things it was the pattern and shadow. Then they believed the Scripture who formerly did not believe it, and believed the word of Jesus which, as the speaker means to convey, they had not believed before the resurrection. For how can anyone be said in the full sense to believe the Scripture when he does not see in it the mind of the Holy Spirit, which God would have us to believe rather than the literal meaning? From this point of view we must say that none of those who walk according to the flesh believe the spiritual things of the law, of the very beginnings of which they have no conception. But, they say, those are more blessed who have not seen and yet believe, than those who have seen and have believed, and for this they quote the saying to Thomas at the end of the Gospel of John, "Blessed are they that have not seen and yet have believed." But it is not said here that those who have not seen and yet have believed are more blessed than those who have seen and believed. According to their view those after the Apostles are more blessed than the Apostles; than which nothing can be more foolish. He who is to be blessed must see in his mind the things which he believes, and must be able with the Apostles to hear the words spoken to him, "Blessed are your eyes, for they see, and your ears, for they hear," and "Many prophets and righteous men have desired to see the things which ye see, and have not seen them, and to hear the things which ye hear, and have not heard them." Yet he may be content who only receives the inferior beatitude, which says: "Blessed are they who have not seen and yet have believed." But how much more blessed are those eyes which Jesus calls blessed for the things which they have seen, than those which have not attained to such a vision; Simeon is content to take into his arms the salvation of God, and after seeing it, he says, "Now, O Lord, let Thou Thy servant depart in peace, according to Thy word; for mine eyes have seen Thy salvation." We must strive, therefore, as Solomon says, to open our eyes that we may be satisfied with bread; "Open thine eyes," he says, "and be satisfied with bread." What I have said on the text, "They believe the Scripture and the word which Jesus had said unto them," may lead us to understand, after discussing the subject of faith, that the perfection of our faith will be given us at the great resurrection from the dead of the whole body of Jesus which is His Holy Church. For what is said about knowledge, "Now I know in part," that, I think, may be said in the same way of every other good; and one of these others is faith. "Now I believe in part," we may say, "but when that which is perfect is come, then the faith which is in part will be done away." As with knowledge, so with faith, that which is through sight is far better, if I may say so, than that which is through a glass and in an enigma.

28. The Difference between Believing in the Name of Jesus and Believing in Jesus Himself.

"Now, when He was in Jerusalem at the Passover, during the feast, many believed in His name, beholding His signs which He did. But He, Jesus, did not trust

Himself to them, because He knew all (men) and because He needed not that any should testify of man, for he Himself knew what was in man." One might ask how Jesus did not Himself believe in those of whom we are told that they believed. To this we must say it was not those who believed in Him that Jesus did not trust, but those who believed in His name; for believing in His name is a different thing from believing in Him. He who will not be judged because of his faith is exempted from the judgment, not for believing in His name, but for believing in Him; for the Lord says, "He that believeth in Me is not judged," not, "He who believes in My name is not judged;" the latter believes, and hence he is not worthy to be condemned already, but he is inferior to the other who believes in Him. Hence it is that Jesus does not trust Himself to him who believes in His name. We must, therefore, cleave to Him rather than to His name, lest after we have done wonders in His name, we should hear these words addressed to us which He will speak to those who boast of His name alone. With the Apostle Paul let us seek joyfully to say, "I can do all things in Christ Jesus strengthening me." We have also to notice that in a former passage the Evangelist calls the Passover that of the Jews, while here he does not say that Jesus was at the Passover of the Jews, but at the Passover at Jerusalem; and in the former case when the Passover is called that of the Jews, it is not said to be a feast; but here Jesus is recorded to have been at the feast; when at Jerusalem He was at the Passover during the feast, and many believed, even though only in His name. We ought to notice certainly that "many" are said to believe, not in Him, but in His name. Now, those who believe in Him are those who walk in the straight and narrow way, which leads to life, and which is found by few. It may well be, however, that many of those who believe in His name will sit down with Abraham and Isaac and Jacob in the kingdom of heaven, the Father's house, in which are many mansions. And it is to be noted that the many who believe in His name do not believe in the same way as Andrew does, and Peter, and Nathanael, and Philip. These believe the testimony of John when he says, "Behold the Lamb of God," or they believe in Christ as found by Andrew, or Jesus saying to Philip, "Follow Me," or Philip saying, "We have found Him of whom Moses and the prophets did write, Jesus the Son of Joseph from Nazareth." Those, on the other hand, of whom we now speak, "believed in His name, beholding His signs which He did." And as they believe the signs and not in Him but in His name, Jesus "did not trust Himself to them, because He knew all men, and needed not that any should testify of man, because He knew what is in every man."

29. About What Beings Jesus Needed Testimony.

The words, "He needed not that any should testify of man," may fitly be used to show that the Son of God is able of Himself to see the truth about each man and is in no need of such testimony as any other could supply. The words, however, "He had no need that any should testify of man," are not equivalent to "He had no need of testimony about any being." If we take the word "man" to include every being who is according to the image of God, or every reasonable creature, then He will have no need that any should testify to Him of any reasonable being whatever, since He Himself, by the power given Him by the Father, knows them all. But if the term "man" be restricted to mortal animated reasonable beings, then it might be said, on the one hand, that He had need of testimony respecting the beings above man, and while His knowledge was adequate with regard to man it did not extend to those other beings. On the other hand, however, it might be said that He who humbled Himself had no need that any should testify to Him concerning man, but that He had such need in respect of beings higher than men.

30. How Jesus Knew the Powers, Better or Worse, Which Reside in Man.

It may also be asked what signs those many saw Him do who believed on Him, for it is not recorded that He did any signs at Jerusalem, though some may have been done which are not recorded. One may, however, consider if what He did may be called signs, when He made a scourge of small cords, and cast them all out of the temple, and the sheep, and the oxen, and poured out the changers' money, and overthrew the tables. As for those who suppose that it was only about men that He had no need of witnesses, it has to be said that the Evangelist attributes to Him two things, that He knew all beings, and that He had no need that anyone should testify of man. If He knew all beings, then He knew not only men but the beings above men, all beings who are without such bodies as ours; and He knew what was in man, since He was greater than those who reproved and judged by prophesying, and who brought to the light the secret things of the hearts of those whom the Spirit suggested to them to be thus dealt with. The words, "He knew what was in man," could also be taken as referring to the powers, better or worse, which work in men. For if anyone gives place to the devil, Satan enters into him;

thus did Judas give place, and thus did the devil put it in his heart to betray Jesus, and "after the sop," therefore, "the devil entered into him." But if anyone gives place to God, he becomes blessed; for blessed is the man whose help is from God, and the ascent is in his heart from God. Thou knows what is in man, Thou who knows all things, O Son of God. And now that our tenth book has come to be large enough we will here pause in our theme.

**Find this and other great works of the Early Church Fathers at lighthousechristianpublishing.com.**

Our Father who art in heaven, hallowed be thy name.
Thy kingdom come, Thy will be done, on earth as it is in heaven.
Give us this day our daily bread and forgive us our trespasses as we forgive those who trespass against us.
And lead us not into temptation, but deliver us from evil, for Thine is the kingdom, the power and the glory. Forever and ever.

Amen

Origen of Alexandra

Hail Mary full of grace, the Lord is with thee. Blessed art thou amongst women and blessed is the fruit of thy womb Jesus. Holy Mary mother of God, pray for us sinners, now and the hour of our death.

www.ingramcontent.com/pod-product-compliance
Lightning Source LLC
Chambersburg PA
CBHW052132070526
44585CB00017B/1792